GW00786581

Slavery, Law and Society in the British Windward Islands 1763-1823

A Comparative Study

BERNARD MARSHALL

ARAWAK publications
KINGSTON • JAMAICA

To my parents
Maria and Casper
and to
Professor Elsa Goveia

... ...

2007   Year of the 200th Anniversary of the Abolition of the African Slave Trade
by Great Britain and the United States of America against the background of
the Overthrow of Slavery by the Slaves in Haiti

Published by
A r a w a k   publications
17 Kensington Crescent
Kingston 5   Jamaica W I

ISBN 976 8189 81 9 (hbk)
ISBN 976 8189 27 4 (pbk)
11 10 09 08 07   5 4 3 2 1

NATIONAL LIBRARY OF JAMAICA CATALOGUING-IN-PUBLICATION DATA
Marshall, Bernard
    Slavery, law and society in the British Windward Islands 1763-1823 :
    a comparative study / Bernard Marshall
        p. : ill. ;   cm.
    Bibliography : p.   . - Includes index
    ISBN 976-8189-81-9 (hbk)
    1. Slavery – Law and legislation – West Indies   2. Slaves – West
    Indies – Economic conditions   3. West Indies – Economic conditions
    4. West Indies – Politics and government
    I. Title

    306.36209729   dc21

Illustrations reproduced by courtesy of the West Indies Collection, The Main
    Library, The University of the West Indies
    -*Front cover image*: An Afro Caribbean Festival "drawn from
    Nature" in the Island of St. Vincent
    -*Image at back cover*: The Voyage of the *Sable Venus* from
    Angola to the West Indies

Book and cover design by Annika Lewinson-Morgan
Set in 10/13pt Book Antiqua with CataneoBT and Cataneo SwashBT
Printed in the USA

CONTENTS

ꝗLLUSTRATIONS

Introduction

The literature on slavery in the Caribbean has grown significantly in recent years. The contribution of historians, anthropologists, economists, sociologists and legal scholars is indicative of the extent to which the subject has become interdisciplinary. However, despite scattered publications by this writer and others on slavery in Dominica, St. Vincent, Tobago Grenada and the Grenadines, and the rare monograph touching aspects of slavery or a particular group in slave society in an individual island, these communities have been virtually ignored. No single comprehensive work exists on these territories to date.

This book is the first attempt to analyse the nature of the slave society in these four communities during sixty critical years of slavery in the Caribbean. It straddles the disciplines of history, sociology, law and political science. It examines the economic, political, social, religious and legal organisation of society against a background of incipient economic decline and shows how it was affected by total dependence upon the institution of negro slavery.

This monograph, though a local case study, is nevertheless an important contribution to the history of slavery in the Caribbean and in the New World in general. In his seminal work *Slave and Citizen: the Negro in the Americas*, Tannenbaum (1946) advances a typology of New World slave systems. Briefly speaking, he divided the slave systems of the Western hemisphere into three groups, the Iberian, the French, and the Anglo-Saxon with the Iberian having a reputation for mildness and the Anglo-Saxon for severity. These differences he explains in terms of institutional forces such as the role of the Church, or legal forces such as the Spanish slave law and an effective slave tradition.

Advocates of this school of thought such as Gilberto Freyre, Stanley Elkins and Herbert Klien have been challenged by Marvin Harris, David Brion Davis, Franklin Knight and others. In his prize-winning book *The Problem of Slavery in Western Culture*, Davis (1966) on the basis of strong evidence concluded that the differences between Latin America and Anglo-Saxon slavery appeared on closer scrutiny to be "far less significant than their underlying patterns of unity". Davis' insight gains support from the experience of slavery in the British Windward Islands during the period of this study. Our analysis indicates that slavery in the British Windward Islands followed closely a pattern that had developed earlier on in the older British West Indies, and was to be repeated later on in the French West Indies and in Cuba and Brazil in the nineteenth century.

This book is a synthesis of two dissertations which have been substantially revised, modified, and to some extent expanded and amplified. The first is a doctoral thesis in History entitled "Society and Economy in the British Windward Islands 1763-1823" written for the University of the West Indies (UWI) under the supervision of Professor Elsa Goveia. The second entitled "Law, Social Engineering and Social and Cultural Pluralism in the British Windward Islands of Dominica, Grenada, St Vincent and Tobago during Slavery" was later written for the University of the West Indies in partial fulfillment of the requirements for a Bachelor of Laws degree. It examined the role and function of law in the four communities and the extent to which the plural society model advanced by the sociologist M.G. Smith was applicable to Caribbean slave society.

In about March 1987 I received communication from the law librarian at the Cave Hill campus of the UWI indicating that Harvard Law School expressed an interest in obtaining a copy of this dissertation and requesting my assent so as to comply therewith. A compelling factor in Harvard's request may have been the fact that I had examined and explored Roscoe Pound's concept of social engineering in my analysis. Pound held the position of Dean of Harvard Law School from 1910 until his death in 1964.

Roscoe Pound has been revered as 'the father of sociological jurisprudence' although he himself admitted his indebtedness to earlier writers such as Jhering. Pound regarded jurisprudence as a technology and he sought to apply the analogy of engineering to social problems. He advocated a new functional approach to law and legal technique directed to social needs in which the judiciary would play a creative role. Pound saw law as an ordering of conduct so as to make the goods of existence and the means of satisfying claims go around as far as possible with the least friction and waste. The focal points of his theory are legal interests, social interests and jural postulates or suppositions of legal reasoning. The task of the sociological jurist is to identify those 'claims or demands or desires' which have pressed or are pressing for legal recognition. He should distinguish individual interests which are asserted in the title of individual life, public interests in the title of politically organised society and social interests in the title of social life. In considering whether one interest ought to be preferred to the other, both must be weighed on the same plane, generally the social plane. Individual interests should be subsumed under broader social interests.

Social interests are defined as general security in health, peace and public order, acquisitions and transactions, security of social institutions, family, general progress in the economic, political and cultural spheres, and in the social interest of individual life with each individual being able to live a human life according to the standards of society. The gravamen of Pound's thesis is that law operates as an arbiter of conflicting interests or an instrument that controls interests according to the requirements of the social order. Pound regarded law as representing the consciousness of the whole society, serving ultimately only those interests which are conducive to the public good.

This thesis has been criticised as being relevant, if at all, to some ideal society that is static, homogenous and cohesive with shared values, traditions and a common cognition of reality. The consensus model as it is described was later challenged by those who advocated a conflict paradigm in the sociology of law of similar genre to the plural thesis as outlined by M.G. Smith who regarded conflict and dissensus as endemic to Caribbean slave society. In his disquisition of the social structure of the British Caribbean to about 1820, Smith (1965) argued that the society was divided into sections each of which practised different cultures. Moreover, the sections were organised in a rigid hierarchy defined in terms of legal and social status differences and held together by force de jure and de facto. This paradigm shares common ground with the conflict school whose proponents contend that far from representing a compromise of diverse interests, law consists of the interests only of specific segments of the population which manipulate the legal system to serve their needs and safeguard their special interests with particular emphasis on coercion and constraint.

Consistent with the above, this case study of the British Windward Islands indicates that the end and purpose of law was not to secure any of the beneficial effects alluded to by Pound, at least from the perspective of the non white groups. Law represented the interest of a specific segment of the population - the white minority. Law operated as an instrument of oppression, brutality, barbarism and dehumanisation of the Afro-Caribbean majority, as the minority ruling class fashioned its own brand of social engineering to support a system of racial inequality and exploitation.

This book is the end product of several years of study and research during which time I have benefited tremendously from the expertise and generosity of several individuals at the several campuses of the University of the West Indies, too numerous to mention. However, I cannot fail to mention the debt I owe to the late Professor Elsa Goveia who supervised the original dissertation. Suffice to say that her patience, guidance, encouragement and criticisms throughout the various stages of the research and writing were invaluable. I am also indebted to Professor Woodville Marshall who suggested the topic of research. Emeritus Professor Dr. Roy Augier, Dr. Nicholas Liverpool, and the late Emeritus Professor Douglas Hall also gave every encouragement and support. My thanks also to the unknown referee who made valuable criticisms of the original manuscript and offered suggestions for its improvement which I have tried to incorporate. Linnette Vassel instead of regarding my unreasonable request for a comment on the manuscript as an imposition, not only cheerfully complied but offered suggestions necessitating a degree of revision. Finally, I wish to acknowledge the support of my family and in particular my wife Joan for the sacrifices they endured occasioned by the time spent on the research, writing and preparation of this book.

I must also acknowledge with gratitude the help of the directors, librarians and attendants at the Library of the University of the West

Indies (Mona); the West Indian Reference Library at the Institute of Jamaica; the British Museum; the Public Record Office; the Library of the Royal Commonwealth Society; the Historical Manuscripts Commission, London; the Institute of Historical Research, London University; Rhodes House Library, Oxford University; Lambeth Palace Library; the Moravian Church Archives; the Archives of the Wesleyan Methodist Missionary Society; and the Archives of the Congregational Council for World Missions, London. Mrs. Kathleen Miles, formerly of the Institute of Social and Economic Research, University of the West Indies (Mona), did an excellent job of preparing the manuscript for the Press.

*A*BBREVIATIONS

    ACCWM   Archives of the Congregational Council for World Missions
    AMC   Archives of the Moravian Church
    AWMMS   Archives of the Wesleyan Methodist Missionary Society
    CO   Colonial Office
    FP   Fulham Papers
    LMS   London Missionary Society
    PRO   Public Record Office

Chapter 1

The 18th century sugar revolution and Black Carib/Kalinago resistance to plantation hegemony in St Vincent

> In the social production which men carry on, they enter into definite relations which are indispensable and independent of their will; these relations of production correspond to a definite stage of development of their material powers of production. The totality of these relations of production constitutes the economic structure of society – the real foundations on which legal and political superstructures arise and to which definite forms of social consciousness correspond.
>
> – Karl Marx, Preface and Introduction to *A Contribution to the Critique of Political Economy* (1859)

In the second half of the eighteenth century Great Britain's possessions in the West Indies were enlarged with the additions of Dominica, St. Vincent, Tobago, Grenada and the Grenadines. Known as the Ceded Islands of the Eastern Caribbean, these were Britain's fruits of victory in the Seven Years' War with France and her sovereignty was acknowledged at the Peace of Paris in 1763, which brought that war to a close. Before 1763, France's rights to the colony of Grenada and the Grenadines had not been disputed, but both powers had not been able to agree on the issue of ownership of Dominica, St. Vincent and Tobago. In 1748, however, they had arrived at a compromise when at the Treaty of Aix-La-Chapelle they agreed to regard these islands as neutral or outside the limits of penetration by either, and that they be left in free, undisturbed possession of the indigenous inhabitants, the Caribs, estimated at sixty families in Dominica and 3,000 persons in St. Vincent.[1]

In recent years there has been a change in the terminology hitherto adopted for classifying the indigenous peoples of the Caribbean. The Caribs who occupied the Lesser Antilles of which the British Windward Islands are a part are now referred to as Kalinago, whereas the Arawaks of Jamaica and the Greater Antilles are designated Tainos. However, while the designation Black Caribs/Kalinago will be used interchangeably, this study for the most part adopts the traditional terminology as it is more convenient so to do, and as it is consistent with manuscript and contemporary sources

France respected the Aix-la-Chapelle agreement only with regard to Tobago. In the case of Dominica and St. Vincent, that power openly violated the agreement. The extent of this violation is demonstrated in statistics of production, acres under cultivation and the French and slave populations of these two islands at the time when British sovereignty was conceded. St. Vincent had a population of 1,300 residents of French extraction and 3,400 slaves. A total of 6,477 acres were in actual cultivation, in tobacco, coffee, and cocoa. Production statistics for 1763 indicated a total of 644,077 lbs. coffee and 1,249,012 lbs. cocoa. In addition there were 249 coffee buildings, 563 horses and 1,999 heads of cattle on the island. In Dominica French residents numbered 1,718 and slaves 5,872 engaged in the cultivation of 3,027 acres. As in St. Vincent, coffee and cocoa were the main crops, with production estimated at 1,690,368 lbs. and 271,650 lbs. respectively. In addition, manioc and cotton were grown in small amounts.[2]

Coffee and cocoa also played a significant role in the economy of Grenada in 1763, with production statistics of 6,000,000 lbs. and 30,000 lbs. respectively. Sugar exports totalled 8,000 hogsheads, but it is important to note that sugar did not dominate the island's economy. Cotton was also grown on the Grenadine islands of Bequia and Carriacou which had a combined population of 150 whites and 500 slaves. Grenada itself had a slave population of 10,351, but on the whole the island's economic potential had been hardly scratched. Only one-third of the land fit for cultivation was in use in 1763. One general point needs to be emphasised: Of the three islands under

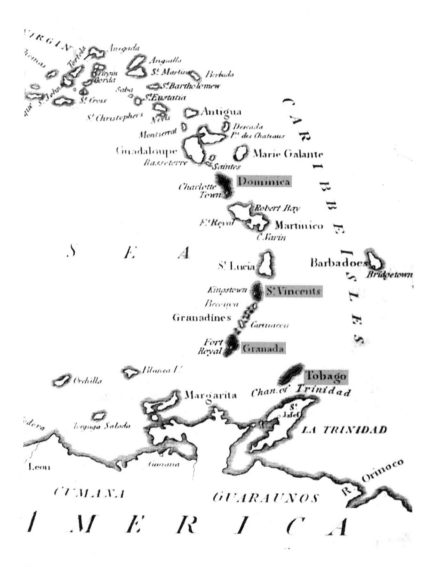

Figure 1 • *The ceded islands of the eastern Caribbean*

cultivation in 1763 only Grenada produced sugar. Yet, as we shall see, by 1773 sugar would become the mainstay of the economic life of these islands, and of Tobago, where there had been no European economic activity before 1763.

Great Britain was anxious for a rapid development of her new possessions and no time was lost in formulating political and administrative arrangements for this purpose. The four colonies were grouped together in a federation with representative institutions – the British Windward Islands Federation – with headquarters at Grenada. This experiment never got off to a good start because of the narrow, selfish interests of its constituent members, and for these reasons it disintegrated after 1771, when Dominica was separated.[4] Such an arrangement, however, was seen by British policy makers as vital for the coordination of defense, internal security, and the control and disposal of land for sugar plantations.[5]

The last was a major preoccupation of decision makers and the task was delegated to the Board of Trade. Accordingly, on October 17th 1763, "Their lordships took into consideration the method of disposing of land in the islands of Grenada, St. Vincent, Dominica, and Tobago and ordered the draft of a representation to His Majesty thereupon to be prepared."[6] Throughout the latter part of 1763 and early 1764, this document passed through several committees of the Board of Trade, the Treasury and the Privy Council, undergoing revisions and amendments before its terms were finally agreed upon.[7]

Perhaps the overriding concern of the Board of Trade in its deliberations on this subject was how to thwart the efforts of individuals and groups in the other British Caribbean islands opposed to the establishment of new sugar colonies in the region. Such persons were motivated entirely by self-interest for the reason that by the middle of the eighteenth century most of the older sugar colonies in the British West Indies were suffering from soil exhaustion which increased the cost of sugar production at a time when output was diminishing. Only those planters with ample capital could afford to carry on economic production and this gave them a virtual monopoly on the home market as demand exceeded supply.[8] This monopoly they did not want to lose and more importantly they feared that an increase in sugar reaching the home market from newly developed territories would lower prices and cut their profits. As a result, they started a propaganda campaign intended to impede the development of the islands. As Professor Pitman writes: "The great planters discouraged the settlement... of even the small islands acquired by the treaty, exaggerating the hardships and anxieties of a planter's life."[9]

In this prevailing state of affairs the Board of Trade expressed the view that such interest groups might be able to achieve their objective by simply and wilfully combining to buy large tracts of land and leaving them idle. Concern was also expressed about speculators, individuals who had no interest in cultivating lands but would buy only for the reason of selling again at a higher price at a convenient time. Measures had to be taken therefore "to prevent the ingrossing into few hands a large proportion of the lands in these islands". As a result they recommended that no one person should be allowed to purchase more than one lot of land in his own name or in the name of others in trust for him.[10]

Another measure designed as a safeguard was the imposition of restrictions governing the actual size of plantation lots to be put on the market. In Grenada, St. Vincent and Tobago it was recommended that these should be generally from 100 to 300 acres in extent with a few exceptions of 500 acres. In Dominica the allotments were to be smaller, generally from 50 to 100 acres in extent with a few exceptions of 300 acres. In making these special recommendations for Dominica the Board of Trade was influenced by the fact that the soil was more suitable in some areas for the cultivation of coffee, cocoa and cotton, crops which did not require large acreages, and by the belief that the island ought to have a large white population in view of what was regarded as its vulnerable position between the French islands of Martinique and Guadeloupe in the event of a renewed war with France. In addition, the island was seen as an important link in communications and commerce throughout the British West Indies. Rapid settlement would therefore lessen its degree of exposure in time of war "to sudden invasion from these (French) islands".[11]

Inducements were also offered to the French inhabitants of Dominica, St. Vincent and Grenada to remain on these islands. Economic and military considerations seem to have played a key role in this decision. The French had already been cultivating sugar in Grenada, and in the other islands their economic activities, of which the Board was quite aware from reports submitted in 1763, could boost the British economy. In addition they possessed slaves and other instruments of husbandry essential to the plantation system and it was for this reason that instructions were issued to military commanders to prevent either the sale or removal of these effects.[12]

As regards the military consideration, it was believed that if the French settlers were allowed to hold property they could be reconciled to an English government, and would form a body of 'Englishmen' who would be ready to defend the islands in the event of a renewed war with France, since they would have something at stake. What was thought to be the vulnerable position of Dominica was again a major consideration. It was believed that the imposition of too discriminatory regulations governing land tenure in the case of the French residents might result in the French government encouraging them to emigrate particularly to Martinique and Guadeloupe. It seemed wise therefore to encourage them to remain by imposing as few restrictions as possible. Hence, in Dominica, St Vincent and Grenada, they were allowed to hold the lands they occupied on leases for periods of 14, 21, 32, or 40 years, provided that they swore allegiance to the British Crown.[13]

These two major recommendations were accepted and they were embodied in the 'Proclamation for the Sale of Lands in the Ceded Islands'.[14] Subject to the safeguards previously stated, all land was to be sold at auction at a price to be fixed by specially appointed Commissioners. Twenty per cent of the purchase money was to be paid down as a deposit and the remainder in instalments of 10% in the first year, 10% in the second year and 20% in each successive year until the whole was paid. A quit rent of sixpence per acre was reserved for the Crown and each purchaser was required to cultivate one acre in every twenty each year, until half the land purchased was cleared. Defaulters were subject to a fine of five pounds for each uncleared acre.[14]

Steps were also taken to speed up the settlement by encouraging the immigration of white people. First, 800 acres of land not suitable for sugar cultivation were to be set aside in each parish for poor settlers, to be divided among them in lots varying from 10 to 30 acres in extent. Secondly, each purchaser was required within three months of purchase, to keep one white man or two white women for every 100 acres on pain of a deficiency fine of 20 pounds per head.[16]

This proclamation, though it angered the group of planters opposed to the extension of sugar cultivation in the region, was welcomed by another group consisting of those planters whose profits were declining under the costly conditions of planting in the islands. The fresh tracts for exploitation in the new islands, it was believed, presented them with an opportunity to recoup some of their lost fortunes. Indeed, they lost no time in manifesting a desire to take advantage of new prospects, and they eagerly sought to acquire lands for sugar plantations, even before the territories were formally vested in the British Crown and also before that government had formulated regulations governing their sale and disposal.

When for instance it was rumoured in the West Indies that Britain might receive Grenada at the conclusion of the Peace Treaty, several planters from Barbados, Antigua and St. Christopher proceeded to the island and began to make conditional agreements with the French residents for the purchase of their estates.[17] As soon as the terms of the preliminary articles of the Peace were known in the West Indies 12 sugar estates with capacities ranging from 150 to 400 hogsheads per annum were bought by these planters and by the end of April 1763 the total had risen to 21.[18]

British merchants resident in Guadeloupe during the British occupation emigrated to Dominica and were given grants of land and allowed to purchase from French residents. Such transactions were either ignored or tolerated by the military commanders[19] and stern warnings and reprimands had to be issued them by the Imperial Government to stop the practice.[20]

The Commissioners arrived in the West Indies in May 1765 and began their duties at Tobago.[21] In the previous year many individuals from the older islands were quite eager to acquire lands in this island especially since it was virgin territory and they had resorted there with their slaves to await the arrival of the Commissioners.[22] However, when Robert Melville, the first Governor-in-Chief, arrived at Barbados en route for Grenada he found out that not only had this disposition changed but that there was also "an universal dread and dislike of that island (Tobago) with nobody interested in going there". The principal reason advanced for this was "the report of an excessive sickness prevailing among the troops" which proved fatal to the early adventurers.[23] Indeed, this situation was eagerly played upon by those individuals opposed to the extension of sugar cultivation and they immediately circulated stories to the effect that "sending people to such a place would be committing murder".[24] The Governor-in-Chief tried to allay such fears but not much was achieved. Those willing to emigrate were what he termed "the lower class of people", for the most part idle and unemployed.[25]

As a result, the sales of lands at Tobago opened under gloomy prospects. Only three bidders appeared at the first auction[26] but from then on the outlook brightened. Four thousand acres had been sold at the end of 1765, 11,096 in 1766 and 14,855 in 1767. By 1771 when the Commissioners reported the termination of transactions in the island, the total acreage disposed of was 57,408.[27]

Before the year 1768, the progress of land sales at Dominica was not as encouraging as at Tobago. At the close of the year 1767, for instance, only 11,217 acres had been disposed of, after three years of sales[28] and this amount was exceeded by sales in Tobago for that year alone. Several explanations were put forward by purchasers resident in this island for the slow establishment of the plantation system. Some, for example, argued that the high prices paid at the first auction had discouraged prospective buyers.[29] Others objected to the restricted acreages offered for sale. Three hundred acres, it was argued, was too small for a sugar plantation, for since the island was mountainous and hilly in parts, there was the possibility that a quarter of this acreage might be inaccessible and unfit for cultivation. The minimum size it was argued ought to be at least 500 acres as in the other islands.[30]

Another objection raised was the state of the island's defences in view of what was thought to be its vulnerable position in the event of a war and the connected problem of the political arrangements made by the home government for the coordination of defence in case of such an eventuality, since orders and directives were to emanate from the Governor-in-Chief in Grenada who was also Commander-in-Chief of the armed forces in the entire government. According to one report submitted in 1765, island defences consisted merely of "four small cannon" mounted on "rotten carriages", placed upon a little barbette battery, and "five thin companys of foot and thirteen men of artillery". This situation was reported to be "so alarming at present to persons otherwise disposed to make purchases here that few are willing to place their fortunes where the danger of loss is so readily apparent".[31]

Throughout 1766 and 1767 the inhabitants bombarded the home government with petitions for rectification of this situation and also called for the complete separation of the island from Grenada as a solution. According to one petition: "In case of emergency in wartime when the Lieutenant Governor must be under the necessity of waiting orders from the Commander-in-Chief, all might be lost before he could receive them or have power to defray the expenses of putting himself in any kind of posture for defence."[32] And further, such a calamity could be avoided by the establishment of "a Council and a House of Assembly as all His Majesty's other islands have excepting the Ceded Islands", and a separate governor with exclusive control over defence.[33]

At the end of 1767 the Board of Trade in response to these demands had recommended a separate governor for Dominica[34] and this decision seems to have had a significant effect upon the sale of lands though the island was not completely separated from the Grenada government until 1770. Sales totalled 12,000 acres in 1768, 12,476 in 1769 and 14,472 in 1770, the year of the separation. In 1771, a record total of 20,401¾ acres were sold and at the end of 1773, when the Commissioners wound up their business, over 95,000 acres had been sold in the nine-year period.[35]

The establishment and growth of plantations in St. Vincent were not as rapid or as successful as in the other islands. This was so because the amount of land available for sale was limited for two reasons. First, 20,000 acres had been gratuitously granted to one Mr. Swinburne and another 4,000 to General Monckton,[36] thus withdrawing about a quarter of the total acreage from the market. Secondly and more importantly was the presence of the descendants of a group of shipwrecked Africans called the Black Caribs – or Kalinago, consistent with the recent classification These people formed "a strong tribal enclave"[37] in the island, and regarding the areas they inhabited as their exclusive property, opposed European settlement.

It is of cardinal importance that this Black Carib opposition to the series of events leading up to the outbreak of what has been popularly termed 'the First Carib War of 1773', and the circumstances surrounding the termination of that war be placed in proper perspective.

Indeed, such an approach is very timely and necessary since to date the popular work on this subject is still that of Sir William Young who published his *History* in the year 1795, using very important source materials, namely the private papers of his father who was Chief Commissioner for the sale and disposal of lands in the islands.[38] To date, this work which has completely distorted the picture has remained virtually unchallenged. In her study on the historiography of the British West Indies, Professor Elsa Goveia did more than justice to this work by describing it as "a piece of settler history",[39] but no one has yet attempted to refute Young's arguments by a thorough re-examination of the available data. Indeed, throughout the work, Young views the Black Caribs as a group of "savages" whose sinister designs against the lives and properties of "innocent" British subjects created a situation in which there was no alternative but to use force against them and remove them from the island at all costs.

It is important to note also the date of publication of this work. That date, 1795, marked the termination of the Second Carib War of 1795 when the Black Caribs were finally subjugated by the forces of General Abercrombie and it was also a time when there was a campaign afoot to expel from them the island so that the areas they occupied might be converted into sugar plantations, an objective which the British settlers had at the outset and which the Caribs had persistently and consistently prevented from materialising. Young's work therefore ought to be viewed as a part of that campaign.

This work, however, despite its distortions is nevertheless a very important one, not only because the author had at his disposal very important source materials but more significantly because his thinking has conditioned that of writers on the subject for centuries and generations. For example, Charles Shepherd[41] devotes a section of his book on St. Vincent to the war of 1773, and he actually follows the line taken by Young. But he like Young could be considered a settler.

Even as eminent a historian as Professor Lowell Ragatz who wrote almost a century after Shepherd accepted without question the arguments put forward by Young and by so doing adopted the settler position of these and earlier writers. For instance, Ragatz accuses the Black Caribs of committing "numerous depredations" on the plantations,[42] but like Young and Shepherd he failed to view such action within the context of provocative British efforts to penetrate the part

Figure 2 • *A family of Caribs in St. Vincent*

of the island they inhabited and displace them from their land. "Matters reached such a point," he continued, "that it became necessary to launch the expedition against them." Persons resident in England who opposed the expedition he describes as "well meaning" but dismisses as "misinformed" and he goes on to argue that the expedition in itself was "actually a necessary preliminary step to the development of the colony".[43]

Again Ragatz sees the "acceptance" by the Black Caribs of a block of land in the northern part of the island at the Peace Treaty, as a result of the fact that their resistance was broken,[44] which seems to imply that the British won a victory both during the campaign and at the Peace Treaty. It is our contention that the British won no such victory and that from all indications the war ended in a stalemate. If indeed the British did in fact win such a magnanimous victory why then did they at the termination of this war get such a negligible portion of Black Carib territory which the Black Caribs quickly reoccupied, and why were the planters so dissatisfied with the treaty? On these issues and others, we challenge existing interpretations and suggest revised and modified conclusions.

The Black Caribs were the survivors of a cargo of an African slave ship bound from the Bight of Benin to Barbados which was wrecked off the coast of Bequia, a small island near to St Vincent. At the time of the wreckage, some Africans managed to reach the island of Bequia but were still in distress because of the lack of adequate supplies of food and water. The Yellow Caribs who were accustomed to resort to this island on their fishing excursions rescued the Africans from their plight and invited them to the mainland of St. Vincent, an invitation which was accepted.[45]

In St. Vincent, these Africans settled down, intermarried with the Yellow Caribs and made a living by hunting, fishing and cultivating cassava for consumption and tobacco for export to Martinique.[46] In the process of time relations between the Black and the indigenous Yellow Caribs became strained and in 1710 the Governor of the French Island of Martinique who acted as arbitrator divided the island between both groups. The Yellow Caribs were assigned the Leeward, and the Black Caribs the Windward side of the island. Those French settlers who were residing on the island in 1763 did so with the blessing of the Yellow Caribs and were confined to the Leeward side[47] since the Black Caribs wanted no Europeans amongst them.

In 1719, for instance, the French Governor of Martinique sent an expedition of 400 men to the island to reduce the Black Carib to submission. When this party attempted to penetrate the Windward side they were greeted by a shower of Carib arrows. The survivors of this ill-fated expedition quickly fled back to Martinique.[48] Again, in 1723,

Figure 3 • Map of the island of St. Vincent

the English monarch George I granted the island to the Duke of Montague. In fact a party of Englishmen actually landed to enforce the claims of the Duke but as a result of opposition not only from the Black but also from the Yellow Caribs, the grant was withdrawn.[49]

When therefore in 1763 the Board of Trade was formulating plans for land disposal, in making recommendations for St. Vincent, it was forced to take into account though somewhat reluctantly, this Black Carib tradition of hostility to settlements attempted by Europeans in the part of the island they inhabited and also their willingness to take up arms in order to prevent these settlements from being made. Indeed, the Board of Trade stated quite explicitly that not only were the Black Caribs "jealous of their property", but that they might be sufficiently numerous to defeat any settlements attempted to be made without their consent."[50] Indeed this was the logic and hard pragmatism which underlay the recommendation that no survey of the lands they inhabited should be undertaken until their consent was obtained, and not considerations of "humanity" as Young makes out.[51]

This recommendation which was embodied in the instructions given to the Commissioners for the sale and disposal of lands had the effect of limiting their activities to the Leeward of the island, which was inhabited by the Yellow Caribs and French subjects. Indeed, the whole of the Windward side with the exception of Calliaqua and certain sections of the Marriaqua valley was either actually inhabited or claimed by the Black Caribs.[52]

Contrary to the prevailing popular belief that the presence of the Black Caribs would scare purchasers from the island,[53] the first sales of land were very successful, with bidders coming from Antigua, Barbados and as far away as North America. At this time, 1765, a total of 7,340 acres had been sold and indeed this figure nearly equalled the combined sales at Dominica and Tobago. At the end of 1767 a total of 12,507 acres had been disposed of since the Commissioners had begun their task.[54]

It was from this time that trouble set in. Indeed, the 12,507 acres sold between 1765 and 1767, represented all the lands on the Leeward side which the Commissioners had been empowered to sell in accordance with their instructions. The original purchasers and others interested in the island were extremely dissatisfied with this situation for two main reasons. First, the Leeward side of the island was very mountainous and rugged and the actual number of cultivable acres was much less than anticipated. Secondly and more importantly, this part of the island was not too suitable for sugar cultivation. It favoured the culture of coffee and cocoa which the French inhabitants grew in significant quantities. Indeed, only the valleys intervening between the hills accommodated sugar.[55]

In contrast to the Leeward side, the Windward side was the most extensive and the finest part of the island. This area was generally very flat, and the soil was regarded as being 'perhaps the best in the world'. In addition it was well watered with rivers which would provide the necessary water power for the sugar mills. It was argued that if the lands here were cut up into sugar plantations the island would in a few years become "a more valuable sugar colony than any possessed by the Crown" with the exception of Jamaica. But in 1767 this was not a feasibility since the Commissioners had no authority to put up these lands for sale because of feared native resistance.[56]

The Chief Commissioner, therefore, in response to settler pressure, quickly sought to convince the British Government not only that penetration into this part of the island was desirable but also how it might be accomplished. He suggested that the Black Caribs be told that the King regarded them as his "loving subjects" and that he would protect them as long as they behaved "peacefully and faithfully" and submitted themselves to the laws in force for the government of free blacks. They should also be asked not only to acquiesce but also to assist the Commissioners in a survey of the areas they inhabited. However, they were to be allowed to choose a portion of woodland for their habitation in a specific area to be designated by the Commissioners. An interim period of five years was to be granted them so that they could reap their crops and remove their belongings to their new habitat. Finally they would be granted compensation at the rate of ten pounds per acre for the areas they presently inhabited.[57]

The British Ministry accepted most of their suggestions and indeed in January 1768, fresh instructions were sent to the Commissioners concerning St Vincent. Subject to Carib consultation and approval, they were authorised to survey in a manner conformable to their former instructions all the cultivable lands between the Rabacca River and Grand Sable. The stipulated compensation for these lands was set at thirteen pounds and four shillings per acre.[58]

These proposals were rejected by the Black Caribs. Chatoyer, one of the most formidable of the Chiefs, gave an outright "no" and refused to entertain any further discussion.[59] But the Commissioners refused to accept his sentiments and indeed, they even violated their instructions by beginning early in 1768 to trace out a road through Black Carib territory as a preliminary step towards a survey of the lands. However, an armed force of Black Caribs prevented them from getting further than Iambou.[60]

Indeed, this and subsequent acts of provocation perpetrated by the Commissioners seem to have escaped the notice of those who accuse the Caribs of committing depredations on the plantations of British subjects. For instance, towards the end of 1768, the Black Caribs made it quite clear that they would be prepared to use force if they were not allowed to enjoy their lands in quiet.[61] But the Commissioners consistent with the customary arrogance paid no heed to this warning in the same manner as they had virtually brushed aside Chatoyer's sentiments on the proposals of a year earlier, and even resorted to the threat of force to accomplish their design.

It was early in 1769 that they made a second attempt to resume this road with the aid of one detachment of the 32nd regiment and four others on standby. Again the Caribs retaliated. They succeeded in cutting off communication between the Commander of this regiment and his forty men whom they held as captives. They then requested the surveyors "to make their escape in the best manner they could by flight", which they did, leaving their baggage and everything else behind.

It was on the next day that the four remaining detachments, all the white men capable of bearing arms, and some slaves marched sixteen miles into the heart of Carib territory in an attempt to rescue the forty men. These were only released after the Black Caribs were given "a clear and explicit assurance", which they had requested that the British "give up all immediate pretensions to interfere with their country and never again attempt to make roads of communication through it".[62]

After this episode the Black Caribs remained relatively free from British molestation until 1770. In this year rumours spread that they had made sales of land to French inhabitants of Grenada. According to these rumours, they had sold 700 acres to a Mr. Pichery and had made an agreement with a Jean Augier for the purchase of a large piece of woodland. The Commissioners interpreted the news of these transactions as an indication that the Black Caribs were really willing

Figure 4 • *Chatoyer of the Black Caribs in St. Vincent with his five wives*

to sell and suggested to the home Government that they rather than private individuals should be the purchasers.[63]

As on previous occasions, the home Government instructed them to put forward proposals for purchase similar to those of 1767, but at the meeting held at Morne Garou with Chief Chatoyer and forty of his men these terms were as on the previous occasion flatly rejected despite the endeavours of the Commissioners "by many arguments to prevail on them to alter their sentiments".[64]

The rejection of these proposals marked the turning point in Anglo-Black Carib relations. It occasioned the settlers to pressure their government for more positive action. In their former petitions the resort to force as a means of accomplishing their design, though stated, was by no means seen as the only possible measure and, in addition, they had urged that the Black Caribs be given compensation either in the form of money or other lands or both. Now they no longer sang this tune. Indeed, after 1771 military force was seen as the only means, compensation was ruled out and the total removal of the Black Caribs from the island was also advocated.

For instance, it was the Commissioners' belief that in future "all treaty and negotiations" with the Black Caribs, "tho on the most just and humane terms", would be fruitless and that it would be impossible to settle the island "without a sufficient force to terrify them into obedience". They argued that the important point was no longer only the sale of lands. The very honour and dignity of the crown was at stake, and also its obligation to protect its subjects from the Black Caribs whose presence in effect constituted an "imperium in imperio".[65]

The British settlers took the same attitude. They argued that the Black Caribs ought to be subjugated since they were a nuisance. Not only were they refusing to allow settlements in their territory but they were also harassing English settlements. It was also asserted that the danger was more real since they were actually being aided and abetted by inhabitants of the French island of Martinique who supplied them with arms and ammunition so that they might gain some advantage in the event of a renewed Anglo-French conflict. They accused the British Government of failure to provide adequate protection for their properties and investments against what they termed Carib depredations and cruelty and concluded by stating that:

> The suffering such a separate empire as these Indians claim within your Majesty's dominions is not only incompatible with the safety of your subjects, but highly derogatory from the honour and dignity of the crown, that lenity and very humane expedient to bring them to a reasonable subjection has long been tried without success.

The continuance of such measures it was urged would only increase their intransigence.[66]

The Governor-in-Chief also supported the jingoistic bandwagon. He had reported that he had intercepted a letter sent to the Black Caribs by the Governor of the French island of St. Lucia. This document was hailed as confirmation of the opinion long entertained by the settlers that the Black Caribs were receiving French support. Therefore, he argued, it was absolutely necessary to use force against them since the "gentle methods" previously used, instead of having the desired effect "were looked upon to have proceeded from timidity." He also argued that conditions were favourable for the deployment of this force since there was no possibility of a war with France, the Spanish war scare had passed and the troops that were stationed in the islands as a result could be mobilised against the Black Caribs.[67]

The British Ministry in deliberating what course of action to take in view of these representations called in for consultations Thomas Hackshaw, James Gordon, C.P. Sharpe, Richard Ottey, William Fitzhugh, all absentee proprietors and Richard Maitland, island agent. Of these men, three were signatories to an earlier petition in which the reduction of the Kalinago people with the aid of military and naval force was seen as possible and desirable.[68] These men were asked whether they thought that the Kalinago should be allowed to stay on the island or be removed from it. If they decided on the latter expedient they were also to choose a place for them to go.[69]

In making their recommendations these individuals deplored the fact that the Black Caribs were in possession of nearly two-thirds of the cultivable and richest land in the island and that they had persistently refused to give up any of it. In addition it was urged that they were not paying taxes or contributing anything to the support of government functions. The British settlers, they argued, could not even make fairly good contributions since their part of the island was generally rugged and broken and the yields from the soil were very poor.[70]

It was further argued that even if the Black Caribs were forced to yield up any of their land by military might, they would reassert their "pretended rights" as soon as that force was removed, or they received assistance from the French. Further the colony would never prosper while the Black Caribs remained in it since their depredations on property created a situation in which mercantile houses were reluctant to extend credit to the island.[71]

These arguments were used in justification for an "absolute and immediate removal" of the Black Caribs from the island. These it was argued should be allowed to choose their place of retreat so long as that place did not "endanger the safety of the other islands". If however they refused to do so, it was suggested that they be given 10,000 acres of land on some part of the coast of Africa or be sent to the desert island of St. Mathow. Finally the Yellow Caribs should be put on the same footing as the Maroons in Jamaica.[72]

Again the British Government yielded to settler pressure. Indeed, that government, after examining the merits and demerits of the arguments advanced came to the conclusion that it was necessary "to take effectual measures for the reduction of them (the Black Caribs) as the only means of giving security to the settlements of his Majesty's subjects". This was to be accomplished by the mobilisation of all the troops in the Grenada Government and Dominica and two regiments from North America. If these forces were insufficient those in the Leeward islands should be sent for and in addition the naval squadron in these parts should be in preparedness.[73]

But this force was to be used only as a last resort. It was hoped that its very presence would terrify the Black Caribs into submission and force them to accept a portion of the island to be decided upon by the Governor and agree to other stipulations of a Treaty similar to that negotiated with the Maroons of Jamaica in 1731. If however they rejected these proposals then that force would be used to remove them from the island to "some unfrequented part of the coast of Africa or some desert island adjacent thereto".[74]

The execution of the whole design was entrusted to a Council composed of the Governor of Dominica, the Commander-in-Chief of the land and sea forces , and the Lieutenant Governor of St. Vincent, with the Governor-in-Chief of the islands at its head. He was specifically cautioned against any disclosure of the proposed measures so that the Black Caribs might not get wind of them and commit acts of hostility before the troops arrived.[75]

The proposed measures were, however, generally known in the island soon after they were formally communicated by the medium of letters sent to individuals by their friends in England, with the only difference that the King had given positive orders to remove the Black Caribs to Africa. The settlers were jubilant as the acquisition of the lands of the Windward side seemed near realisation. But this mood of jubilation quickly changed to one of disappointment when the Governor-in-Chief issued a proclamation embodying the first part of his instructions, asking the Black Caribs to accept the treaty. "Such is the temper of the people," he wrote, "nothing else than a total extirpation of these poor infatuated people would be satisfactory."[76] As the Chief Commissioner then in the position of Governor of Dominica put it, the general opinion in the island was that "Delenda est Carthago", and all reports seemed to justify this notion.[77]

The Black Caribs, however, were quite aware of the fact that the settlers had long adhered to this doctrine and would have liked to put it into execution. They were also aware, in view of the fact that the secret instructions leaked out, of what was contemplated against them. According to the Governor-in-Chief, shortly after this news leak they made frequent trips to the French islands of Martinique and Guadeloupe, returning with arms and ammunition. In fact even before the terms of the proposals were formally communicated to them and at a time when six companies of the 68th Regiment had arrived in the island they made it quite clear to the Governor-in-Chief, that they were determined not to yield up any portion of their lands, "which lands were transmitted to them from their ancestors and in defence of which they would die".[78] They reacted in the same tone when the propositions were officially communicated. They promised to "behave themselves well" if they were left in peaceful possession of their lands, but they were also determined to "let the consequences be what they would as "not an inch of their territory" would be given up. In view of this refusal and despite their determination the British troops that had been mobilised began to advance into Black Carib territory and the war of 1772 began.[79]

The foregoing analysis of the series of events leading up to this war should indicate quite clearly to the reader who was responsible for the outbreak of hostilities. Sir William Young however places the responsibility on the Black Caribs. "It was not," he writes, "until after eight years of patient forbearance by the British Government that the contumacy of the Caribs under the French influence, step by step, led to the necessity of control and the war of 1772."[80] But the available evidence indicates that this argument cannot be accepted. So too is the argument that the Black Caribs had no legitimate right to the part of the island that they claimed since they were not the original inhabitants and in fact were the usurpers of the legitimate Carib heritage in St. Vincent.[81] But even if this was correct, that in itself did not give Great Britain any moral obligation to dispossess them of these lands. In fact the aim of that government was not to restore these lands to the Yellow Caribs but to sell them to its subjects for sugar cultivation.

The argument that the Black Caribs were in their actions influenced by the French also needs examination. It is true that they would have welcomed moral support and even supplies of ammunition from the French to resist English attempts to forcefully remove them from their territory. For contrary to what Young writes, the years prior to 1772 were not characterised by "patient forbearance" as the attempt to trace the road in 1769 with military assistance demonstrates. But the important point is that the available evidence indicates that the decision not to budge was theirs and theirs only. Indeed, they did not need the French to tell them what to do in this respect and it needs to be recalled that they had previously resisted attempts at encroachment by these same French men whom it was now claimed were their advisers.

Indeed, the entire argument that the Black Caribs were in fact responsible for this war can only be accepted if we admit that they had no legitimate right to their lands and that the lands rightfully belonged to Great Britain. But the available evidence indicates no basis for such a claim. In fact as a Black Carib/Kalinago supporter in England put it, since the Kalinago had a legitimate right to their lands, at the Peace of Paris in 1763 France ceded to Great Britain only that part of the island inhabited by its subjects, which was the Leeward side.[82]

In an article published in *The Scott's Magazine* this anonymous writer appealed to Lord Dartmouth, Hillsborough's successor, "to put a stop to the murderous commission sent out by your predecessor to extirpate them". "The administration was berated for "reviving the Spanish cruelties at the conquest of Mexico, to gratify avaricious merchants, land holders and venal commissioners", and a passionate plea was made that the expedition against the Kalinago be immediately called off before it became the subject of a parliamentary inquiry.[83]

The campaign did in fact become the subject of such an inquiry. This was demanded by the opponents of Lord North's administration and as a result it was finally resolved that the expedition was founded in injustice and inhumanity. Major Dalrymple, the officer in charge of military operations, was immediately instructed to negotiate a treaty with the Black Caribs if he had not already effected their reduction, or if the campaign had progressed to a point where in his opinion the treaty would guarantee the safety of the island. The stipulations of the proposed treaty were that the Black Caribs be left in full and peaceful possession of their lands, that they accept full allegiance to the British Government, allow roads of communication through their territory and that if at anytime they were disposed to sell any portion of their lands they would do so only to such persons as were authorised by the king.[84]

The whole affair was examined after the receipt of reports of the conduct of the campaign in St. Vincent dated October 9, 1772 and indeed these reports were by no means satisfactory as they indicated that the Black Caribs were getting the upper hand in the conflict.[85] Indeed in this campaign the Black Caribs did have an advantage. Few Englishmen had ever been allowed access to their territory and this access was for the most part limited to specific areas and on specific occasions such as the conference held at Morne Garou in 1771. Englishmen therefore had little opportunity of familiarising themselves even with those parts of the country in which they were allowed, let alone the whole of the Carib territory which was for the most part inaccessible. So while the troops were strangers to the terrain, the Black Caribs knew it well even in the dark, and in addition they were good strategists and fighters.

So effectively did they combine these advantages that when early in October 1772 the British had lost three men in attempting to cross Iambou and all the huts built as posts in their attempted penetration had been burnt down, the Governor-in Chief despaired of success. Indeed, this mood of pessimism was reflected in a despatch to the Home authorities:

> I flatter myself, we shall soon be able to give your Lordship some satisfactory account of our proceedings, tho I must confess the conduct of the Charibbs is more serious and formidable and I see greater difficultys in the execution of His Majesty's Commands tha[n] I expected. I very much fear their reduction will be a work of time, for they possess a country very inaccessible, and seem to have a knowledge how to avail themselves of this advantage.[86]

A hurricane in the Leeward islands added further complications to the situation as the ships of the naval squadron were disabled and so unable to rendezvous at the island. Indeed, so critical was the situation that additional reinforcements were requested.[87]

It was three months after this adverse report was received that the British Government finally decided to call off the expedition. When that Government instructed General Dalrymple to negotiate a treaty to end the war it was pointed out that the objectives of that treaty were the "welfare and happiness" of the Caribs and not their extirpation. Mention was also made of the administration's desire "to end the bloodshed on both sides" but great concern was also expressed at the fact that "the King's troops were preparing to enter upon a service hazardous in the execution and uncertain in the event".[88]

The proposed treaty however was not negotiated until February 1773. That this was so because the General was in Carib territory and did not receive the information in time seems unlikely. So too is the speculation that the treaty was proposed to the Caribs prior to February and rejected. It seems more likely that the General, in accordance with his instructions did not think it politic to negotiate before February in the hope that more would be gained by either pressing for a complete victory or a decided advantage so that in either case he could drive a harder bargain in the negotiations. By the end of 1772 his forces were divided into two bodies, one stationed at Majorca and the other at Grand Sable. At this time he complained that he had suffered many casualties as a result of the actual fighting, diseases, and also that the country was becoming more and more difficult to penetrate.[89] Early in 1773, his forces had still got no further than Grand Sable and with increasing casualties he probably despaired of complete military victory. As for the Black Caribs their mobility in this vicinity was restricted as a result of posts constructed by the

Figure 5 • Meeting between General Dalrymple and Chatoyer in St. Vincent 1773

General. In short at this time the war seemed to have reached a point of 'stalemate' and with neither side being able to declare outright military victory both parties agreed to sit down at the bargaining table. However, in retrospect, the eventual peace treaty and its immediate aftermath suggests that the Black Caribs/Kalinago were the immediate victors if there was one.

At the Peace Treaty the boundaries of the Black Caribs were pushed inward from the River Colonarie to the River Byera. Only a negligible portion of their land or roughly 2,000 acres was ceded to British settlers.[90] Not only were the colonists thoroughly disappointed but the Black Caribs vacated this portion only with reluctance and finally resettled it in 1775. Plantation lots disposed of at this time totalled 95,134¼ acres in Dominica, 57,401 in Tobago, 74,081 in Grenada and a mere 17,595 in St. Vincent. With regard to lands held on lease by French inhabitants, the acreage in Grenada was 14,200, Dominica 8,874¾, and St. Vincent 4,096.[91]

The year 1773 can also be regarded as the take off point for the sugar revolution. Indeed, the islands with the notable exception of St. Vincent had from a settler viewpoint developed remarkably well. This development was characterised by two main features – a massive importation of slaves and the consequent rise and expansion of sugar plantations, a process which had taken place earlier on in the older British West Indies and was to be repeated in Cuba in the 19th century. Between 1765 and 1773 Tobago imported 7,342 slaves and in the latter year alone 1,495 were imported.[92] Dominica's slave population had also more than doubled itself, with the total being 15,753 of which 5,295 were imported between April 1772 and January 1773.[93]

Sugar plantations developed rapidly because the British planters who monopolised most of the land displayed, not surprisingly, a tendency to devote their acreages to sugar rather than to any other crop. Of 46,261 acres of cleared land in Grenada, in 1773, 32,011 of these or nearly two-thirds were cut up in 334 sugar plantations.[94] In Tobago, 3,445 of a total of 9,601 cleared acres were divided into 103 sugar estates of which 41 had already begun production.[95] And in St. Vincent and Dominica where sugar was not produced before 1763, so keenly did the planters concentrate on this crop that it topped the export lists of the islands in 1773, with coffee and cocoa dropping to second and third places respectively.[96]

This concentration on sugar was given a boost in 1774 when the coffee producers who were mainly old French residents were hard hit by a fifty per cent drop in prices received for their berries on the German market. They were unable to make ends meet or to find alternative markets where they could sell at a profit and facing bankruptcy they sold their estates and emigrated. The estates were eagerly bought by English planters and converted into sugar plantations.[97] This occurrence represented the culmination of what to all intents and purposes was a remarkable transformation of the economy of the British Windward islands. As we have seen before 1763, it was the cultivation of coffee, cocoa, cotton and spices rather than sugar cane that dominated economic activity in the islands. All this was now replaced by an agricultural system based on sugar cane monoculture. By 1774, the foundations of a society and economy based on the twin props of sugar and slavery were laid.

CHAPTER 2

The erosion of the economic infrastructure

At a certain stage of their development the material forces of production in society comes in conflict with the existing relations of production or what is but a legal expression for the same thing with the property relations within which they had been at work before... With the change of the economic foundation the entire immense superstructure is more or less rapidly transformed.

– Karl Marx, Preface and Introduction to *A Contribution to the Critique of Political Economy* (1859)

The establishment of sugar plantations was quite a huge undertaking involving considerable expenditure for the land, plantation buildings and equipment and the purchase and maintenance of the labour force. In the second half of the eighteenth century, for instance, a sugar estate in St. Vincent consisting of 442 acres of land and 261 slaves required an outlay of £74,035.[1] Such large sums of money, the planters borrowed from mercantile houses in the metropolis to be repaid with interest and of course they hoped to make a profit on their investment.[2] This however they could accomplish only if the economic system remained relatively stable, or possessed the capacity to absorb dislocations effectively. This did not, however, turn out to be the case.

As early as 1772 for instance, the planters were hard hit by a credit crisis in the metropolis which resulted in the cutting off of loans for the plantations.[3] Again, after the fall in coffee prices in 1773, many planters who had borrowed and invested heavily in this crop because of the then existing high prices were unable to meet their obligations to creditors and went bankrupt.[4] Indeed, these were two early indications of the vulnerability of the economic system which depended on outside sources for its very existence and survival.

Perhaps the most important single factor contributing to this situation was the outbreak of the American Revolution and its consequences. This event precipitated the economic decline of the British Windward Islands by disturbing and interrupting one of the three basic trades on which the plantation economy depended – a trade with the mainland colonies of North America. The other two trades vital to the plantation system were a trade in slaves with Africa, and an export trade in tropical staples, mainly to Great Britain. However, the net effect of the American Revolution and its aftermath was that supplies of essential goods became scarce and terribly expensive making the West Indians high cost producers. The high cost of production in turn impaired their ability to compete on the market with other colonial territories producing similar crops.

All of this happened because the American trade was in one sense the most vital to the existence of the plantation system. The planters in the British Windward Islands as their counterparts in the other British West Indies devoted most of their acreages to the cultivation of staple commodities for export. Little land was put in food or in pasture to raise cattle, mules and horses which were essential in certain activities on the plantations. Neither did they attempt to conserve timber resources. During the period of settlement large numbers of trees were felled to make way for sugar plantations. As a result, the British North American colonies became the chief suppliers of food such as Indian corn, corn meal, beef, pork, rice, flour and saltfish, the last being of especial significance since it was one of the principal components of slave diet. In addition to food, the British North American colonies supplied large quantities of lumber, shingles, hoops and staves for making hogsheads, horses, cattle, mules bricks, candles, naval stores and rope. These commodities in turn, the West Indian colonists paid for in rum, molasses and sometimes sugar.[5] The planters' dependence on regular supplies of these commodities was vital and, in addition, the prices at which these were obtained became "an element of first rate significance in determining the cost of production and transport of the staple crops of the islands".[6]

The planters in the British Windward Islands were quite aware of this as demonstrated in an address of the Assembly of Grenada to the King just before the differences between the American colonists and Great Britain had reached the state of armed struggle. "Our existence," they declared, "depends upon a regular and constant supply of North American lumber and provisions", which could not be had from any other source "so quickly, regularly or cheaply." In view of their apprehension "of the worst consequences from any obstruction to that assistance and support" they demanded that Britain immediately compose and terminate the disputes between Parliament and the North American colonists.[7]

The fears of the plantocracy were soon realised after the outbreak of hostilities. In St. Vincent, for instance, lumber which sold at 90 shillings per 1,000 ft. before the war had risen to 800 shillings. Shingles which sold at sixteen shillings and sixpence per thousand had risen to one hundred and thirty-two shillings, white oak staves from one hundred and thirty-two shillings to six hundred and sixty shillings and saltfish from fifteen shillings to seventy shillings per cwt.[8] It should be clear that such huge price increases significantly increased the cost of production. Scarcities of lumber and provisions were also reported from all the islands.[9] The inhabitants of Grenada managed to survive for a time on captured lumber and provisions from North American vessels[10] but by 1778 the island was on the verge of a famine.[11]

The war itself was disastrous to the islands in other respects. Freight rates for example soared from three shillings and sixpence on a hundred-weight of sugar to ten shillings and sixpence.[12] Enemy ships captured vessels laden with imports, which included sixteen slavers bound for Dominica.[13] Vessels destined for Great Britain with tropical staples were also captured, and so serious was the menace that large supplies of sugar ready for shipping lay stored up on the plantations.[14] Before the close of the war, the islands were all captured by the French. The period of French occupation was generally disastrous. In Tobago, for example, the invaders burnt sugar estates and many planters were forced to give up their estates to creditors.[15]

In 1784, at the termination of the American Revolutionary War, the islands were returned to Britain at the Peace of Versailles. But the effects of the war were still to be felt and indeed would continue to be felt for the entire period covered by this study. Even though the increased charges paid for North American commodities had fallen, prices on the whole had not reverted to their pre-war levels.[16]

Planter appeals for a resumption of normal trading relations after the war fell on deaf ears. The Americans had also hoped for such a resumption[17] but British policy-makers decided that they could not have their cake and eat it too. By new Orders in Council promulgated in 1784, the West Indian colonists were allowed to import only specified items from the United States. The list enumerated included lumber, livestock, grain, flour and bread but these were to be carried in British vessels only. American saltfish, beef and pork were excluded and the colonists were told to place their principal reliance for these and all other commodities in future on British North America and Ireland.[18] After this defeat they sought for the establishment of free ports[19] when they believed that the American traders would be admitted to them but in this too they were disappointed, as the British government remained inflexible in its policy of excluding the Americans from the carrying trade of the islands.

The new regulations caused severe hardships in the islands and some of the colonists resorted to smuggling. American goods, for example, were smuggled into Dominica and St. Vincent from the French islands of Martinique, Guadeloupe and St. Lucia, and sometimes openly landed from American vessels in the ports with the connivance of custom officials.[20] Again, the governors were granted a discretionary power to open the ports to the Americans if a really genuine need existed, and the planters frequently and successfully pressured them to do so,[21] especially after 1794 when their hopes for a more regular trade were dashed to the ground with the refusal of the American Congress to ratify the Jay Treaty.[22] But even though these measures provided some relief, prices still remained high at the close of the eighteenth century.[23]

Between 1793 and 1803 when the American traders were frequently admitted to the ports by proclamations issued and renewed annually by the colonial governors,[24] the planters were provided with an invaluable outlet for their sugar, rum and molasses. Between 1794 and 1804, for instance, St. Vincent exported 708 hogsheads of sugar, 33,562 puncheons of rum and 6,296 puncheons of molasses to the United States.[25] In fact, in this period shipments of rum and molasses to the United States exceeded those to Britain and British North America.[26] In 1804 however, this outlet was closed as a result of the imposition of tighter regulations causing the planters great frustration and hardships.[27]

This was so because the planters viewed the United States not only as a supplier of cheap and plentiful commodities but also as a market and a profitable one too for the sale of plantation products. Demand in Britain for rum, for example was limited partly because the British Army and Navy, the heaviest consumers preferred foreign spirits such as brandy, which were cheaper,[28] and in addition Great Britain had increased the duties.[29] Rum was also shipped to British North America but here too, demand exceeded supply and prices were low. Annual consumption in British North America, for instance, was estimated at 2,500 puncheons or just about the combined production of two of the small Grenadine islands.[30]

In 1806, the average price the Tobago planter received for a puncheon of rum sold in Canada was between five pounds and seven pounds, and for the same quantity of molasses two to three pounds, and it was alleged that these prices did not even equal the cost of production in the island.[31] When it is considered that by 1807 the production of rum had expanded considerably, the need for alternative markets such as the United States, where, as the Dominica proprietors angrily protested, the product could be sold "at a rate which affords the planter a tolerable recompense for his labor"[32] could be appreciated. Sugar was in no better predicament. Between 1776 and 1807 the sugar duties had increased by 325%[33] and at this time, British revenues took by far the lion's share of the proceeds of the sale of this product. As a result the net revenue of the Grenada planters, for instance, declined by about one half in the space of 15 years.[34]

It was partly for this reason that the planters in the British Windward Islands, as their counterparts in the other British islands, had welcomed the destruction of the French colony of Saint-Domingue in 1793. The withdrawal from the market of the huge supplies from this

Figure 6 • Map of Grenada

colony created such a scarcity that prices were high. For a time it seemed as if the tide of economic decline was turning and once again the planters began to plan to make fortunes. But this period of prosperity was short-lived. Even while the world market for sugar was so favourable, the British government, concerned at the high prices in the metropolis intervened in the interest of the British consumer to bring them down by suspending the drawbacks and bounties whenever the average price in Britain rose above 50 shillings per

Figure 7 • Map of Dominica

hundredweight exclusive of duty, and also by the importation of sugar from the East Indies.[35]

But the planters still continued to expand production of new canes such as the Bourbon and Otaheite capable of producing higher yields than the old Creole canes. In 1798, for instance, it was reported that the inhabitants of Dominica were "all getting rich, owing to the wonderful produce of the Otaheite cane".[36] The planters of Tobago were also said to be "doing wonders with the Bourbon cane",[37] and indeed by 1807 the production of sugar had doubled. These large amounts of produce coupled with the reduction of prices in Britain and the unsatisfactory state of the market for rum, seemed to have increased the desire for alternative ones where surpluses could be more easily disposed of.

As Professor Goveia has pointed out, the great advantage of the American Trade was that it provided such alternative outlets.[38] Not only were the Americans good consumers of sugar and rum but at this time their carrying trade to Europe was decidedly on the increase and was conducted on cheaper terms than British shipping could afford. Again, when during the Revolutionary Wars at the end of the eighteenth century the frequent capture of British vessels at sea by France resulted in a decline in exports to the continent, the Americans who were regarded as neutrals were doing a lucrative business transporting the cargoes of both neutral and enemy colonies to Europe.[39] This increased the anxiety of the planters for a regular trade with the Americans.

The anxiety of the planters to increase their shipments to Europe at this time was heightened by the fact that the high prices on the world market were welcomed as a relief from years of depression. Indeed, before the destruction of Saint-Domingue, British West Indian sugar because of its uncompetitive price had been virtually squeezed out of the European market. A report submitted to the Privy Council in 1788 indicated that the cost of production in the French West Indies was 25 per cent less than in the British.[40] The French were thus able to sell their sugar at a much cheaper price than the British could afford to and the net result of this was that the British West Indian product remained largely confined to the British market with whatever re-exported being heavily dependent on a system of bounties and subsidies. The scarcity and high prices after 1791, however, allowed British West Indian planters to compete but the anticipated results were not realised. For not only did the suspension of bounties minimise profits, but so too did the importation of East Indian sugar and the re-export of foreign sugar warehoused in Britain without payment of duty.[41]

Again, with the resumption of war between Britain and France in 1793, the produce of colonies captured by Britain was imported into the mother country on the same terms as that of the British West Indies.[42] Another important reason for the low profits was the fact that the British West Indians were not the only producers attracted by the high prices on the market. So too were the Spanish, Portuguese, Dutch and Danes,[43] and so, after the first years of scarcity, the planters found themselves face to face with cheaper rivals. Then in 1799 continental demands fell off due in part to a financial crash, in which 82 firms that handled the British West Indian product went out of operation. This caused a sharp decline in the re-export of sugar to the continent, confining it mainly to the protected market in Britain which was also glutted with large amounts of foreign produce from the captured colonies of Demerara, Surinam, Martinique, St. Lucia and the Danish colonies.[44] The inevitable result was a fall in prices. Finally, with the institution of the Continental System in 1806, there was a further falling off in exports to the continent and by 1807 the position of the proprietary class had become critical.[45]

The planters in the British Windward Islands were extremely hard pressed. On one hand, the price of everything that they had to import had increased tremendously.[46] But while the prices of imports had risen drastically, that of exports had fallen in nearly the same proportion. In St. Vincent, for instance, the planter received a net value of £30 for each hogshead of sugar in 1798, but in 1799 the price received was only £12. In 1798 he received 7/- for each gallon of rum sold but only 4/- in 1799,[47] and 2/-6 in 1807.[48] Annual operating costs for a sugar estate with a labour force of 100 slaves was estimated at £4,902. 15/-, but the commodities produced fetched only £3,573.[49] This situation was typical of the other islands as a whole.

The plantocracy in the British Windward Islands was partly responsible for the economic distress that they experienced in 1807. Ever since the last decade of the eighteenth century, the measures adopted in Britain for price reduction should have indicated to them that it was unwise to expand production at such a rapid rate. Again they very well knew from their experience in the American Revolutionary War when their sugars could not reach the market, that wars generally disrupted overseas trade. But they paid no heed to such warnings, apparently because of their pre-occupation with exploiting to the limit a favorable price inflation even though the pursuance of such a policy had ruined the coffee producers in 1774. At that time the Governor of Dominica attributed the distress of the coffee planters in that island to their "setting out upon too unbounded expectations from the profit of coffee... which... carried them into schemes too enlarged for their abilities and credit".[50]

This same mistake was repeated after 1791, since high prices had become essential to the existence of the plantation system. When in 1792, the British government suspended bounties and subsidies, the Legislature of St. Vincent sent a strongly worded memorial to Parliament protesting the measure, because as one planter, put it, "it was only by such occasional instances good fortune [the destruction of St. Domingue] that we could retrieve our estates from debt and cultivate them in future".[51] This statement was applicable to the plantocracy in the British Windward Islands as a whole.

The years after 1807 were economically disastrous for the plantocracy. The continental blockade which drastically curtailed exports to the continent, for instance, would not be lifted until 1814. Again, commercial relations with America, already hampered by earlier restrictions were even more curtailed by the imposition of the Embargo and Non Intercourse Acts of the United States Congress in 1808.[52] The inevitable result was a serious shortage of food, lumber and staves, for making hogsheads. Dominica, which was hit by hurricanes in 1813 and 1814, was most seriously affected by the food shortage and many slaves perished. Sugar could not be shipped because of a lumber shortage[53] and in St. Vincent the planters were forced to resort to pulling houses down to make casks.[54] Not only did the planters experience shortages but high prices as well.[55] Indeed, these price increases were hard to bear at a time when the price of all British West Indian staples was depreciated. If we are to believe the Tobago proprietors, by 1811 they were not even making a sixpence return on each hogshead of sugar shipped from the island.[56] At this time, all the Legislatures addressed memorials to the home government asking for relief.[57]

With the breakdown of the Continental System in 1814, exports to the continent were resumed. But the long awaited relief was not realised. First of all, Great Britain reduced the drawbacks payable on re-exportation and subsequently discontinued them altogether.[58]

Secondly, the British West Indies were faced with two serious competitors, the Spanish colony of Cuba, and Brazil. The development of the sugar industry in these two territories had been relatively recent and they had the advantage of rich fertile soils and consequently lower production costs. According to Ragatz, while British West Indian sugar could not be profitably disposed of for 53s. per hundredweight after the drawbacks were discontinued, "Cuban cultivators grew opulent with theirs bringing a mere thirty shillings".[59]

The British West Indians blamed the government for their inability to compete. The Tobago planters, for example, argued that Cuba and Brazil were able to flood the market with cheap sugar because they had access to a trade in slaves which Britain had denied to its colonies in 1807.[60] But the available evidence indicates that access to the slave trade would not have been the solution to the problems of the British West Indians especially when we take into account the factor of soil exhaustion. In Dominica, for example, the repeated hurricanes in the eighteenth and nineteenth centuries made the soil sterile both for sugar and coffee by 1816[61] and in view of this situation it can be said that some of the islands had too many slaves. On the Grenadine island of Union Island, for example, where cotton alone was produced and where the total slave population was 652, the annual production on average for the years 1819 to 1822 was 283 small bales. In 1823 one half of the slave population was deemed enough to keep up the existing rate of production.[62]

The cheap and plentiful sugar of Cuba and Brazil not only squeezed the British grown product out of the European market; it also denied it access to the American market after 1823 in which year the British government relaxed its policy of excluding the Americans from the carrying trade of its colonies. Between 1816 and 1819, 5,000 slaves had died from starvation in Dominica alone[63] at great economic loss to the proprietors and the plantocracy in the British West Indies as a whole greeted the resumption of the trade with enthusiasm. But their hopes were not fulfilled. In St. Vincent, for example, the Americans refused to accept sugar in payment for lumber and provisions since it was possible for them to obtain it "cheaper at Cuba and the Brazills".[64] Neither did they accept rum since during the years when the restrictions were in force they had brewed their surplus grain into a liquor that sold at half the price of the British West Indian product.[65]

Indeed, by this time, the position of the plantocracy was even more critical. Their inability to compete effectively in the European and then the American market confined the bulk of it to the protected market in Britain. This monopoly, however, was threatened as early as 1814 when at the close of the Napoleonic Wars, the sugar territories of Mauritius, Demerara, Essequibo and Berbice were added to the British Empire. To make matters worse, Great Britain imported large amounts of East Indian sugar after 1815[66] which undersold the British West Indian product even though the preferential rates set against it in 1792 were still in force.[67]

The plantocracy in the British Windward Islands expressed extreme resentment at this situation. In Grenada, for example, the view was expressed that the British West Indies were of right entitled to a preference in the British market and that such countervailing duties should be imposed on the East Indian product as would ensure them a fair price for theirs.[68] The Dominican proprietors presented a petition stating similar views and further accused Britain of breaking "the irrevocable compact of mutual monopoly with its colonies".[69]

But as Eric Williams points out, the era of monopoly and preference for the British West Indies was fast coming to an end.[70] In their petitions the plantocracy argued about how valuable their enterprise was to the British economy, but as far as the British were concerned their monopoly of the market was too expensive. British self-interest dictated the monopoly had to go.

It is not surprising therefore that by 1823 bankruptcy was general throughout the British Windward Islands. In Dominica, for instance, even the most productive estates were not bringing their owners any return on their investments and others could not even meet operating costs.[71] Between 1808 and 1823 a total of 799 slaves were sold for debts and 2,197 were removed chiefly to Demerara and Berbice[72] where prospects seemed to be more promising. The proprietors in Tobago could not even pay the taxes on their estates.[73]

The St. Vincent plantocracy were also "in a state bordering on bankruptcy" and many estates were taken over by creditors.[74] In 1795, war with the Caribs had left in its wake, 53 estates burnt and destroyed.[75] In Grenada too, at the same time, a revolt involving whites, mulattoes and slaves did considerable damage to estates.[76] To tide the planters over their difficulties in these two islands, Parliament in 1796, authorised loans of £15,000 in Exchequer Bills to be repaid at the end of 1798 and extensions of time were subsequently granted until 1804 was given as the final deadline.[77] Some of these debts, however were not liquidated as late as 1806[78] and the plantocracy of St. Vincent became even more indebted after a volcanic eruption on the Windward side of the island, which eruption from the perspective of the Black Caribs would have represented punitive and retributive justice.

This was so as this was the area from which the Black Caribs had been expelled following their defeat in 1795. A controversy had delayed the establishment of sugar estates until 1811[79] in which year, the planters borrowed huge sums from merchants in Britain. A loan of £35,000, for example, had been made to two planters to finance an estate to be repaid in yearly installments up to the end of 1818.[80] But suddenly, the volcanic eruption wrecked everything, covering the ground with larva to the depth of ten inches and "destroying every appearance of vegetation".[81] Cultivation was not resumed until 1818 and only with extreme difficulty.

The sugar plantations in the British Windward Islands started to decline very soon after they were established and, indeed this decline was in some respects as rapid as their growth. This decline as we have shown was due to a combination of factors such as the loss of the American Trade, soil exhaustion in the case of Dominica, and inability to compete with non-British tropical territories, but there was also the hardships imposed by Britain's fiscal and economic policies, wars, and natural disasters such as hurricanes and the volcanic eruption in St. Vincent. But there were also other forces at work. The plantation system itself, as it functioned in the British Windward Islands, contained inherent structural weaknesses which if corrected might have helped to alleviate or mitigate some of the problems. But instead the planters adhered tenaciously to prevailing practices, ideas and assumptions. These will be discussed in chapter 5.

CHAPTER *3*

The failure of the federal idea 1763-1775: The interplay of commerce, law and politics

Law is the tool of the ruling class.
– Quinney (1974)

The disposal of lands in the British Windward Islands was not the only major problem that confronted British policy makers in 1763. Another equally important was that of administration. British administrators took into account the physical and spatial extent of the islands. Dominica, the largest, is 305 square miles in extent, St. Vincent 150, Grenada 133 and Tobago 114. In addition to the above they are situated at what was thought to be reasonably accessible distances from each other in an age when the sailing boat was the only means of communication. Hence, the question arose whether for administrative purposes each should be allowed under the representative system to govern itself separately, or whether all should be unified into a single state.

But there was the further question as to what form this unity should take. Should it be based on separate assemblies controlled by a single governor who would possess nominal authority only? Or should there be, despite the existence of the separate assemblies, one general federal assembly to which each island would send delegates, and possessing legislative authority which would be recognised as binding the four islands?[1] These were the questions on which the Board of Trade had to decide and Lord Egremont the Secretary of State submitted proposals for its consideration.[2]

Egremont expressed a preference for "an united general government" rather than "small independent ones" and therefore he suggested that "the plan of the Leeward Islands may be adopted and pursued, as far as the difference of circumstances will permit". Further, executive authority should rest in the hands of a Governor-in-Chief, and, although each island should have a separate assembly, there should be one general assembly composed of representatives of the various islands.[3]

In his opinion, this arrangement would provide the best guarantee for internal and external security:

> Whatever danger in time of peace might arise to any particular island, from a sudden commotion among slaves, Charaibbs or other low and worthless people no assistance in troops or stores, could be expected from the governor of any other island, as he would certainly be unwilling to send away, any considerable part, of the force allotted for his garrison, as it would be at his own peril and taking upon himself all the consequences which might happen during their absence – In short, the moving of troops, military stores, or provisions from one island to another, in any case cou'd not be regularly done, and with due authority unless by the orders of one Commander in Chief intrusted with general authority for the security of the whole...
>
> One general establishment for the islands with a particular Lieutenant Governor... plainly affords *a greater security* for each island both in peace and war.[4]

This arrangement would be the most suitable one, if the interests of the Crown and the cultivation of the lands according to the regulations were to be ensured:

> With regard to civil matters the expediency of having one *general governor and Lieutenant Governor* for these islands as well as *a particular one* in each, seems no less evident – for unless a person with chief authority unbiased by local connexions or views and earnestly zealous to promote real good of each settlement without injury to the rest and above all to maintain the interests of the mother country (which will be but little regarded in competition with present gain) I say unless such a

person makes visits, from time to time to the several settlements and exerts himself in conjunction with the particular Governors or Lieutenant Governors – the revenue of the Crown – the interests of Great Britain, as well as its laws – Justice among its inhabitants – good order among the slaves – cultivation of the granted lands according to regulations and many other essential points will be much expos'd to suffer.[5]

A further argument for unification was administrative convenience:

If these islands are form'd into one general government; the business of them both civil and military would be much less various and distracting to the officers in England than if in separate independent ones because it will be the duty of the Chief Governor to receive from time to time, reports or informations from the several Lieutenant Governors, to transmit them with his own observations to England and to communicate (as well as enforce if necessary) such orders as may be sent to him in reply – In other cases when it may seem unnecessary or prejudicial to wait the arrival of orders, it will be his duty to give such directions in the interim as he judges to be best for the publick service as may safely be answer'd for.[6]

Unification would also reduce the expenses of administration:

And lastly I shall only add, that besides being more *compleat, respectable,* and *secure* it will be less expensive to the publick, then such establishments of independent Governors and Lieutenant Governors to each island, as cou'd be rely'd on without inspection or controul.[7]

It is significant to note that underlying some of the reasons given by Egremont for unification, was the belief that local jealousies and conflicts which might arise to defeat the intentions of Government if each island was given a separate independent establishment, could be contained and frustrated in a federation. Indeed he did not see that in a federation these local jealousies and conflicts could lead to disintegration, although he did not rule out the possibility of separation at some stage in the future.[8] In this and other aspects he was truly optimistic, even though the example of the Leeward Islands federation should not have given cause for optimism. The federation he argued, should work smoothly as communications at least should pose no problems. Indeed, the islands were even better off in this respect than the Leeward Islands:

It seems only necessary to add, that by the happy situation of these islands with regard to the trade wind and usual current there maybe a quick and continual intercourse kept up between them, an advantage wanting in the General Government of the Leeward Islands.[9]

Yet, ironically, local jealousies and problems of communications were two of the most important factors contributing to the failure of the federal idea.

Most of Lord Egremont's suggestions were accepted by the Board of Trade, and indeed they formed the basis of the plan that was finally approved. In their report to the king on this subject, the Board of Trade stated that:

We are of opinion that the erecting of all these islands into one general government, with a subordinate Lieutenant Governor in each as is now practised in the Leeward Islands, will be better adapted, as well as to the application of military power to the protection of the whole than either the separating of them into distinct governments or leaving those of St. Vincent, Dominica and Tobago under the commission of the Governor of Barbados.[10]

Grenada was chosen as the seat of Government and the residence of the Governor-in-Chief, although Lord Egremont had recommended Dominica instead, because he felt that it was strategically situated, "for distressing the French colonies on the right and left (in case of war) and of cutting off all communication between them".[11]

By letters patent dated October 4, 1763, General Robert Melville was appointed Governor-in-Chief of the new colony, and he was specifically instructed to summon and call general assemblies of the islands 'jointly and severally'.[12] He was further required "frequently to visit the other islands, in order to inspect the management of all publick affairs and thereby the better to take care that no disorderly practices may grow up contrary to our service and the welfare of our subjects".[13]

Melville arrived in his new government in January 1765 with the intention of putting into effect the plan of a General Assembly but he was confronted with a number of problems. One was the claim of the French naturalised Roman Catholic subjects of Grenada to vote and stand as candidates for election to the Assembly and nomination to the Council, without subscribing to the declaration called the Test. Some limited concessions were granted by the British government when in 1766 they were given the right to vote[14] and two years later the further right to put up three of their number as candidates for election to the Assembly.[15] Higham argues that this problem of Catholic representation was "one of the main distractions" which prevented Melville from giving his attention to the federal assembly,[16] but even though this might have been so, no matter how zealous Melville might have been it would have been almost impossible for him to succeed in implementing a scheme which public opinion clearly did not want.

A second problem was the lack of qualified freeholders in all the islands with the possible exception of Grenada. This island as we have seen was the most exploited of the group and it was the first to attract purchasers.[17] In the other islands the quantum of qualified freeholders would be determined by the progress of the sales of land subsequent to the arrival of the Commissioners who did not reach the West Indies until March 1765.[18] In addition, the progress of land sales was initially very slow. At the end of 1766, Tobago had only 20 freeholders, Dominica 7 and St. Vincent 36.[19] To complicate the position further all the purchasers did not remain resident in the islands. Although by early 1768 for instance, 77 individuals had purchased lands in Tobago only 20 of these were actually resident in the island. Of the remaining 57, four were residing in Britain and the others in St. Vincent, Grenada, Barbados and the Leeward Islands.[20]

But the major problem that confronted General Melville was deep insular prejudices especially at Dominica. It was mainly because of these that the proposed general assembly never met all and in the end each island was allowed to go its own way. The outer islands as Higham points out, strongly objected to any federal assembly at Grenada,[21] but he ignores the important fact that a significant body of opinion in Grenada did not want it either. In this sense, the stand that Grenada took assumes a certain degree of importance. It was the first island to have a separate establishment, and this was so not simply because it had enough freeholders for this purpose. It is also possible that this event strengthened the less vociferous islands in their determination to have separate establishments, rather than a few delegates to a General Assembly, although even without Grenada's stand this is what they preferred.

On the new proposed constitution, there was a division of opinion at Grenada between the local residents and the absentee merchants and planters, and both groups presented petitions to the British administration in 1765 expressing their different views. Again, Higham does not mention this important point. The petition of the residents with 47 signatures was presented to Melville on April 19,1765.[22] While expressing no objection in principle to a federal assembly, they also asked that a particular assembly be immediately convened for the island in order that "a variety of evils" might he rectified. They wanted first of all to change the Capitation Tax, a legacy of French rule in the island, and which they complained was "unequal, ineffectual, liable to evasion, and burthened with exemption", for some other efficient mode of taxation. This was very urgent, as there was a "variety of absolutely necessary public expense" to be defrayed in building churches and paying clergymen, constructing a government house, Court house and other public buildings, and repairing and mending the roads. There were no impediments tending to militate against the institution of the Legislative machinery that was necessary for the implementation of these plans, since unlike the other islands, Grenada had "a sufficient number of protestant freeholders and merchants to form a particular assembly... consisting of as many members as those of Barbados, Antigua or St. Christopher".[23]

They further stated that Grenada was entitled to this as of right especially as they had already paid the 4½ percent export tax. But when the outer islands had a sufficient number of freeholders, those, it was stated, would be free "to join such as may be elected here to form a very full general assembly".[24]

But although there was no objection in principle from the local residents to a Federal Assembly which they saw as something possible in the future, it is clear that they were not prepared to accept it at all costs. Their main concern centered around contributions to a common revenue fund to defray the expenses of the public offices shared by the islands.[25] Grenada was financially better off than the other islands as it was the most developed and most prosperous in 1763, and was at this time the sole contributor to the salaries of the public officers. The residents were not at all satisfied with this arrangement: "The other ceded islands share in the benefits arising from the establishment of public offices; and (we) therefore submit... whether, in point of equity, they ought not to pay their proportions towards these establishments."[26]

It was projected that at the expiration of "a little time" they would be in a position to do so, as two of them were already yielding "a very considerable produce", and if a general assembly was convened in the future, their delegates would have the right to fix their own quotas. But until this question of quotas was fixed by a general assembly, they wanted an assurance that "so much of the expense of the establishment as exceeds the just proportion of Grenada... may be... reimbursed by the Treasury".[27]

Two significant points emerge from this petition. First, the island was concerned more with protecting its own local interests rather than with a larger whole. Indeed, this explains the demand for a particular assembly to solve what was regarded as its immediate and pressing needs which might be jeopardized if it had to wait on the calling of a general assembly. Secondly, it seemed to be suspicious of the intentions of the other islands on the question of contributions towards the establishment. The fact that it asked the Treasury for reimbursement for the sums expended above what was thought to be its fair share, seems to indicate that it felt that these sums would or might not be refunded by the other islands whose economic developments it was watching closely. Indeed, these feelings of suspicion and preoccupation with local interests were the main reasons why the federal assembly never got beyond a paper scheme.

While the local residents expressed no objection in principle to a federal assembly and seemed to indicate that they were willing to accept it sometime in the future so long as it did not mean the assumption of any unfair obligations, the absentee proprietors and merchants took a completely different view, and expressing strong objections to any federal assembly at all, they petitioned for the establishment of 'a complete legislature', conformable to the powers vested in the Governor-in-Chief.

To the reasons given by the local residents, they added the precarious situation of many titles to land, the need for an established rate of interest, and for a fund for surpressing the Maroon slaves who were impeding the progress of the settlement of the island by acts of sabotage:

> These and other inconveniences, can only be remedied, we presume, by calling a distinct and separate assembly for the island of Grenada; *the plan of a general assembly being in our apprehension subject to many objections from the distance and situation of the other islands, and liable to produce great diversity of interests, which may impede or wholly prevent the regulations necessary to each particular island.*[28]

At first, Melville did not know that the absentee merchants and planters were averse to the calling of a general assembly. Indeed, with some justification he interpreted the petition of the local residents as a sign that the island was committed to the federal issue and so he wrote home in April 1765 announcing with optimism his intention of calling the general assembly.[29] It was in the reply to his despatch that he was informed of the absentee view point, and specifically cautioned not to take any action "but upon the best and matured deliberation".[30] At this time both petitions were being considered by the Board of Trade and its recommendations to the King could be regarded as a sort of compromise although they favoured more the absentee viewpoint. The Board of Trade argued that the reasons given by the absentees for the formation of a distinct assembly "do appear to us to have great weight", and that Melville should be instructed to establish a distinct and separate assembly for the island. But as they saw it, the establishment of the separate assembly did not mean separation since the initial plan was that each island should have a separate assembly which would be permanent and lasting, whereas the general assembly would be of temporary duration meeting only on occasion.

The Committee of Council for Plantation Affairs accepted this view and Melville was instructed to form a distinct and separate assembly for Grenada alone.[31] Soon after, the Grenada election ordinance was drafted to this effect because "the emergencies of government in Grenada, are so great and pressing, as to make in [sic] indispensably necessary to call together the representatives for Grenada and the Grenadines before the other islands have a sufficient number of freeholders to enable them to send representatives to the General Assembly".[32]

The powers of the Assembly were limited to Grenada only. Indeed, it was made quite clear that:

the representatives of Grenada and the Grenadines, assembled in this island, without representatives from Dominica, St. Vincent and Tobago, shall be deemed, and held to all intents and purposes, as an Assembly for Grenada and the Grenadines only, without having any power, or exercising any authority whatever, over the above aforesaid islands, until they shall have been called to send their representative to the said Assembly.[33]

The anxiety and determination of the other islands to have separate assemblies of their own was increased following the establishment of the Grenada Assembly. In September 1768 the Privy Council agreed on the establishment of separate councils and assemblies under a Lieutenant Governor in each island,[34] but Melville had already established them. This was due to local pressure from the individual islands concerned who saw in separate councils and assemblies a greater degree of protection and security for local vital interests than could be ensured in a federal assembly.

Indeed, each island seemed to be jealous and suspicious of the intentions of the other. Early in 1765, the Lieutenant Governor of Dominica wrote home complaining of "that jealousy which manifests itself too strongly between the several new colonies in these parts, as well as between these collectively and our former settlements."[35] The Governor-in-Chief was quite "uneasy" when he found out that the Grenada absentees did not want a federal assembly at all, but early in 1766 he realised that the planters in the other islands were "averse to it even for a short time". Opinion in St. Vincent was that in a federal assembly which had obligations regarded as binding, the island might be forced to assume unjust and unfair obligations which might adversely affect its local interests. Objections were also raised against spending what was regarded as unnecessary time at Grenada for meetings of the federal assembly.

On those two objections, Melville was careful to give clear and specific assurances. On the first, he pointed out that he would "not assent to any arrangement but what seems quite fair and equal to all the islands" if any such thing was suggested, and on the second he made it quite clear that he would "when the assembly takes place, endeavour to have all the business relating to the distant islands done within as small a compass of time as possible, so that their representatives may not be long detained (unless they chuse it) from their private affairs".[36]

The inhabitants of Dominica expressed fears similar to those entertained by the planters of St. Vincent. In an effort to mitigate these, Melville despatched the following correspondence to the Lieutenant Governor of the island:

> As to all laws respecting justice, internal police and the government of slaves, and such like matters, I apprehend that there would be a pretty general concurrence and dispatch, especially as I should imagine that many of the laws which have been found best in the neighbouring islands might with some few alterations (where necessary) be very well adopted by us and continue in force at least till experience should show their faults and dispatch. And as to taxes, should any have been thought necessary by the representatives they must have been laid on particularly for each island, for their particular purposes, and with regard to my assent without which no law would be enacted, the majority of the representatives for the island taxed would have had the proper weight.[37]

Apart from what he regarded as the "trifling expense" towards defraying the "extraordinary charges" of the representatives of the various islands "for a short time" at meetings of the General Assembly, "no inconvenience or detriment could possibly happen".[38]

But the advantages and safeguards which Melville hinted at were not sufficient to allay the fears and suspicions of the other islands. What they wanted was separate assemblies of their own. Melville was quick to realise this and so, soon after the first meeting of the new Grenada Assembly in April 1766 he decided to make a tour of them "to gain... a knowledge of the real present circumstances and disposition of the various inhabitants", after which he would "establish their legislatures to their advantages and satisfaction" as soon as each had enough freeholders.[39]

At the end of 1766 a petition signed by forty-eight inhabitants of St. Vincent was presented to Governor Melville asking for "a separate Legislature establishing a Council and House of Assembly of Representatives". They claimed "that from the want of a power of taxation among us, no fund can possibly be raised to satisfy the exigencies of the island". There was "a heavy load" of public debt remaining unpaid for the past two years, and it was urgent that it be discharged before it further accumulated. In addition, they needed to construct and repair roads to facilitate communication between the various parts of the island, to build gaols, a court house and other public buildings.[40] A Federal Assembly was not the solution to these problems: "We daily experience many other great inconveniences... from the want of a separate legislature *composed of residents and persons thoroughly acquainted with its conditions, who only (we conceive) can consider of and form proper laws for its Government.*"[41]

Melville quickly responded to the wishes of the islanders. In May 1767 he issued the writs for the election of members to the Assembly which met for the first time on May 12.[42]

Grenada, being the most developed and populated island of the group in 1765, could not wait on the islands which were less so, for the formation of a general assembly, and so had gone ahead and established its own to solve its immediate needs, and for most part unconcerned with the larger whole. Following Grenada's lead, St. Vincent with its own problems to solve and also being more peopled than either Tobago or Dominica, had gone ahead too and established its own Assembly. After St. Vincent, it was Dominica's turn, but before we discuss the movement here, we will look briefly at that in Tobago.

Towards the end of 1767 a petition signed by twenty-eight of the inhabitants was presented to Melville asking for the establishment of a separate council for the island. The absence of some sort of legislative machinery it was argued, was impeding the progress of the development of the island, which "soon would grow into consequence" if some such apparatus was established.[43] But the establishment of the Council was seen only as a temporary expedient, since there was at this time not enough inhabitants to form a complete legislature. In the meantime however, the council would "make such regulations as may be deemed expedient under the present circumstances... until a regular civil government and constitutional legislative power shall be established".[44]

Melville agreed, and decided to constitute a council of twelve persons for three months in the first instance since in his view the requisite measures "cannot amply be effected but by persons constantly resident in the said island (Tobago) and perfectly cognisant of the particular circumstances and situation thereof".[45]

Soon after the establishment of the council, however, Melville was besieged by repeated representations from the inhabitants calling his attention to "the pressing necessity" for the establishment of a separate Assembly, but at first he declined because in his opinion there were still too few resident purchasers in the island.[46] But the continuous pressure necessitated a personal visit to the island to view the actual situation and by the middle of the year he had issued writs for the calling of the Tobago Assembly.[47]

Although objection was expressed to the proposed federal assembly at St. Vincent, Grenada and Tobago, nowhere was this objection as vociferous, bitter and intense as at Dominica. It is significant to note that St. Vincent, Grenada and Tobago, seemed to have had no objection to some kind of unity. What they did not want was this unity to be manifested in the form of a federal assembly. They did not object to a chief governor resident in one island so long as they had their separate assemblies and councils. It must be admitted, however, that this unity would be only partial and not effective as the chief governor's authority would have been nominal only. But even this nominal unity was objected to by a significant body of opinion in Dominica even though it was favoured at first by some residents. Hence as in Grenada, there was in Dominica for a time, what might be called two parties expressing different views on the federal issue. But whereas in Grenada, the parties differed as to how this unity should manifest itself, in Dominica the struggle manifested itself between those who desired unity and those who wanted the island to be completely separated from the government of Grenada.

The inhabitants of Dominica expressed fears that the island's interests would be adversely affected so long as it remained a part of a federation in which the seat of government was stationed in another island. Soon after the first Lieutenant Governor arrived in the island in 1765 he received "complaints of the oppression or neglect of this colony in favour of that which is the seat of government".[48] Indeed, the inhabitants seemed to have been firmly convinced that the proposed federation would be beneficial only to the island which was the seat of government. In support of this contention they cited the example of the federation that had formerly existed in the French West Indian Islands of Grenada, Guadeloupe and Martinique with the last named island being the seat of government. As a consequence: "It (Martinique) has been brought to its highest pitch of culture these forty or fifty years past, whereas the former are very little more than half cultivated to this day... and... the same causes will generally speaking have the same effects."[49]

That Martinique's economic superiority was due to the fact that it was the seat of government is debatable. The point is however that the inhabitants of Dominica believed it and were determined that what had happened to Grenada and Guadeloupe should not happen to Dominica. But the belief was that the island was already suffering under Grenada's hands. We have seen how initially the settlement of the island was slow. This was so not merely because the island was not as suitable for sugar cultivation as the others, or because the allotments for sugar plantations were too small, or because the price of land was too high.[50] The main reason was that it was felt that certain essential preconditions for a successful settlement such as defence, and also the economic development of the island as a whole, could never be ensured while the island remained a part of the Grenada government. The island, it was argued, "will advance at a snails pace" unless it was made a separate government.[51]

The distance of the island from Grenada was used as a strong argument for separation. Strong objections were raised at the fact that the Governor-in-Chief and the Council "round which everything moves", and the Superior Courts and Records were "distant from this place between 60 and 70 leagues", and "nothing of the least moment can be done here without going or sending there, although it often costs a man who has anything to transact as much time and money as it would to go to London".[52] Although, vessels plying between the two islands usually made the distance in four, five or six days, there were times when this same distance took four, five or six weeks "owing to the currents and calms". The situation was even worse in the hurricane season which generally lasted for three months, when there was "little or no communication" between the islands.[53]

The inhabitants were terribly aggrieved because of the expense of going to Grenada to transact business, and the inconveniences to which they were subjected because of the inadequacy and infrequency of communication. But on this problem of communication, even more important than routine business matters, were considerations connected with defence and security, especially in the event of a war. We have seen how the inhabitants were particularly concerned over this subject of defence.[54] Despite the fact that plans had been drawn up for the defence of the island since 1765, there had been "not... a single shilling laid out upon any kind of fortifications", for "defending the property of the people who might settle here", and this caused great uncertainty.[55] They did not know whether the plans had been approved of as there was no word from Grenada on this head. Even the Lieutenant Governor had earlier on expressed his "utter ignorance... of every part of His Majesty's instructions concerning the government of these islands", and complained of the delays and inconveniences he experienced as he had to refer everything to the Governor-in-Chief at Grenada with which communication was difficult.[56]

If it was dangerous and risky to await orders from Grenada concerning the defence of the island in peace time, it would be even more dangerous and riskier if there happened to be a sudden rupture of the peace: "In case of emergency in wartime when the Lieutenant Governor must be under the necessity of waiting for orders from the Commander-in-Chief, all might be lost before he could receive them or have power to defray the expenses of putting himself in any kind of posture for defence."[57] This situation could only be avoided by the establishment of "a Council and a House of Assembly as all his Majesty's other islands have excepting the ceded islands", and a separate governor with exclusive control over defence.[58]

The separatist movement intensified after Prince Ruperts and Roseau were declared Free Ports late in 1766. At this juncture, a striking insularity motivated by the desire for economic and commercial gain was strongly manifested. Indeed as early as July 1763, a few months after formal cession of the island had taken place, the military commander wrote home suggesting that a free port should be established in the island, and it is significant that the first settlers to arrive in the island were merchants.[59] The military commander was "very desirous of promoting their commercial views", and so at their instigation the first site he chose for a settlement was changed because in their opinion it was "ill situated for trade".[60]

During the time he was stationed in the island, Lt. Colonel Dalrymple impressed upon the home government the necessity of establishing free ports there. "There seems", he wrote, "a good field of commerce open to us from our late connections with our neighbours which may be advantageously carried on underhand but much more so if the port was open".[61] Actually, he deliberately encouraged this illicit trade, taking precautions that the French carried "nothing away from us that is hurtful to the national interest".[62] This trade flourished after 1763. In 1765 Lt. Governor Scott had to make application to Governor Melville at Grenada for assistance in checking the progress of this contraband trade which, he stated, "has been very considerable from this island".[63]

This illicit trade with the French islands of Martinique and Guadeloupe involved the exportation from the island of North American commodities, slaves and British manufactures, and the importation of cotton. And the balance of trade was clearly in Dominica's favour. In July 1766 it was said that in the four months before, the merchants imported 2,000 bales cotton from the French islands but at the same time they exported 7,000 barrels beef, 3,000 barrels flour, 12,000 slaves and:'a great quantity of fine broad cloath with metal buttons, Manchester velvets and fustians, Irish linens, checks osnaburgs and cutlery, wares and iron mongery, printed linens, shoes, stockings, tea and refined sugar, beer porter, cheese, beans, hats, sadley wares and household furniture.[64]

In all, the cargo of 70 New England vessels which had come to the island had been transhipped by the local merchants to the French islands, and it was said that the demand was so great that if they had thrice the quantities of slaves and provisions all would have been disposed of, even though the French had guardas costas at Martinique and Guadeloupe to prevent this trade.[65] Hence the urgent need for a free port; for if this trade were legitimised not only would it expand greatly,[66] but the possibility existed that it might be extended to the Spanish Islands.[67]

But the desire for a free port was not confined to Dominica alone. Indeed, other British West Indian islands were also interested in acquiring this privilege, and it was a time when absentee merchants and planters were manoeuvring in Britain to get free ports established in those islands in which they were interested. The inhabitants of Grenada were just as interested as those of Dominica in securing this privilege. Grenada was admirably situated for trade with the

Spanish territories as Dominica was for that with the French. Indeed, as early as 1763 the demand for British manufacturers brought Spanish traders to the island who engaged in contraband with the inhabitants with the connivance of the civil commander. "I have hitherto," he wrote, "given it all the encouragement in my power and will continue to do so" until the home authorities directed otherwise.[68]

It is possible in this contest for free ports lay the seeds of much of the friction between Dominica and Grenada. The Dominicans felt that if this trade was allowed in the West Indies, their island would "from its situation alone... have very near the whole of it" and because of this other islands might "murmur".[69] But this did not matter, because what was important was the fact that it would cause the island to become in a few years "as opulent, formidable and more flourishing, both as to produce and trade, than any of the islands, excepting Jamaica and Saint Dominique".[70]

The news that Prince Ruperts and Roseau were made free ports in 1766 "caused great rejoycings" in the island, but it was said to have had "quite a different effect upon our fellow subjects in our sister islands", because they did not get this concession. Grenada was one of the islands that was mentioned as being jealous of Dominica in this respect.[71] But despite this felicitation the inhabitants of Dominica took strong objection to certain clauses in the Free Port Act. One was the duty of 36/- sterling to be imposed on every slave imported into the island. The other was that which subjected all the island's produce except certified rum and sugar imported into Britain to foreign duties. It was felt that these clauses "would render abortive, or at lease cramp in a great degree the advantages intended to this island by making it a free port". But more so, the opinion was expressed that these clauses were inserted at the instigation of the "friends" of those islands which were dissatisfied and jealous of Dominica[72] and so wanted the "excellent plan" of free ports altered to the island's disadvantage.[73]

It is significant to note that at this point, the separatist movement changed its position. Indeed, before this event no one called for complete separation of the island from the Grenada government. But soon after the arrival of the Free Port Act, it was everybody's opinion: that one thing ought to be done – that is, the erection of the island into "a separate and independent government".[74] Of course they gave clearly discernable reasons why this was so, but it seems reasonable to suggest that the current belief, that Grenada, the headquarters of a federation of which the island was a part, had "connived" with the other islands in getting the objectionable clauses inserted in the act, reinforced old fears and strengthened the separatists in their determination to have nothing at all to do with that island.

Hence, at the beginning of 1767 a petition was sent to the King asking that the island be entirely separated from the government of Grenada and be "given a Legislature of Governor, Council and House of Assembly elected by the people". It was argued that because the island was a part of the Grenada Government, its inhabitants were denied the British constitution, which as British subjects they had a right to enjoy. For since 1763 no Courts of Justice were held for the trials of criminals as a result of which "murderers, robbers and dangerous disturbers of the peace" escaped with impunity leaving them "a prey to the rapacious band of villany" since the Governor-in-Chief who was Chancellor and keeper of the seals resided in Grenada where only suits in Chancery and Error were triable. Persons involved in these suits were unable to attend because of the "tempestuous passage" and above all "the time it must necessarily take them from their occupations and family". This almost total stop to the course of justice and the general "state of confusion and unhappiness", could only be rectified by the establishment of a regular civil government in the island.[75]

The incidence of crimes in the island however might not have been as great as was made out, and was probably grossly exaggerated in the hope of extracting the concessions demanded. For the real objection against travelling to Grenada to attend courts had very little to do with cases of this kind. Indeed, they arose out of economic and commercial considerations, considerations which became more important when free ports were established. But in this petition they did not say so even though they used the establishment of the free ports as an argument for separation:

> As by an Act made in the sixth year of your Majesty's reign relative to the trade of this island, it is put upon an entire different footing with your Majesty's other West Indian Colonies, your petitioners most humbly apprehend a separation from the government of any other island would be the more necessary.[76]

Indeed it was felt that the free ports would not operate smoothly because the Lieutenant Governor would have little power to decide disputes which might arise, and that it would be prejudicial to the parties concerned if these had to be tried at Grenada. Very soon after the arrival of the Free Port Act, an argument used for the separation of the island from Grenada was that:

> among the concourse of different nations that will undoubtedly flock here to settle or trade, disputes will happen, and cases that cannot well be decided by the Governor-in -Chief, or the Council at Grenada; from whence will arise a hindrance in business and tedious delays that are too often detrimental to trade.[77]

The establishment of the free ports also made it the more necessary that something should be speedily done about the defence of the island which it was felt could never be ensured while it remained a part of the Grenada Government. But now, in the concern over defence, the emphasis was not laid only on what might happen in wartime, but probably more so, on what could happen or rather what was actually happening to the trade of the island in peacetime. We have seen how before the arrival of the Free Port Act the islanders were engaged in a lucrative illicit trade with the French islands, and the belief was entertained that if this trade were made legal it would increase.[78] But the Free Port Act gave rise to smuggling. Indeed it was because of the fear of smuggling that all Dominica's produce except certified rum and sugar entering Britain were classified as foreign. The opinion was clearly expressed that because of this "the planters will rather risk smuggling their coffee, etc. over to the French, than send them home to Britain".[79] This trade was of course beneficial to the planting interests, but it could adversely affect the mercantile interests since raw cotton exported from the island to Britain was processed and re-exported to the island for export to the French islands.

But the merchants were not affected as much by this as by the illicit entry of French manufacturers. Attempts were made to smuggle many French manufacturers such as brandy, soap, silks, wine and other luxury articles into the island, and these entered into competition with similar British products. It was said that the persons engaged in these operations "often succeed", because of the island's "almost total want of external as well as internal security". What was needed therefore, was a legislature to raise funds and make laws to protect the island's trade, and a separate governor who would also check the progress of this illicit trade. And the island had "for a long time past, persons of character, reputation and property... more than sufficient to form a complete legislature".[80]

In their struggle for separation they were aided by the merchants of London and Liverpool who were their partners in the free port trade. Both these groups presented supporting petitions on their behalf although at the same time they were looking at their own economic interest. The merchants of London held the view that the free port trade could only be successful if the island "had all the advantages that might be given to it for the security of the merchants trading thither".[81] But these advantages were sadly lacking. Indeed it was forcefully stressed that "Dominica being dependent on Grenada or any other island, for the determination of suits at law, and consequently property must obstruct, and indeed in a great measure defeat the good intentions of government in making it a free port.[82] It was also observed that:

> the present necessity of transferring suits of law to Grenada for final issue, has already damped the spirit of settlement at Dominica, as the agents and factors of your petitioners are in case of appeal, obliged to follow their suits in person to Grenada; at great expense and hazard, as well as loss of time, which no trade can support.[83]

Therefore, in order not to "defeat the good intentions" of the British government in making the island a free port, it was essential that it be given a government and a legislature "independent of Grenada or any other island".[84]

The Liverpool merchants also deplored the inconvenience of referring suits to Grenada for final issue. Grenada they argued, was "too remote to obtain the speedy redress requisite in every case of justice... which, in the many instances of small debts, is clogged with an expense that renders all application impracticable.[85] Furthermore "these disadvantages which distress the colonists of Dominica, extend to the merchants of this port, since the inability they labour under of recovering their own debts, prevents them from making their due remittances here".Hence it was imperative that regular courts be established in the island.[86] In this connection it is pertinent to observe that the political directorate in Jamaica, Barbados and Trinidad and Tobago in misconceived advocacy for a proposed Caribbean Court of Justice as a final Court, as if cognisant of the eighteenth century objections and concerns which are still relevant today has attempted to temper and contain same by recommending that the said Court be an itinerant Court. It is important to note also that save and except for Tobago for whom Trinidad purports to speak, St. Vincent, Grenada and Dominica, have not signed any instrument signifying intent to be a constituent component of the proposed Court in a manner that would dispense with appeals to the United Kingdom Privy Council.

Although this petition was not as radical in its demands as that of the London Merchants, like that petition, it was asking for the same thing – the separation of the island. For the call for regular Courts of Justice meant the establishment of similar courts as in those islands which were separate and independent, especially a Court of Chancery in which a Governor presided. Even if a separate Court of Chancery was set up with a Lieutenant Governor in the chair, the island would be to all intents and purposes independent, since the Governor-in-Chief would have nominal authority only.

Faced with these strong demands, Secretary of State Earl Shellburne referred the matter to the Board of Trade for a decision. Before coming to any final decision however, the Board called in for consultations Mr. Shaw, agents for the merchants, traders and inhabitants, several absentee proprietors and merchants, and other merchants with interests in the island.

During the discussion, the suggestion was put forward by the Board that all that was needed to remedy the inconveniences was the establishment of a separate council and House of Representatives and separate courts as was the case in the Leeward Islands, and that there was no need to burden the island with taxes for the support of a separate governor. It was stated that some of the "principal proprietors" who had signed the petition for a separate governor and government "appeared to acquiesce in this opinion", but at the same time they were careful to point out that they had no other objections to a separate governor except those arising out of considerations of the cost. But the merchants disagreed with this view, arguing strongly that a separate governor would help to check the progress of the illicit trade with the French, which had of late increased considerably.[87]

But although the Board of Trade accepted the planter viewpoint, it strongly endorsed the mercantile view:

> Although we do agree in opinion that many of the grievances and inconveniences stated in the several memorials...may be remedied by the establishment of a separate Council and Assembly and by constituting separate Courts of Judicature; yet we humbly submit, that these grievances and inconveniences though they are objects of your Majesty's care and attention, are not however the only considerations in this important question; there are others of great weight arising out of the peculiar situation and commerce of the island.[88]

These they listed as the situation of the island between Martinique and Guadeloupe which in time of war exposed it to "constant and imminent danger", and in time of peace, facilitated contraband trade which the French were only "too eager to avail themselves of". So although the free port opened up prospects of commercial gain, these would not be realised unless regulations were "most carefully and as strictly enforced" to prevent the extension of "that prejudicial trade".[89] When these factors were taken into account:

> we cannot be of opinion, that it is expedient or adviseable, that the government of it should continue to be administered and the military force necessary for its protection, commanded by a person, whose residence is in another island, so remote in distance, and the communication with which, is, from the nature of the seas, and the situation of the possessions of France, so tedious and precarious, and therefore we think that it is necessary for the security of this important island, for the interests of the proprietors of land there, and for the advantage and improvement of commerce, that it should be erected into a separate government, independent of Grenada or any other island whatever, and with a separate Governor having authority both civil and military, competent to every emergency which can happen.[90]

Earlier in 1767 Governor Melville had expressed a willingness to establish a separate Council and Assembly in the island, but he regarded it as impracticable as there were only seventeen or eighteen resident freeholders.[91] He was definitely opposed to the complete separation of the island from his government and he made this quite clear to the home authorities early in 1768 when he heard what the

Board of Trade had recommended: "However proper such a measure may become some time hence, it would be for the present premature."[92]

Indeed it was because of this consideration that he speeded up his plans for the formation of the Council and Assembly in 1767 after he heard what was intended, and after a request from the inhabitants:

> I shall accordingly do it confiding fully that should even a separation take place (as suddenly as has been pushed by for some, and is reported to be intended) yet that so great an affront to myself or injury to the colony cannot happen from a just and enlightened administration as to reverse a constitution which I may have legally formed according to the powers vested in me with the General Council and for the best purposes, as well as in compliance with the very general and earnest wishes of the colony – beside that it would (I apprehend) be no ways inconsistent with a separation of government should that be judged necessary.[93]

Before the end of the year 1767 he had formed a Council and called an Assembly. The creation of the separate Assembly "will best convince everybody here that the scheme of a mock Board of Trade and frequent embassies is not approved of as some here have the confidence to assert".[94]

But Melville was doomed to disappointment. He was severely censured by the home authorities for establishing the Assembly when he knew that the island's constitutional position was under consideration, and it was decided to investigate the whole policy he was pursuing with regard to the constitution of his government. He was called home to justify his actions[95] and his deputy was instructed to prorogue all Assemblies pending the receipt of further instructions.[96] Again the establishment of the Council and Assembly gave the separatist movement a forum to express their dissatisfaction with the constitutional position of the island, contrary to Melville's expectations.[97] The Assembly had to be dissolved in January 1768,[98] and again in February when it was reconvened, because there arose "such matters of difficulty and contest from the remaining agitations of party spirit" over the constitutional position of the island.[99]

In this contest over the constitution it appears that whereas the majority of the members of the Assembly favoured immediate and complete separation, the Council did not. Both parties rigidly adhered to their different points of view, but according to Melville there was the possibility of some accommodation being effected through the efforts of Mr. Pringle, the President of the island. But the rumour that a change of government was absolutely decided upon by the Board of Trade, coupled with the arrival of a 'mischievious lawyer' from England, "overset every sober idea and worked up the Chamber of Commerce, and those of their body in the legislature, to such a pitch of elevation and violence, that no terms of arrangement could be received", and the Council and Assembly refused to meet for the transaction of public business.[100]

This situation continued for about two months, until Lieutenant Governor Young assumed command of the civil government of the island. He was instructed by Lord Hillsborough to intimate to the contending parties his intention of assisting them towards the separation of the island from Grenada so long as they were all agreed on the expediency of the measure, and were prepared to raise a salary for the support of the governor.[101] Both groups subsequently drew up petitions and in these there was a striking unanimity, although Melville had felt otherwise and had expressed the view that "Some of the most sanguine promoters of that measure have begun to cool, declaring that the island is not yet ready for it, nor able to bear such charges."[102]

The Council called for "a separate government, unconnected with any other".[103] The Assembly asked for "a separate and independent government distinct from any other island".[104] In both petitions, the inconvenience of attending courts in Grenada and the danger to which the island was exposed in wartime were forcefully argued. These were the two main grounds on which the Council based their claim, especially the danger of attack in wartime from the fact that vessels from Grenada would have to pass near the French islands. They said nothing at all about the free port trade.

The free port argument, however, was used strongly by the Assembly which was composed mainly of merchants who it must be remembered were the first settlers to arrive in the island.[105] It is true that in their petition mention was made of the fact that 12,000 acres were sold in 1768, that this was the largest amount sold so far, and that this was due to the fact that people were encouraged to settle because of the hope that the island would be made independent. But the main emphasis was put on the free port trade, a trade which:

induced many persons of opulent fortunes to become settlers here as Merchants and planters, who would never have ventured their lives and fortunes in a new colony so immediately situated between two of the most powerful French islands were they not in the hopes of being independent of any other island for the formation of their laws and the completion of every other legislative business whatsoever.[106]

Further:

that notwithstanding the natural and acquired advantages of this island, it has not arisen to that increase of population and commerce, it might otherwise have justly pretended to owing to its being dependent on another island and which is and has been productive of much expense, and great inconveniences to the inhabitants; tending, as they justly apprehend, to defeat the many advantages... it should enjoy.[107]

A supporting petition was presented by the absentee proprietors in London[108] and because of the continued pressure[109] the home government yielded early in 1770. After the investigation into Melville's conduct was over, he was ordered as soon as he returned to his government to tell the inhabitants that it had been agreed to set up "a separate and distinct government" in the island.[110]

No attempt was made by the British government to establish a federal assembly for the three other islands after Dominica was made a separate government. When William Leyborne succeeded Melville as Governor-in-Chief in 1771, the Board of Trade in drafting his commission commented that "As the Grenada government does in the general form of it assimilate to that of the Leeward Caribbee Islands, we have accordingly framed the drafts upon the plan of the Commission and instructions given by Y. M. to William Woodley, Esq., Governor of those islands, nor do they in any respect materially differ therefrom."[111]

Yet, as Higham points out, the Commission omitted the crucial words 'jointly and severally', the essential feature which differentiated the Leeward Commission from that issued to all other colonial governors.[112] In effect this meant that the plan to establish a federal assembly had been abandoned and the reason for this must have been a recognition of the fact that the prevailing mood of public opinion was clearly against it. So rather than attempt to implement a scheme that had already been objected to, the Board opted instead for the loose association of three colonies under a Governor-in-Chief. But even this partial unity was soon to disappear under pressure from the people of St. Vincent for their own governor, and as a result of the vicissitudes of war.

The inhabitants of St. Vincent asked that the island be separated from the Grenada Government when they were experiencing difficulties with the Black Caribs. After the war of 1772, the Black Caribs had by the resultant treaty of February 1773 agreed to cede 1,990¾ acres of land to the British and their boundaries were pushed further inwards from the river Colonaire to the river Byera.[113] But although they had agreed to this on paper, they were not prepared to respect it in practice.

Three months after the treaty had been signed, the Governor-in-Chief after a visit to the island, reported that the Black Caribs had returned to their old quarters, building new huts, falling off wood and cultivating their lands again, without any apparent intention of returning to that part of the island allocated them by General Dalrymple'.[114] He did in fact hold consultations with Chatoyer and several other chiefs in an effort to induce them to remove, but not much was achieved:"Tho' some of them promised to go to Windward others seem'd determined to remain in their grounds with a firmness that surprised me." Nothing short of the use of force would induce them to remove.[115]

Early in 1774 the Black Caribs were still occupying the lands which according to the terms of the treaty they had agreed to vacate, and from which they had been subsequently requested to do so. In March of that year when Governor Leyborne paid another visit to the island, the 70th regiment stopped there on its way to England. He saw this as a good opportunity to attempt to effect the removal of the Black Caribs.[116] Accordingly, he held consultations with the Chiefs and gave them a period of eight days within which they were to remove to the portion of the island allocated them. Shortly after, the 70th regiment, acting under his instructions, burnt some 415 houses leaving only an occasional hut for the occupation of a few Caribs who were to reap the crops within the eight day period.[117]

It is not clear whether the Black Caribs had removed at the expiry of the eight day ultimatum. But even if they did so at that time, it was not long before they went back. In May 1775, the Lieutenant Governor reported that the Black Caribs had "resettled on all the lands...

ceded by the treaty, in many places fully as numerous, and in all as openly as they were before the treaty".[118]

It is also not clear whether Governor Leyborne remained in the island to see if the eight-day ultimatum would be obeyed. The important point, however, is that the inhabitants seemed to have believed that the problem was not being effectively dealt with since there was no one with chief authority constantly on the spot to devote full attention to it. That official resided in Grenada and had to deal with not only the problems of St. Vincent but those of Tobago and Grenada as well. He could not be everywhere at the same time – and in fact in Grenada itself he had inherited two constitutional problems which needed urgent solution.

The first centered around the claim of the Assembly to have sole control of the levying and disbursement of public funds, and the connected right that all moneys raised should be paid into the hands of a Treasurer nominated by that body, rather than to a Receiver General appointed by the Governor. This privilege it claimed shortly after it came into existence and it refused to pass any money bills unless its demand was met.[119] Indeed "so fixed and united were their determinations against the Receiver General", that Melville had been forced to give in to their demands in 1767, or otherwise "not a shilling would have been raised".[120]

Shortly after Governor Leyborne assumed command however, Lord Hillsborough expressed the view that that method of raising money was "liable to great objections and inconveniences", and he instructed him to induce the Assembly to give up its claim.[121] For his guidance, he sent a copy of Instructions that were earlier issued to the Governor of Jamaica during a similar dispute, which stated that he was not to give his assent to any law for raising money which did not expressly declare that the money would be paid to the Receiver General.[122]

But the Assembly refused to give up its claim. When for instance, they passed an Act granting the Governor a salary, they tacked onto it a clause that the money raised by that Act should be paid to a treasurer of their nomination, and the Governor refused his assent.[123] Subsequent efforts to induce them to accept the imperial point of view were fruitless.[124] This dispute dragged on for the entire period of Governor Leyborne's administration with the result that no money was raised to discharge the public debts of the island and it was not until 1776 that an Act to this effect was passed.[125]

The second problem centered around the claim of the French naturalised subjects who were Roman Catholics for political rights equal to those enjoyed by the British colonists as agitated for under the previous administration of Governor Melville. However, up to the time that Governor Leyborne assumed command only the right to vote had been conceded. The rest of the instructions had not been carried into effect because the British born subjects had opposed them on the grounds that no one had a right to fill positions of trust without subscribing to the declaration called the Test, and when the governor announced his intention of implementing them, they made it quite clear that they would continue to oppose them. This had the effect of alienating the French naturalised subjects to such an extent that the colony became virtually divided: "The breach between his Majesty's old and new subjects is of such a nature, so little intercourse between them, such a thorough want of confidence and in short so rooted an enmity that I see but very little hope of a reconciliation."[126]

Towards the end of 1771 Governor Leyborne attempted to admit a Roman Catholic to the Council and although all the Protestant members showed their disapproval by walking out of the chamber, the measure was nevertheless carried through.[127] Early in 1772 he had admitted another Catholic to Council, three to the Assembly, and in each parish he had appointed one Catholic to be a Justice of the Peace.[128] The British born subjects became thoroughly angry as a result of this action. Such was their resentment that it was thought unwise to appoint a Catholic as Assistant Justice in that year,[129] and when an attempt was made to do so in 1776 they unanimously opposed it.[130] The Protestant members of the Council continued to declare that the admission of Roman Catholics to that body was illegal;[131] in the courts Protestant jurors were reluctant to sit on the same bench with Roman Catholic jurors[132] and, as Edwards writes, with "the most zealous of the protestant members of the Assembly declining to attend, it was seldom that a house could be formed".[133] The result of all this he continues, was that: "Public affairs soon fell in the utmost confusion, and in this state of faction and perplexity the island continued until its recapture by the French in 1779."[134]

This was the situation which confronted Governor Leyborne in Grenada at a time when it was reported that the Black Caribs in St. Vincent had been resettling the lands which they had agreed to vacate, collecting arms and ammunition from the French islands, and strengthening their fighting force which numbered 1,600 with runaway slaves.[135] At this point the inhabitants immediately asked that the island be made "one separate independent government", because "[it] *alone fully demands and is well worth all the attention that a Governor in Chief can bestow on it and which particularly from the unsettled troublesome situation of affairs in Grenada,* and the diffused extent of that command, *it cannot possibly now receive from* the Governor in Chief".[136]

It is possible to suggest, however, that they might have believed that the Governor-in-Chief had regarded the problems of the island which was his residence, as being more urgent and of more immediate concern to him. Therefore if the Carib problem was to be effectively dealt with the island ought to be given its own Governor, and this was further seen as "the most effectual method of securing to the mother country all the vast benefits which may be reaped from this colony".[137]

The British administration took no immediate decision on this proposal. The inhabitants, however, kept up their struggle as the Carib resistance continued,[138] and finally on January 26, 1776 St. Vincent was made a separate government "in view of troubles with the Caribs".[139] The separation of St. Vincent from the Grenada Government meant that only Tobago and Grenada remained in the union. But in 1776 the American Revolutionary War broke out and before it ended all the islands were captured by France. At the peace negotiations between England and France in 1783, England succeeded in regaining Dominica, St. Vincent and Grenada, but lost Tobago to France.

In 1783, therefore, of the four islands which had formerly constituted the Grenada government, only three remained in British hands. Of these, two (Dominica and St. Vincent) had already been made separate governments. Only Grenada did not have this status, but the island with which it shared a common governor was lost to France. It was therefore made into a separate government. It seemed only right in the circumstances existing in 1783 that this should be so. For it seems likely that any attempt at this time to establish even a loose association of the three islands, even if Grenada wanted it, would have been undoubtedly opposed by St. Vincent and Dominica for two reasons. First, such an arrangement would have necessitated a lowering of their constitutional status, a status which Dominica had since 1770 and to which St. Vincent had only recently been elevated. Secondly, and undoubtedly more important, was the strong sentiments shared by the inhabitants of both islands, especially Dominica, that their vital interests could not be ensured in such a constitutional arrangement. Therefore, when in 1793 Tobago was recaptured by Britain,[140] that island was given its own governor as the three islands which had formed part of the original federation had already been constituted into separate and distinct governments.

The reasons for the failure of the federal idea should have emerged sufficiently clearly during the course of this discussion. Indeed the difficulties of communication and more so the local jealousies proved to be invincible obstacles. But if any one factor can be isolated as being of special significance, it is commercial jealousy. In Grenada a significant body of opinion felt that federation had really nothing to offer the island. Even the less radical group felt that federation might be a drain on the country's financial resources. It is possible to suggest that both groups entertained these notions because their island was the most prosperous of the group, and they saw no reason why they should help the less developed islands which might rival Grenada in future.

The outer islands were also thinking solely in terms of their own economic development and prosperity, and especially in the case of Dominica the feeling was that this would be jeopardized in a federal assembly or even in a loose association. Hence, island councils and assemblies, and in some cases separate governors seemed to guarantee to the islands concerned a greater degree of protection for these vital economic interests than a federal assembly or a common governor could. Finally, while one cannot criticise British policy makers for attempting to impose a constitution on the Leeward Islands pattern, one can criticise them for being a bit too optimistic about its success. That comparison was not only "misleading"[141] as Higham points out, but the working of the model should have given rise to disillusionment rather than optimism, since by 1711 the narrow, selfish interests of its constituent components had reduced it to ineffectiveness.

CHAPTER 4

The legal / judicial and political systems

The legal system is first and foremost a means of exercising political control available to the propertied, the powerful and the highly educated. It is the weapon and toy of the hegemonic bloc of classes and class factions whose rough consensus it sustains. As such it lies hidden beneath a shroud of discourse, ritual and magic which proclaim the Wisdom and Justice of the Law.

– W.G. Sumner, *Reading Ideologies: An Investigation into Marxist Theory of Ideology and Law* (1979)

We have seen in the previous chapter how the plan for a joint legislature for the four islands comprising the Windward group fell to the ground. Indeed, beset with many problems since it was first mooted, the scheme was finally dropped after the separation of Dominica in 1770. Despite Dominica's secession, however, there was still up to 1776 some partial unity among the three other islands and from then between Tobago and Grenada until they were captured during the American Revolutionary War.[1] Administratively these were under the jurisdiction of a Governor-in-Chief who resided at Grenada and his was the office of highest rank in the islands. In St. Vincent and Tobago the office of highest rank was that of Lieutenant Governor. In the absence or death of the Lieutenant Governor the civil command devolved temporarily upon the President in his capacity as most senior member of the Council.

Before the emergence of separate political structures, attempts were made to establish a common administration for the whole group. Thus the islands shared the three patent offices of the Secretary Register and Clerk of Crown, the Provost Marshall and the Naval Officer. In addition they shared the revenue offices of the Receiver General of Casual Revenue and the Collector and Comptroller of Customs. All these offices were in the hands of absentees and were divided up among the islands through the practice of deputation.[2] Indeed, Lord Egremont had recommended a federal government for the group partly because of his belief that the public offices would have been patented out and shared among the islands as was customary.[3] Each island therefore had its own Deputy Receiver, Deputy Marshall, and Deputy Secretary. The office of Deputy Secretary carried with it a certain degree of prestige and importance because of its emoluments. In 1773 its profits amounted to nearly £2,000 and it was said that this sum exceeded "considerably the net profits of the last year, almost by one half", and indeed its annual value was "very certain".[4]

This practice of patenting out offices to individuals and moreso individuals who were frequently absentees had the effect of making the administration weak and at times ineffective. It meant that the representative of the Crown had very little control over his administration since the holders of patentees were responsible to those from whom they held their deputations and not to the Governor. On this problem, Governor Melville wrote as follows in 1770:

> The Clerks of the Councils in these islands are usually the substitutes of the Deputy here of the patentee Secretary residing in England; and sometimes (as in cases of sickness or absence) only persons acting for these substitutes, whose payment comes from the Deputy Secretary, and is such as they settle between themselves. The Clerks of the Assemblies are of their nomination and receive such salaries as they are pleased to grant... By these circumstances and the instructions relating to the patentees and deputies, your Lordship will be able to judge, pretty exactly, of the authority which the Kings Governor has over them.[5]

In 1792 the Deputy Comptroller and Commissioner of Customs and the Deputy Secretary of Dominica were granted leave by the holders of the offices who made provision for the discharge of their duties in their absence without consultations with Governor Orde. Orde subsequently protested to the home authorities about the problems that could be created from such a situation in which patentees had the power to grant leave and provide for the performance of their duties "without the control of the Governor" for, he wrote, "a Governor [may] be left to cooperate with men, not duly appointed and qualified, unknown and disagreeable to him, unacquainted with their duties; and only with such means of subsistence as the generosity of their employers only afford".[6]

Yet, despite this warning the practice continued with serious effects upon the administration. For instance, Griffin Curtis who was appointed Secretary Register and Clerk of Crown in 1795, left the island three years later and in1818 he was still absent.[7] In 1813 Governor Ainslie thought it fit to suspend him from his duties[8] but on appeal he was reinstated by the home authorities.[9] Because of his prolonged absence and his frequent changes of deputies, it was said that there had been no correct minutes of the Court of Vice Admiralty which fell under his portfolio since 1804, and everything was in "the utmost irregularity and confusion".[10] This deplorable state of affairs continued until 1818 in which year Curtis tendered his resignation only because the emoluments of the office had fallen off.[11]

In addition to separate groups of officials and separate legislatures, the islands had separate Courts. Each island had its Chancery Court, proceedings in which were based on practice in England and over which the Governor presided. These Courts were frequently used by debtors to secure injunctions against proceedings by their creditors and the Master and Examiner were nominated by the Governor.[12] Each island also had its Court of Vice Admiralty presided over by judges recruited from the local resident whites, whether they were legally trained or not. For instance, Mr. John Audain, a clergyman who was "not a person of competent abilities to discharge the duties of the office", was Judge Surrogate of the Vice Admiralty Court in Dominica in 1803, a time when many enemy vessels had been seized in the Napoleonic wars, and because of his lack of legal training it was feared that "sentences not perfectly legal may take place".[13]

In addition to its Chancery and Vice Admiralty Courts, each island also had a full complement of Courts for dealing with civil and criminal cases. At Grenada for instance, there was a Court of Common Pleas, Kings Bench and Grand Sessions of the Peace. The Court of Common Pleas heard all civil actions between subject and subject and was initially composed of one Chief Justice and four Puisne Judges. The Court of Kings Bench and Grand Sessions was a Court of criminal jurisdiction only and heard cases where the King on behalf of the public was the plaintiff. The judges consisted of the Members of the Council, and the judges of the Court of Common Pleas with the oldest member of Council sitting as President. The island also had a Court of Complaint for the recovery of debts under £10, and a Court of Error.[14] However with the decline in numbers of the white population due to absenteeism, it became extremely difficult to recruit the numbers required for these Courts and so adjustments had to be made to cope with this situation. Formerly the Court of Error consisted of the Governor and not less than five members of the Council. In cases where any member of Council was a party to the trial, three other members were required to sit. But at the end of the eighteenth century members had to be limited to the Governor and three other persons.[15] At the same time too, and for the same reasons, it was deemed politic to merge King's Bench Grand Sessions and Common Pleas into one Supreme Court of Judicature.[16] The judicial system was completed by a Court Merchant staffed by justices of the Court of Common Pleas, for the trial of all actions for debt not exceeding £200 involving persons trading to the island.[17]

In 1776, the Secretary of State had expressed the view that he wished to see all the law offices in the islands "filled with men of knowledge in their profession and integrity in their lives".[18] But despite this hope the administration of justice became heavily dependent upon the work of untrained judges. For instance, in most of the islands the office of Chief Justice was held for the most part by men with no legal training. In St. Vincent, Drewrey Ottley whose only qualification was that he was a planter, held the office of Chief Justice from 1767 to 1793 and again from 1799 to 1804.[19] When he died, his successor William Taylor who held the office from 1805 to 1811 also had no legal training.[20] When in 1805 Elphinstone Piggot was appointed Chief Justice of Tobago, he was the first barrister ever to hold the position.[21] His predecessors, Walter Robertson and John Balfour were both untrained.[22]

This deplorable situation is no longer the prevailing norm in the Commonwealth Caribbean in that save and except for the Justices of the Peace who preside at the Petty Sessions Court and exercise a limited civil and criminal jurisdiction, the Resident Magistrates and the Judges of the Supreme Courts and the Courts of Appeal are all legally trained. However, the prevailing practice of making most judicial appointments to the Bench from the Civil Service on grounds inter alia of length of service tends in effect to sacrifice competence and scholarship to seniority and sentimentality.

It was indeed very difficult to get qualified men to fill these positions as the emoluments were generally unattractive. When for instance, John Balfour was Chief Justice of Tobago he received no salary, only an allowance of £200 per year.[23] This was supplemented by fees but these were also very inadequate. As Chief Justice Ottley of St. Vincent said, "no professional gentlemen would be expected to give up the emoluments of his profession for an appointment of much trouble and responsibility without emolument."[24]

The above observation of Chief Justice Ottley is as relevant today as when it was first made, notwithstanding the fact that the emoluments of the Chief Justice and indeed all Judicial Officers cannot be said to be unreasonable in all the circumstances and taking into account Caribbean realities. However, leaving aside the question of financial reward actual and/or potential, the prevailing civil service ethos, autocracy, authoritarianism, the abuse of and corruption of power as well as perceptions of political interference generally inhibit any consideration of aspiration to judicial office by members of the private bar, who cherish their independence of thought and action, principles which are hallowed and incompensatable and not to be sacrificed to any apparent notion of judicial security of tenure whatever that may connote. Indeed, the last imbroglio between the President of Zimbabwe and the Chief Justice as well as other members of the Judiciary, threatened by the President with removal and/or early retirement for failure to give judicial decisions consistent with governmental policy is a timely reminder to the Caribbean people. It is also significant that in an article in the *Daily Observer* of March 14, 2001, the Attorney General of Trinidad and Tobago sought to defend himself from charges of attempting to influence a decision of Justice Archie who threw out motions brought by two junior ministers of the then Basdeo Panday administration.

Three years after the restoration of Tobago to Britain, the President complained to the home authorities about the disadvantageous effects that the lack of trained judges was having upon the island:

> There is a variety of points of litigation arising in Courts of Law which can only be decided by professional men; and nothing can be more injurious to the commercial and general credit of a colony than to have the decisions of its courts of justice depending upon persons not educated to the bar, and who have never had opportunities of acquiring any professional knowledge either in theory or practice.[25]

He was of the opinion the situation was truly critical as there were "many difficult causes arising from irregular grants, and other disputed proceedings under the French government [which] must inevitably be decided in a Court of Justice".[26]

In an attempt to rectify this situation, the Legislature voted £500 per annum for the salary of the Chief Justice provided the incumbent was a Barrister with ten years experience.[27] The home government also agreed to supplement this with an extra £500 to make the office more attractive. But this did not initially have the desired effect because as Chief Justice Balfour pointed out no gentleman "of respectability in his profession could support himself in the island in the rank of Chief Justice on a salary of £1000 per annum independent of the expense of coming here and making an establishment".[28]

In 1788 the Legislature of Grenada realising the evils of having such an important office filled by untrained men, passed a resolution to the effect that it should be filled by a person of "integrity, ability and experience". They voted £1000 as an annual salary and had success in getting a barrister to accept the position.[29]

But although the Legislature might have wanted someone of ability and experience it seems that they did not want someone of integrity. Rather, it seems as if they wanted someone whom they could manipulate as they chose, someone who would give the kind of judgments that they liked whether or not these were just according to the merits and demerits of the case. Critics of the proposed Caribbean Court of Justice have voiced this concern in Jamaica in connection with a possible motive for the abolition of Appeals to the United Kingdom Privy Council and the replacement of that Court with the Caribbean Court.

Indeed the legislatures were in a fairly strong position in this respect since they were the ones who not only chose the incumbent but fixed his salary usually for not more than a year. Realising the evils of this, Governor Shipley in 1814 suggested that a fixed and permanent povision should be made by the legislature for the incumbent, so that he would not feel indebted for the amount that he received "to any personal canvas or personal favour".[30] For instance, Richard Ottley who was appointed Chief Justice at this time had actually started to perform duties before his salary was fixed and had to decide on cases in which some members of the assembly were defendants. As the Governor rightly feared "his situation must be embarrassing when compelled to decide on the property of those who perhaps in a few days afterwards are to fix the quantum of his emoluments".[31] In short if he wanted a fairly lucrative salary he had to be careful not to 'offend' those defendants who were members of the Assembly. In this connection it is pertinent to observe that despite provisions for security of tenure for judges and other 'safeguards' in Commonwealth Caribbean Constitutions, the perception persists that the independence of the Judiciary smacks more of appearance than reality.

In fact, Governor Maitland had earlier on in 1805 attempted to avoid the evils that might result in the judicial system because of the influence of the planter class. He had suggested to the home authorities that the Chief Justice should be "some gentleman distinguished by good sense, learning and integrity, who is a perfect stranger to all the inhabitants, and to any of the proprietors resident in England". The appointment of such a person, he argued, was "essential for the well-being, and happiness of the colony".[32] Clearly then such a person had to be recruited from abroad and not from the local resident whites as was customary. In retrospect, it can be said that these observations of Governor Maitland appear prophetic and are of extreme relevance today in view of the arguments advanced in favour of the retention of the United Kingdom Privy Council as well as expressed fears of interference and manipulation by the political directorate in the affairs of the proposed Caribbean Court of Justice.

The home government agreed with Governor Maitland and appointed Mr. George Smith an English barrister, under whose administration an edition of the laws of the island was published in 1805.[33] The assembly voted him a salary of £2000 per annum.[34]

Chief Justice Smith was indeed a man of integrity and so there was little place for him in a corrupt slave society. In this society with a political system dominated by a small oligarchy of white slave owners who were determined and accustomed to build up their power and prestige by any means no matter how unjust or unfair, it was very difficult for someone who either rejected or refused to conform to these values, to be comfortable. If he was not prepared to conform then he should leave. Chief Justice Smith was forced to take the latter alternative.

This happened in less than two years after Mr. Smith's arrival on the island. One Mr. Adye who had been Chief Justice before Mr. Smith, and who was also a member of Council, was defendant in a case that was being tried by one Mr. Ottway who was also a member of the Council. The plaintiff was one Mr. Westmoreland who in 1797/98 acted as Clerk to Mr. Adye and had brought an action against him in 1806 to recover a sum of money that Mr. Adye owed him as his salary. Chief Justice Smith anticipating an absence from the island instructed Judge Ottway to let the trial abide his return. But the case was nevertheless tried and initially, the jury decided to award damages to the plaintiff in the sum of £170.16.4.

However, when Chief Justice Smith returned to the island he discovered that after the jury had so decided Mr. Adye was permitted to proffer arguments to show that the Statute of Limitations should be applied to the case. The plaintiff's housekeeper who was a coloured woman was then allowed to give evidence in which she stated that she had gone on behalf of her master to Mr. Adye's home to request payment of the money owed and that she was told to call back in a day or two. But Judge Ottway ruled that the evidence of a housekeeper was insufficient in law to take the case out of the Statute of Limitations because, in the opinion of Chief Justice Smith, he was certain that the error in the law on this point would not be detected. When the plaintiff appealed and a new trial was convened, the final verdict was given in favour of Mr. Adye against the plaintiff with Judge Ottway voting in favour of his own decision.[35]

Chief Justice Smith was infuriated because he felt that a deliberate miscarriage of justice had taken place, since in his opinion the argument of Judge Ottway that a housekeeper's evidence was insufficient to take a case out of the Statute of Limitation was invalid, and that the other justices had accepted this argument which influenced their voting because they were ignorant of the law. He therefore made the revolutionary suggestion that the votes and opinions of Assistant Judges who were not qualified ought not on a point of law to have equal weight with those of the Chief Justice as long as he was a legally trained person.[36]

The Governor agreed with these sentiments. Since on points of law there was "much uncertainty" even among the most learned judges, he argued, then the decision of a man who never studied law at all, on a legal point, could only be "a vague and hazarded opinion" which, even though it might be given with the best intention, should not be received with any confidence "because it is delivered without any clear understanding of the science it is assured to proceed from".[37]

But these ideas were too far-reaching to be adopted in a slave society in which deliberate misuse of power and corruption were features of everyday life. The Council and Assembly unanimously opposed the suggestions. Since the cession of the island in 1763, they were given a British constitution and a judicial system that was sanctioned by the British Government. Hence they were prepared to resist "any innovation subversive of our happy constitution.... Every judge has and ought to have an equal voice and authority", and the Chief Justice "can and ought to be no more than primus inter pares".[38] Is this view held by the judiciary in the Caribbean today? And further, "The proposition for abrogating the rights and privileges of the Assistant Judges in order that the absolute powers of the Court may be centered in one man, betrays an attempt and desire incompatible with that indifferent and unambitious disposition which is ever the characteristic of a good and great judge."[39] Lastly, no precedent existed for this "even in the worst times" in England.[40]

Although the Council and Assembly based their rejection of the new suggestions on what appeared to be strictly legal and constitutional grounds, it is possible to suggest that there were other considerations. They were annoyed because Chief Justice Smith was indirectly striking at the abuses in the judicial system. For the incident which gave rise to Chief Justice Smith's suggestions indicates clearly how the influential whites used the political and judicial process at their disposal to their own advantage and against the less well off of their class just as they used it to enforce the political and social subordination of the free coloureds and the slaves. Although the evidence indicates that the clerk had a good case, yet, because he was a person of small consequence in the society compared with Mr. Adye who was a large planter and a member of council, he was denied legal redress.

In the Caribbean today the judicial system still tends to discriminate in favour of what we in Jamaica call 'the big man', a term correlative with race, class, complexion, social status and other invidious distinctions emanating from slavery. The late Peter Tosh's call in song for "equal rights and justice" is an expression of this reality today as it was then. In this situation there was little that Chief Justice Smith could do, except leave the island. It is significant that his successor Richard Ottley whose judgments were notorious[41] lived in peace with the inhabitants on a lucrative salary of £2500 per annum.[42]

In addition to separate legislatures, separate groups of officials and separate courts, each island had its own Militia constituted by an Act of the Local Legislature. It was generally composed of all able-bodied white men between the ages of 16 and 65 and free coloured men of the same ages who served in inferior positions. It was composed chiefly of foot soldiers sometimes with a section of cavalry and artillery.[43] The main function of the Militia was to quell any local uprising particularly among the slaves, even though its numbers were quite small compared to the total slave population. For instance, in1816 the total strength of the Militia in Grenada was 700, 150 of whom were generally inactive due to sickness[44] whereas the total slave population was 21,699,[45] which would give a ratio of about one free adult to every 31 adult slaves. But as a standby in case of need, there was additional defence provided by the British Government.

The British Government maintained a naval dockyard at English Harbour in Antigua on which the islands were dependent for naval protection[46] and there were garrisons of regular troops stationed in

Tobago, St. Vincent, Grenada and Dominica. But the islands were also expected to contribute towards their defence by providing grants of money and black labour to work on the fortifications, and quarters and rations for the troops. As Professor Goveia points out, this system had the advantage not only of making available a reserve of imperial force, but also of spreading the cost of imperial defence over the Empire.[47]

But the Legislatures were by no means always willing to assist the Imperial Government in measures for the defence of the Empire. Indeed, even when the West Indies had become a battleground during the American Revolutionary War the Legislature of Grenada refused a request from the Governor to purchase provisions for the troops stationed in the island.[48] When however there was an imminent fear that the island might be captured, the Legislature reluctantly granted 150 slaves to work on the fortifications for a period of twenty one days.[49] Again, after Dominica was captured in 1778 and the fear became more real the Assembly voted £4400 for the maintenance of the signal and alarm posts, for hiring an advice boat to cruise for intelligence and for the purchase of arms.[50]

The Legislature of St. Vincent was more recalcitrant. Indeed, that island repeatedly complained about the heavy burden of its defence costs. Even after the capture of Dominica in 1778 the Assembly refused to vote money towards defraying the expenses of an armed sloop to patrol for intelligence because they were "deeply encumbered in unnecessary expense".[51] The Assembly also at this critical time refused to provide rations or pay for the troops stationed in the island arguing that "the present circumstances of the colony will not permit" them to incur the heavy expense.[52] It also at this time refused to pass a Militia Law,[53] and it is probable that this recalcitrant attitude contributed to the ease with which the island was captured by the French in 1779.

Even after the restitution of the island in 1784, the Assembly showed little signs of abandoning its intractable position. For instance, in 1787 it refused to provide expenditure towards the construction of fortifications at Old Woman's Point, despite representations from the Governor.[54] In 1789 a circular despatch was sent out by Lord Grenville, impressing upon the Legislatures the necessity of assisting in the erection of fortifications in the islands. The

Legislatures were to grant Negro labour, Negro artifices, mules or horses for the carriage of materials, and money for the purchase of any lands that were necessary for the works.[55] As a result, the Legislature showed some signs of yielding as it voted 150 Negroes to work on the fortifications at Berkshire Hill,[56] but it refused to provide Negro artifices and mules.[57] When the Legislature was again asked to pay the salaries of the troops stationed in the island it again refused. In view of the fact that they had already voted Negroes for the works:"We are sorry we cannot consistent with the duty we owe to our constituents raise any further taxes than are absolutely necessary for the internal expenses of the colony."[58]

The responsibility for the defence of the islands was divided up between the Imperial Government and the local legislatures even though the latter did not seem to accept their responsibility. Authority over the troops was divided up between separate military commanders representing the British Government in the islands. Up to 1784 the troops stationed in the islands were under the command of a military official, but they also received orders from the King's representative in the civil government. In that year the Imperial Government decided to appoint one military official as Commander-in-Chief of the forces serving in the Windward and Leeward Islands, with other officials under his control in charge of the local forces in each island. It was the duty of this official to see about what works were necessary for local defence but the Governors also had under the terms of their commissions some control over local defence. Again the lines were not clearly drawn and this situation led to friction. For instance, the Governor of Dominica complained in 1784, that Governor Matthew of Grenada, the official in charge of the troops on the Windward and Leeward Islands had sent orders to Captain Brereton in charge of the local forces "without", as he protested "any command to communicating them to me". He further complained that plans were being drawn up for the erection of military works "without my being either consulted or acquainted by the Commander in Chief". Hence he asked the home government for a ruling on the subject so that "by a clear line drawn we may know our respective duties".[59]

Apart from this partial unity in military matters which did not work smoothly, the islands were separate and distinct entities. Each had its own separate political system with its separate legislature, its separate courts and its separate militia. Each island also had its own system of local government in the parishes managed by the Vestry Boards, whose members were elected by the white freeholders in each parish. The rector of the parish church was always a member of the Vestry Board of the parish. The Vestries levied and collected taxes for the support of the Minister. They also distributed funds for poor relief and were responsible for the maintenance and repair of churches and chapels. They also appointed Wardens whose duty it was to see to the upkeep and maintenance of the streets, public walks and other conveniences.[60]

But despite the lack of cooperation and the existence of separate institutions the political systems of the islands showed striking similarities. In each island for instance it was dominated by a small oligarchy of white slaveowners or men with an interest in slaveholding who were prepared to build up and maintain their power and autonomy by any means, and were hostile to outside interference in matters which they regarded as being of their own local concern. This hostility was most strongly manifested when the Imperial Government attempted to legislate on the subject of slavery.

In 1815 for instance, in order to prevent the illegal importation of slaves into the islands in contravention of the Act of Abolition, the British Parliament after criticism by the African Institution[61] decided to adopt a policy making compulsory the registration of all slaves. Such a system had been earlier introduced into the Crown Colony of Trinidad by an Order in Council of March 26, 1812.[62] The Directors of the Institution however had believed that the colonies with representative institutions would never introduce it of their own volition and hence they suggested that Parliament should take the initiative since it had jurisdiction over the colonies and possessed full legal right to establish the regulation.[63] It was this right that the colonists questioned when the proposed bill was drafted and circulated.

They argued that the right of the British Parliament to legislate for the colonies was restricted to external matters only such as trade and navigation. It had no such right to legislate on the subject of slavery since it was an internal matter and their constitutions gave them the power to make laws for the public peace, welfare and good government. That right lay with the legislatures themselves. The St. Vincent Legislature declared that

> any interference by the Imperial Parliament... in the interior regulations of the colonies will be a violent infraction of those original rights under which British subjects were induced to settle in them, and should be opposed by every legal or constitutional means for if once such a precedent is established the Colonial Assemblies will soon dwindle into absolute insignificance, and in fact become worse than useless.[64]

The Dominica Legislature also deprecated parliamentary interference as being "dangerous in the highest degree". No such right, it was argued, "ever did or could exist in any colony which enjoys an independent legislature".[65] The Grenada Legislature also argued that the island had been given the right to frame laws best suited to internal policy by the Proclamation of 1763. Hence, they "cannot without a palpable dereliction from their duty consent to any Legislative interference of the mother country in the internal concerns of the colony".[66] The Tobago Legislature also, for similar reasons viewed "with dismay, this commencement of interference on the part of Parliament of Great Britain".[67]

Faced with this united opposition, the Imperial Government postponed action on the matter and later expressed the hope that the Colonial Legislatures would pass registration acts of their own volition. This they did[68] but they nevertheless won a victory as their point was conceded.

The Councils and Assemblies were the forums used for the type of political expression just described and indeed these organs enjoyed a large measure of independence throughout the period of this study. The Commissions that were issued to the individual governors gave them the power to nominate and suspend Councillors. The power of suspension in itself should have given them some influence over the conduct of members but this was not the case as it was always difficult to find enough candidates for nomination even though the required complement for a quorum was limited to seven. In 1822 Governor Brisbane of St. Vincent admitted that he could not adhere strictly to the rules governing the quorum:

> because as is the case at present members of Council are continually going from the colony on account of ill health and various other causes –

there are now no less than five members of council absent in England, and several from their great ages, would be quite unable to render assistance upon any emergency.[69]

The Governor was further instructed to choose his councillors from among the wealthier inhabitants of the colony but this also became impossible and in many instances property qualifications had to be disregarded. In 1804 for instance, President Campbell reported from Tobago "that a sufficient number of persons, duly qualified as to property, could scarcely be found to form... the Council". Only five members of the Council were at that time resident and apart from these there was "literally no person, qualified as to property" in the island. He was therefore forced to appoint what he termed "some respectable individuals... otherwise extremely well qualified", one of whom was a doctor.[70]

In St. Vincent between 1809 and 1820, and for the same reasons, Governor Brisbane was forced to appoint to seats in the Council four men who had no sugar estates. Two of these he described as "lawyers of eminence", the only qualifications of the others being that they were "not inferior in the estimation of society to any other inhabitants of the country", having land and houses in the capital:

> That in my opinion renders them as well qualified by independent circumstances to fill the situations I have placed them in as the generality of West India proprietors – few of whom remain in these colonies, but such as are compelled to do so, by embarrassed circumstances or ruined fortunes.[71]

In this situation Governors had to act with great caution when using their powers of suspension because the possibility existed that they might be left with no Council at all and this would bring the machinery of government to a virtual standstill. Indeed such a situation did occur in Grenada in 1771. In February of that year the home government had given instructions to Governor Melville to appoint one Mr. Chanteloupe, a French naturalised Roman Catholic to the Council.[72] The Protestant members of the Council were not in favour of this measure and, indeed, when earlier on Governor Melville's Deputy had attempted a similar manoeuvre, all except two members walked out of the Chamber.[73] Governor Melville however left the island before he carried out his instructions and the responsibility for the admission of the Catholic devolved upon his successor Governor Leyborne. He knew that his attempt would be opposed but he was nevertheless determined to go ahead declaring that "I will not sit still and hear the King's authority put at a defiance under the apprehension of such an event." When the measure was proposed, the five councillors who were the only ones present on the island walked out of the Chamber and he suspended them.[74] As a result of his action he was left without a Council.

But on the whole, suspensions were quite infrequent and when they occurred they were in most cases reversed by the home authorities. For one thing, popular opinion was seldom on the governor's side. The victim generally received the sympathy of his colleagues, and this was important in view of the fact that a Governor who acted against public opinion could find it difficult to get cooperation from his Council. When for instance, Governor Lindsay wanted to suspend President Robley because among other things he had during his temporary command appointed one Stewart to office on condition that he received half of the emoluments of the post,[75] only two of the six councillors present voted in favour of the suspension.

With regard to the Assembly, the Governor had less power in dealing with that body than he had with the Council. His chief weapons were negative rather than positive such as his refusal to assent to bills or his use of the power of dissolution in the hope that a more tractable assembly would be re-elected. But as in the case of the use of his power of suspension, his power of dissolution was limited by the impossibility of finding suitable persons for re-election. As Lieutenant Governor Morris of St. Vincent pointed out:

> dissolutions of Assemblys for opposition to measures, seldom answer the end proposed, either the same members generally are rechosen, or others of like sentiments elected; bringing with them an increased degree of acrimony, and distrust of every future measure whatever, or the new assembly bears too much the aspect of, and ever will be branded as a packed one, and of course not only lose the confidence of, but are often looked upon, however unjustly as the reproach of a colony.[76]

When, in fact, the Lieutenant Governor of Dominica dissolved the Assembly in 1792 for persisting in its refusal to meet for the transaction of public business,[77] almost all the members that were chosen at the subsequent election for the new Assembly were members of the previous one.[78] Hence dissolutions not only encouraged reprisals rather than submission but generally turned out to be ineffective in practice. In that self same island a later Governor complained of his "torments in this miserable and misguided colony [where] such a perverse and self-sufficient set of beings hardly ever got together".[79] When the "nest of fools" comprising the Assembly refused to allow him to scrutinise their proceedings, he suggested that the "block-heads" should be deprived of the privilege of keeping journals, and that the island be administered as a Crown Colony.[80] In 1819 when his difficulties had not subsided he again expressed his desire to be transferred "to a more congenial government",[81] and he was finally sent to Antigua. It was not long before his successor the Earl of Huntingdon found out that it was almost impossible for him to be on good terms with the people or avoid disputes with them.[82]

But it was extremely difficult for any Governor to avoid disputes. Indeed, under the old representative system these were seen as a means of adjusting the balance between the imperial and the colonial interests. The position of the Governor was one of extreme difficulty. He occupied a dual position as representative of the crown and head of the local government. In this first capacity he had to uphold the Imperial interests to see that Imperial policy was carried out. In the second he had to supervise all branches of local administration. But local and imperial interests frequently clashed since the colonists were not prepared to accept without question policies made in Britain which it was the duty of the Governor to carry out, and it was extremely difficult for him to do this without offending his Legislature. As Hume Wrong points out, he was placed in a perpetual dilemma, having always to bear the burden of such struggles;[83] and in many instances the colonists won the day.

Sometimes the colonists resorted to mass protest action against imperial policy. When for instance in 1776 the Lieutenant Governor of St. Vincent was instructed to secure from the Legislature an imperial tax of 4½% on exports, no sooner were the writs issued for choosing an Assembly "than the publick papers teemed with letters, and hints strongly recommending the freeholders not to chuse men known to be inclined to load the colony... with the 4½%".[84] Indeed so serious was the opposition that when the Assembly met it was thought wise not to put forward the suggestion.[85]

During the American Revolutionary War the colonists again expressed their dissatisfaction with Imperial policy by refusing to pay quit rents at the rates demanded. The Chief Baron of the Exchequer Court to which delinquents were brought refused to prosecute any such cases on behalf of the King.[86] A multitude of hand-bills were circulated and island-wide meetings were held in which people were encouraged "to disobey all process of any and every Court which might be issued for compelling the paying of quit rents at the rate demanded". They even decided to use violence if necessary,[87] and threatened to tar and feather Archibald Ingram, the Receiver, if he did not hand over his boxes and collect the dues at the rates they set. Ingram was held in execration by the majority of the inhabitants and left the island to avoid trouble.[88] Indeed one of the planters was quoted as saying he would join Washington's army "sooner than pay his Majesty's quit rent at £3.18.3".[89]

But these were not the only forms of obstruction. In some cases an island legislature might refuse to vote the required laws or the necessary taxes as Tobago did for two years,[90] and Grenada for eight,[91] thus bringing the machinery of government to a virtual standstill. But there were less serious forms of obstruction which could frustrate the plans of the Imperial Government and nowhere was this more marked than in the field of defence where their failure to cooperate was a matter of serious consequence for the success of imperial policy.[92]

As Professor Goveia points out, these obstructive tactics were the manifestation of a colonial relationship in which the island legislatures enjoyed considerable power without responsibility.[93] They were designed to impress upon the colonial government the feelings and viewpoints of the colonial societies on certain vital matters. In keeping with this policy each island appointed a Colonial Agent in Britain to protect and further its interest with the Imperial Government. Some agents were paid salaries as low as £100, and their work was directed by Committees of Correspondence appointed by the local legislature.[94] They were good though at times ineffective spokesmen for the colonial interests on such questions as slavery, trade regulation and imperial preferences and they were aided by the organisations of absentee merchants and planters who formed a powerful vested interest.[95]

The population of the British Windward Islands consisted of a tiny minority of whites, a somewhat larger proportion of free people of colour and large mass of negro slaves. Only the British born whites were eligible for full participation in the political process. The French naturalised subjects were allowed to vote, but except in Grenada, and only for a time, they were not eligible for seats on the Councils or Assemblies. The slaves of course were denied any participation at all in the functioning of the political system; they were regarded merely as property to be represented by their white masters. Their descendants, the free people of colour, were also without political rights. In all the islands they were denied the franchise and they were regarded as ineligible for any public and parochial office or for commissions in the militia.[96]

The general exclusion of the French naturalised subjects and the free people of colour and slaves from participation in the functioning of the political system meant that the number of persons qualified to do so was extremely small. Indeed, very early in the second half of the eighteenth century, following the transformation of the economy to sugar there was a mass exodus of whites from the islands. Their place was filled by large numbers of negro slaves who were brought in to do agricultural work,[97] but who as time progressed were used in a variety of other occupations.[98] The disproportion between the races was increased by the absenteeism of the planters. Indeed, throughout the period the richer planters were constantly retiring abroad, visiting their estates intermittently. Alexander Campbell, a member of the Grenada Council and an owner of estates in St. Vincent, Grenada, Tobago and the Grenadines, was one of those temporary absentees. Between 1763 and 1790 he spent half of his time in Europe and the other half in the West Indies, visiting his estates only once a year.[99]

But Alexander Campbell was not unique in this respect. In 1772 the machinery of government almost broke down in Grenada, as most of the members of the Assembly were absent in Europe.[100] For a period in 1792 only two members of the Council were on the island, "the private affairs of others having scattered them to different countries".[101] In 1804 three members who had retired abroad, one as early as 1799, and the others during 1800 and 1801,[102] were still absent and it was understood that "neither of those gentlemen mean to return to this island at least with any intention of a longer residence than will afford them an opportunity of inspecting their properties here".[103] In 1816 one governor reported that "the very few resident proprietors there are in this island is a circumstance very seriously to be lamented".[104] In 1810 Governor Young reported from Tobago of the "little embarrassment... created in my administration from the contingency, so repeatedly occurring of privy councillors, on the plea of ill health, or of business leaving this island for Europe". Two members had been absent for more than four years and a third had recently gone "on what leave of absence from the Crown I am not apprized".[105]

The effect of these repeated absences was that the number of whites eligible for participation in the political system was further reduced. Yet despite this, the representative system functioned, and elections were contested even though the number of voters was extremely small. Indeed, it might be misleading to call some of the contests for seats on the Assembly elections. In such an 'election' in the parish of St. Davids in St. Vincent held in 1779 and in which two candidates were returned out of a total of four contestants, the winning candidates received nine and six votes respectively.[106] In another such 'election' in the parish of St. John in Dominica in 1768, only seven persons were on the voters roll.[107]

The only exception to this sad picture was an election held in Grenada in 1768 in which 21 members were returned by 526 persons.[108] The position got worse during the nineteenth century as the white population dwindled in numbers. For instance, in an election in Dominica in 1818 a candidate was elected for the town of Portsmouth by one voter, and the governor was of the opinion that there were not more than twelve voters in the whole parish, and that this was representative of the island as a whole.[109] It was found necessary at times to admit men without any property qualifications at all, and men whose interests were entirely different. For instance, of three men nominated to the Council of Dominica in 1772, one was the Chief Engineer of the island; another's only qualification was that he was the son of the first president of the island; and that of the third was that he was "sensible and useful".[110]

It was the same thing with the Assemblies even though the electoral laws favoured control by owners of substantial property. At Grenada for instance a candidate seeking election to the Assembly had to be a free white male over 21 years old, a natural born or naturalised subject, and a Protestant, who possessed a freehold property of at least 50 acres in extent, or land or houses in the capital which produced an income of £100 per annum.[111] But faced with a declining white population the island virtually abolished its property qualification. In an Election Act passed in 1812 it was declared "advisable and just", that the qualifications for members standing as candidates for election, if disputed, should be queried by the Assembly after the election had taken place and not before by the Returning Officer as was customary.[112] It is not surprising therefore that five years later it was reported that:

> Many of the members of the Assembly were become members thereof who are merely the agents or managers of estates belonging to proprietors resident in Great Britain, and not possessing any freehold estate of their own.[113]

This, however, might be regarded as an inevitable outcome of an earlier development. As early as 1772 Governor Leyborne complained that "the persons elected are mostly of very small property... [as] those that have weight and property... are off the island".[114] The position was similar in the other islands. In 1816 the Assembly of Dominica consisted of five proprietors only, eight merchants, four attorneys of estates, one surgeon and an estate manager. Apart from the five proprietors, only two or three of the other members held the necessary fifty acres, which were not even in cultivation.[115] At the end of the period of this study the situation got even worse. In January 1824 Governor Huntingdon reported that:

> many who are returned as members are possessed of no property but merely a grant of fifty acres of land obtained as a qualification, and not in the least cultivation, yea in many instances, the land never seen or been visited by them.[116]

In 1822 Governor Robertson reported from Tobago that the House of Assembly was "composed of very different materials from former times", as so many of "the principal inhabitants" had left the island. All the members of the Privy Council except one were recruited from the Assembly, which he contended had not more than five legally qualified members... some of the rest were even of the lowest description originally, who were brought in at different times for sinister purposes under fictitious qualifications.[117]

Faced with a small and declining white population the white ruling class had been forced to admit to its ranks other white men without wealth to strengthen its hold on the political system. Earlier on those less well off whites such as managers and overseers and tradesmen were not eligible for seats on the Councils and Assemblies. They were generally relegated to minor offices such as jury service.[118] But these whites who were admitted to positions of power and prestige which were previously denied to them were all British born Protestants, the Roman Catholic subjects were still excluded even though they were a fairly well off and dynamic group.

This exclusion dated from the assumption of British control. In St. Vincent although the Roman Catholics as in Grenada were given the right to vote, this right was challenged by the British subjects. In 1779 Governor Morris wrote home asking the administration to send out

some very explicit orders confirming the privileges granted to the new adopted subjects, which it is the study of all the English of the colony to rob them of by illegally assuring them that they are obliged to take the test, and to renounce their religion, or else they have no privilege whatever, and still less right to vote for a representative.[119]

– although in some parishes they represented nearly half of the freeholders and even more in others.[120] Indeed, in an election in the parish of St. David in 1779 two protestant members who were returned were declared ineligible to sit in the Assembly because they were elected by a majority of French votes.[121]

The protest movement of the free coloureds for participation in the political process is discussed elsewhere in this study.[122] However, as late as 1830 a directive from the home government to the Legislature of Dominica for the passage of an Act granting political rights to the free coloureds was "totally rejected by the Board of Council".[123] But before the emancipation of the slaves the whites had been forced to concede political rights to the free coloureds in every one of the Windward Islands.

One might ask why the whites who were bitterly opposed to this measure and were traditionally hostile to any attempts by the Imperial Government to interfere in their local affairs submitted in this case, to the demands of that government. The answer to this seems to lie in the fact that the political system was being gradually undermined by forces of change. Although the whites still had a monopoly of political power, their control over the political system was slender. For this control arose out of their control over the economic and social life of the islands they governed. But this society was based upon an economy that was dominated by the large plantations and the sugar industry which by 1823 was tottering to the ground under the impact of rising production costs and the inability to compete with cheaper producers.[124] This threat to the economy was, as Professor Goveia points out, a threat to the whole slave society and hence a threat to the political power of the oligarchy who controlled it.[125]

The wealth of the West Indians had during the eighteenth century enabled them to exert considerable influence upon the shaping of Imperial policies affecting the islands. Indeed, many of the wealthy sugar barons held seats in the British Parliament and acted as a powerful vested interest. But the decline in their economic position in the first three decades of the nineteenth century was paralleled by a decline in their political importance as a pressure group.[126] Confronted with attacks from the humanitarians for reforms in and finally for the abolition of the slave system, and also with demands from the free coloureds for political rights, both of which were backed up by the British Government, there was very little that the legislatures in the British Windward Islands could have done to resist as they lacked political clout.

CHAPTER 5

Slavery and the plantation system

By extending the working day... capitalist production... not only produces the deterioration of human labour power by robbing it of its normal moral and physical conditions of development and activity, but also produces the premature death of this labour power itself. It extends the worker's production time within a given period by shortening his life... The Emancipation Act... forbade the planters to work any negro slave for more than 45 hours per week... But capital was by no means soothed.

– Karl Marx, *Capital: A Critique of Political Economy*, vol. I (1863)

The history of slavery in the British Windward Islands is indissolubly and inextricably linked with the establishment and expansion of the sugar industry. Ever since 1773 sugar had gained a position of first rate importance in the plantation economy – a position which it maintained throughout the period of this study to the almost total neglect of other kinds of economic activity.

For instance, in St. Vincent after 1773 tobacco cultivation was carried on by the Black Caribs only and following their expulsion in 1797 it was most likely abandoned.[1] A report from the island in 1788 also revealed that the culture of coffee and cocoa was being neglected by the planters.[2] By the last decade of the eighteenth century it was only the old French residents who grew cocoa in Dominica. Only two or three estates were reported producing indigo and small quantities of ginger, and tobacco was grown exclusively by the slaves.[3]

Coffee and cotton managed to survive for longer periods in some of the islands but in most they played rather insignificant roles. Up to the end of the eighteenth century, Tobago was famous for the production of "a most valuable long wool cotton" and indigo "of a superior quality" but by 1807 the island produced "little cotton, less coffee and no indigo".[4]

Indeed, this concentration on sugar was given a boost by the abortive sugar boom of the 1790s when prices were high. It was precisely at this time that Mr. Robley, the largest cotton grower in Tobago abandoned its culture and changed to sugar instead.[5] At the same time too, 3,000 acres of land in St. Vincent were diverted from cotton to sugar.[6] As a result of these developments, at the end of the period of this study the islands of St. Vincent, Tobago and Grenada, the last being the greatest sugar colony of the group, were almost totally dependent for their existence on the cultivation of sugar. Only Dominica was exporting cotton in fairly significant quantities.[7]

The advent of sugarcane monoculture was accompanied by an exodus of small white planters, mainly the old French residents who either could not compete with or were bought out by the large sugar planters especially after the coffee crisis of 1773. The Lieutenant Governor of St. Vincent saw the dangers of this and called for caution as early as 1774. He suggested that small plots of land should be either sold or granted to settlers with the express stipulation that these should never be planted in canes since "the profits of that culture (were) inducing and generally ending in the swallowing up in it all the inferior settlements of cocoa, coffee, indigo, ginger, cotton etc., to the great dispopulation of white and other free settlers of the middling class".[8]

But his advice in this respect was not followed and as a result the small white population dwindled in numbers. In 1765 for instance St. Vincent had a population of 735 French proprietors.[9] By 1811, it was reported that this group had almost "totally disappeared", because of "the buying up and consolidating the small settlements into extensive estates and changing the cultivation of the island from coffee, cocoa, manioc, etc. into sugar".[10]

While there was a sharp decrease in the white population, there was a corresponding increase in the numbers of slaves and this significantly changed the racial composition of the islands. Before the introduction of sugar the proportion of blacks to whites in Dominica and St. Vincent was approximately two to one and three to one respectively. By 1773 the Dominica ratio was five to one[11] and by 1791 that of St. Vincent had risen to fifteen to one,[12] a ratio which had been achieved in Tobago as early as 1773.[13] At the end of the period of this study, blacks outnumbered whites in even greater proportions.

Sugar was undoubtedly the most heavily capitalised plantation industry during the eighteenth century. The planters in the British Windward islands borrowed the necessary capital from London merchants on mortgage at interest rates which were as high as 15% in Grenada. These sums were repaid from the crops of sugar which were sent directly to the merchants for disposal. The planters became indebted to the merchants in all their business transactions since they also acted as agents and charged extra fees for commission and brokerage.[14]

This system of credit was mainly responsible for what Professor Goveia describes as "the chronic indebtedness of the planters".[15] Even when the planter received a high price for his staple he was not financially well off. In 1776 for example, the total value of Grenada's exports was £600,000 and this figure was surpassed only by that of Jamaica for the entire British West Indies but in spite of this it was reported that "the planters are not yet opulent" as most of the profits went to the factors who received up to 20% for interest and commission on sales.[16] Two years later the island owed a debt of £200,000 sterling to London finance houses, exclusive of instalment payments on the lands.[17] This situation was typical of the other islands as a whole.

But the accumulation of debts was partly due to the extravagance of the planters manifested for example in the form of conspicuous consumption at dinner parties. Mrs. Carmichael, describing a dinner in St. Vincent in the 1820s wrote as follows:

> The dinner was like all West Indian dinners – a load of substantials, so apparently ponderous that I instinctively drew my feet from under the table, in case it should be borne to the ground. Turtles and vegetable soups, with fish, roast mutton... and turtle dressed in the shell, with

boiled turkey, boiled fowls, a ham, mutton and pigeon pies, and stewed ducks concluded the first course; ducks and guinea fowls with a few ill made puddings and tarts, etc. formed the second course... A good deal of wine was drank... the wine is of the best quality, and malt liquor particularly London Porter...[18]

With increasing economic difficulties in the 1820s, dinners "took a more rational turn" before Mrs. Carmichael left the island. But even the small dinners that were substituted were so expensive that they were held only "on great occasions".[19]

The indebtedness of the plantocracy was also due to the prevalence of absenteeism – the practice of retiring or spending long periods abroad, while leaving the management of their estates to overseers and attorneys. While abroad these absentees wasted large sums of money which should have been spent instead on their estates. Such a famous absentee was Sir William Young, a proprietor of estates in Tobago and St. Vincent. After the devastation of his estates in St. Vincent during the Carib War in 1795 he was granted a loan of £10,000 in Exchequer Bills for renovation. In 1804 he still owed £7,000 and was faced with arrest for recovery of this sum. This was because "instead of retrenching every domestic expense beyond what was necessary for decent subsistence" he engaged in "a run of vanities and extravagance". This ruined him. He was subsequently forced to sell the furniture in his Harley Street mansion, rent that house, sell his plate, and "the valuable books of my library" as the debts, which were "due in part to my own imprudence", accumulated.[20]

While most absentees lived in a manner similar to that of Sir William Young, their agents in the West Indies lived in a similar fashion at their expense. But the greatest evil of absenteeism was the effect it had on the management of plantations. All the available evidence indicates that most plantations operated by agents were mismanaged. The inference need not be drawn, however, that the plantations would have been better managed if the owners were resident. As both Houses of the Grenada Legislature admitted in 1788, the plantations suffered because of "arbitrary methods of management and expenditure by the proprietors if present or their representatives when absent".[21]

It cannot be denied, however, that the system of absenteeism led to gross mismanagement, frequent abuses and depreciation of the estates. The overseers and attorneys for example believed that one indicator of their efficiency was the quantity of sugar shipped each year and all the evidence agree that in pursuance of this policy they forced the slaves to work harder than usual with serious consequences. Charles Peters, a Protestant Clergyman in Dominica, accused the agents of absentees of "oppressive conduct" towards the slaves, and saw them generally as a group of men whose interests were "most effectually promoted by means tending to the ruin of the plantations". He pointed out that on one estate 90 slaves out of a gang of 160 died in the short space of two years and this he attributed to overwork and under-feeding by unscrupulous agents in an effort to increase output.[22] When instances such as this occurred, the proprietor was inevitably faced with the alternatives of either finding replacements before those that died had repaid him on his investment or leaving his estate underhanded.

Another disadvantage of absenteeism was that managers would rob their employers. Sir George Young, speaking from experience in Dominica and Grenada, accused the managers of under-feeding the slaves, buying sick and disabled slaves, and charging them to the proprietors as healthy prime ones, while pocketing the difference. He was further of the opinion that absenteeism had the effect of depreciating the value of the estates by as much as one-fifth yearly, and asserted that "the overseers or managers who have been but little time upon any of them, became rich and frequently more so than their masters".[23] Also in 1788 the Governor of Dominica estimated the net income from a plantation managed by a resident proprietor to be £2,000 per annum and went on to point out that less than half this sum would be made were it absentee managed.[24] This seems to suggest that the profits of absentees were generally less than those of resident proprietors.

The disadvantageous effects of absenteeism coupled with the lavish style of life of the planters made it impossible for them to carry on sugar production profitably except when prices were high. But even when profits were being made, money that should have been reinvested in the estates was often used instead to provide property settlements for members of their families in the form of wills and legacies. In 1820 for instance, the two estates of the Gregg family in St. Vincent and Dominica produced a net income of £2,000, but legacies to be paid out amounted to £4,400.[25] But the difficulties the planters experienced are not to be attributed solely to man-made causes such as ostentation and absenteeism. Indeed, the sugar industry itself was subject to forces which man could not have controlled.

Cane diseases such as the blast, the borer and the grub affected many estates.[26] The mountainous lands of Dominica were infested with rats which did extensive damage to young canes.[27] Tobago and Grenada suffered from a plague of ants which made their nests in the roots of the cane which they damaged to such an extent that the plants did not receive sufficient nourishment. As a result the plants became sickly and stinted and did not provide good quality juice for sugar making. The islands were not ridden of these pests until 1780 when a hurricane accompanied by huge torrents of rain destroyed them[28] but up to this time they had done considerable mischief. In Grenada, they destroyed large sections of the plantations and as late as 1788 not all had been restored to their former states of cultivation.[29]

While the hurricane of 1780 wiped out the ants it also did extensive damage to the plantations. In addition hurricanes in the West Indies were generally followed by a scarcity of basic foodstuffs, high prices, starvation, and high slave mortality No island however suffered as severely from these tempests as Dominica. One European who lived there noted that at the approach of the hurricane season "the apprehensions of the people increase as they know too well that... they hold their lives and properties by a precarious tenure."[30] In 1787 for instance, three hurricanes destroyed the entire crops of coffee and sugar and all the ground provisions for the slaves. The island was at that time on the verge of a famine as the restrictions on trading with the United States added to the scarcity and high cost of food.[31] In 1806 again plantation buildings were razed to the ground and in the capital, Roseau, "many houses and many buildings of wood were totally removed from the places where they stood".[32] Hurricanes struck again in 1813 and 1814 and the disaster was even more severe as the river Roseau overflowed its banks and swept away about two-thirds of the houses in the capital.[33] Up to 1820 the island continued to suffer from these visitations and so serious was the shortage of food that an estimated total of 5,000 slaves died from actual famine or diseases connected with it.[34]

In addition to hurricanes, fires were a common cause of destruction. This was so mainly because West Indian towns were constructed chiefly of wood. In addition, these wooden structures which the Governor of Grenada described as being "little more than paper buildings"[35] were situated close to each other in long rows thus enabling a fire to spread from one to the other with devastating swiftness. In 1772 for instance, a fire destroyed the entire capital of Grenada in the space of seven hours, causing "the total ruin of many who were in affluent circumstances but a few hours before" and leaving in its wake an estimated damage of £132,846,191.[36] In 1792 another fire left damage estimated at £100,000, and the total loss to the island as a whole in a space of 23 years of fire was conservatively put at £1,000,000 sterling.[37]

The capital of Dominica was also destroyed by fire in 1780[38] and again in 1805 during an invasion by the French. Estimates of the losses were put at £202,857. 12. 3.[39] The cost of reconstruction as in the case of hurricanes had to be borne by the sugar industry which was the mainstay of the economic life of the island. But the sugar industry was unable to withstand these successive shocks and after an appeal made abroad for relief, Parliament made a grant of £50,000 to the victims.[40] Soon after this, as we have seen, the hurricane of 1806 created widespread destruction and by 1817 such repeated visitations had made the soil sterile and unproductive. Hence, in an effort to diversify the economy, the legislature asked for the establishment of a free port to trade with the French islands in American provisions, lumber and other commodities, but this was not granted.[41]

But while the planters would have liked the establishment of free ports as a possible means of diversifying the economy of the island they refused to entertain notions about diversification in the agricultural sector itself. They seemed wedded to the theory that land was of little use unless it was planted in canes and to this they rigidly adhered deviating only when forced by natural or geographical circumstances they could not control. This concentration on sugar was to a large extent responsible for the agricultural techniques practised by the planters. For it meant that supplies of cattle and horses were severely limited because of the inadequacy of pasture land for their subsistence. This in turn meant that tasks which could have been easier performed by these animals had to be done by the slaves.

As early as 1791 for instance it was argued that as cattle in Dominica bred well, the deficiency of these "valuable animals" could have been made up in a few years if sufficient land was reserved for pasturage.[42] Similar views were expressed by the Governor of Grenada.[43] But the conservative outlook of the majority of the planters militated against the implementation of such suggestions. As late as 1807, Sir William Young the Governor of Tobago, in his "Prospectus for the Institution of an Agricultural Society" in that island was still calling for the establishment and improvement of pasture lands for cattle and horses so that there would be enough of these animals to take over some of the tasks which the slaves were performing. Young, making the further point that "every good negro's time and work is become more precious",[44] was undoubtedly influenced by the abolition of the slave trade. The cry he echoed, however, brought response from one planter in Grenada only who planted 400 acres of land in guinea grass.[45] The available evidence suggests that the overall general negative response might have been due to a belief that keeping the slaves constantly at hard work was a necessary factor in maintaining order and subordination. If they were replaced in some tasks by cattle and horses, then that order and subordination would be more difficult to obtain.

It was this assumption which in part seems to have influenced the attitude of the majority of the planters towards the use of the plough as an agricultural instrument, although they never admitted it. In 1788 it was only in Grenada that this type of equipment was in use and it was limited to a small part of one estate.[46] Some planters argued that the soil in the islands was in general mountainous and that there were few areas fit for ploughing. Others used as a further objection the difficulty of teaching the slaves to use the plough.[47] A proprietor of estates in St. Vincent, Grenada and Tobago further added that the plough would be of little benefit since the expenditure necessary for procuring cattle, horses and a skilled ploughman would be twice that of slave labour. "Ploughs," he concluded, "have been often tried and found by experience not the answer",[48] thus giving the impression that the matter was thoroughly investigated.

All these contentions were, however, refuted by the Governor of Grenada. The argument that ploughs were of little use, he declared, "admits of further proofs", since "experiments have not had sufficient or fair trials" and the matter was "given up on slight investigations".[49] This testimony indicates that there was no general interest and is corroborated by other testimony which indicates that this was so because of the need to keep the slaves at hard work as a means of maintaining order. When questioned by the Investigating Committee on Slavery and the Slave Trade as to whether he was familiar with any notions entertained by the planters against the use of the plough, Robert Foster replied: "I have understood... that it was the general opinion that if negroes were not constantly kept at hard labor, they would become insolent and unruly".[50]

The shortage of pasture lands caused indescribable hardships upon the slaves. It meant that they had to gather fodder wherever they could to feed the cattle. This practice called 'grass picking' was indeed a severe imposition upon the slaves. They were generally put to this task after the day's labour in the field was over but at times they were sent at noon in the two hours allotted for meals and rest.[51] It was for this reason that Matthew Terry of Grenada described the practice as an "oppressive" one.[52] In addition it was at times difficult to collect adequate amounts at reasonable distances from the plantations. The slaves were therefore forced to travel long distances in search of it, sometimes without success, and they were flogged if they failed to bring in the required amounts.[53]

Because of the shortage of pasture and the consequent shortage of cattle, mules and horses, the slaves were given the arduous task of transporting heavy baskets of animal dung as manure, to the cane pieces. Even when they were assisted by mules and horses, the heavy loads were transferred from the animals to the slaves as soon as the slopes became "too steep for these".[54] The Grenada Legislature claimed, however, that cattle and other stock were continually penned on the cane pieces so that manure was never too far distant from the holes, and that where this was not so, mules transported the dung in boxes.[55] But this claim was denied by their own agent who asserted that the practice of penning stock was far from universal and that on most estates the slaves carried out the manure to the fields on their heads in baskets capable of holding 15 to 30 pounds.[56]

Before manure was applied however, the slaves prepared the fields for the reception of the plants. This practice called 'hoeing' was generally agreed to be "a harder species of labour than most other works of the plantation".[57] In tough lands like those in Dominica this work imposed a great physical strain on the slaves and it was precisely for this reason that Mr. Laing, an old French planter, suggested that the plough be used in this branch of agriculture.[58] This was the view held by this class as a whole which lamented the absence of ploughing "malgré les grands advantages qu'offre cette methode".[59] Yet, on the whole, ploughs were non-existent and land was prepared for planting by the cumbersome, inefficient time-consuming and laborious method of digging holes with the hoe.

The field intended to be holed was first lined out and marked with stakes at reasonable distances to guide the slaves in hoeling. The soil was then turned up by hoes to a depth of four to six inches and formed into holes about five feet by four feet square or other dimensions "according to the fancy or judgement of the planter".[60] Then the loose soil would be hauled up to form the banks of the cane holes, after which manure was applied and three or four cane tops inserted.[61] Such a planting system necessitated the mobilisation and use of a large supply of unskilled labourers who were equipped with the simplest and crudest agricultural instruments. When questioned on the possibility of introducing European instruments of husbandry in cultivation in 1788, as a means of lightening the labour of the slaves the Grenada Legislature replied that they had no use for anything else besides the hoe and the bill: "On the whole, we do not apprehend that the introduction of any other European instruments of husbandry is likely to abridge or lighten the labour of the slaves, or that the severity of that labour renders any such introduction necessary."[62] This distaste for agricultural innovation was widespread. The hoe and the bill it appears were the major European instruments of husbandry used in cultivation for the entire period of this story. As Ragatz writes: "obsolete methods were the legacy of one generation of planters to another; custom all but reigned supreme".[63]

In the Windward Islands as in the other British West Indies, sugar was grown by methods of intensive culture. After planting the canes had to be frequently weeded, stripped, moulded and constantly fertilized especially in Dominica where by the last two decades of the eighteenth century the planters complained that the soil was becoming fast impoverished and exhausted.[64] Since the planters were unwilling to introduce labour saving devices, such intensive methods necessitated a large labour force. But on the contrary the density of slaves employed in agriculture in the Windward Islands was comparatively low. According to Professor Goveia the planters at St. Christopher in the Leeward Islands seem to have owned two slaves for every three acres in cultivation which would give a ratio of one slave to two thirds of an acre.[65] The picture was completely different in the Windward Islands and nowhere was this ratio achieved at any time during the period of this study. Estimates submitted to the 1788 Investigating Committee indicate that the planters in Grenada, St. Vincent and Dominica owned one slave for each acre in cultivation,[66] and early in the nineteenth century the picture was even worse in Tobago. In 1807 that island had a slave population of 15,350 engaged in the cultivation of 30,537 acres, or roughly one slave to every two acres.[67] This suggests that the work load of the slaves in the British Windward Islands was greater than that of their counterparts in the Leewards and probably Barbados and Jamaica.

In 1790, for instance, it was reported that not even three estates in Grenada were sufficiently handed and that 15,000 more were needed to sufficiently slave the cleared lands and those that were unimproved but fit for cultivation. St. Vincent was said to be in need of twice the present number and Dominica of three times as many.[68] For this reason the planters were unwilling to give up the trade in slaves which they further saw as the only reliable and economic method of recruiting their labour force. The alternative of breeding was totally unsuccessful throughout the period of this study and so after abolition in 1807 the planters still complained about a shortage of labour which they argued was responsible for diminishing production.[69]

The maintenance of the slave system was one of the most difficult tasks the planters had to face. In the early years of the establishment of the sugar industry in the British West Indies when slaves could be purchased cheaply, and when sugar prices were high slave labour proved to be economical. But at the time of the introduction of the slave system in the Windward Islands sugar production was not as profitable as it had been during the seventeenth century. During the eighteenth century, the sugar industry was generally in a state of decline and only the abortive boom of the 1790s saved some planters from total ruin. Again the planters of the British Windward Islands did not reap all the fruits from this boom because of Britain's fiscal and economic policies and also the devastation of St. Vincent and Grenada during insurrections in 1795.[70] As we shall see, slave prices increased steadily during the eighteenth, and early nineteenth centuries at a time when the planters' margin of profit had virtually disappeared. Indeed, instead of being faced with an acute shortage of labour which up to a point was true, the larger problem, on the contrary, was that the planters were unable to maintain their slaves from the proceeds of the sugar industry.

Of the territories in the Windward Islands where sugar cultivation was carried on only Dominica had a density of fewer than 100 slaves to the square mile in 1823. Grenada had the highest of over 200, St. Vincent was next with 134, Tobago had 108 and Dominica a mere 62.[71] The lower density for Dominica was due in part to the heavy exportation of slaves as the sugar industry became more and more unprofitable.[72] But the main reason was that here sugar never had such a stranglehold of all the arable lands as in the other islands and, in some cases coffee, which needed fewer slaves was more important than sugar. However, the density for all the islands must have been higher since none of them had ever been in a state of full cultivation. And the need to purchase and maintain these numbers was one of the most important factors contributing to the high cost of production which made the sugar industry increasingly unprofitable during the period of this study.

The recruitment of the slave population by fresh purchases from the ships was becoming more and more expensive as time progressed. At Dominica for example the planters purchased field slaves in the 1760s for £26.10/- but in 1788 the price had increased to £38, and slaves with special skills such as tradesmen or artisans fetched £150. In the last decade of the eighteenth century when the question of abolition was being discussed, the price for a field slave soared to 50 guineas.[73] By 1804 the price had increased to £165 sterling.[74] But this was not the end of the planter's expense. For he had to spend heavy sums insuring them, he had to provide them with food, clothing, lodging and medical assistance and he had to replace them when they became incapacitated or died.

Since the slave masters believed that it was cheaper to buy slaves rather than to encourage natural reproduction they did nothing to facilitate such a process even in the changed conditions consequent to abolition of the trade. For the three-year period 1797 to 1800 there were 1750 births and 1523 deaths in Dominica,[75] which represented a natural increase of 227, but this was an exception rather than the general rule. Included in the slave population of Grenada in 1820 were 4,731[76] slaves who were most likely born in the island. Towards the end of the eighteenth century, provisions were made in Tobago whereby female slaves were to be excused from labour in proportion to the number of off spring they had borne, with a total exemption for mothers who gave birth to six children. This practice it was said was also implemented in Dominica on the Gillon Estate.[77] Similarly, at Grenada an Act of 1797 exempted mothers of six from all labour and their owners from taxes.[78] In 1811 it was reported that of late years the Tobago planters in an effort to increase the slave population were encouraging slaves to marry – offering as inducements, materials to build houses and the time to do so.[79] At first sight it may be tempting to regard such incentives as indicative of a commitment to pro natal policies in an attempt to encourage natural reproduction as a means of ensuring a labour supply in the long run as suggested in other Caribbean slaves economies.[80] However, leaving aside the fact that such piecemeal measures were insufficient and failed to address fundamental issues there was in practice a divergence between the actuality and the rhetoric as demonstrated in the following Table:

Slave Population at specified years

	1805	1807	1808	1810-11	1823[81]
St. Vincent	16,500				20,122
Tobago		17,123	16,302	16,040	13,671
Grenada	29,942				25,310
Dominica	22,083				15,050

The figures show a noticeable decrease in the slave population except in the case of St. Vincent. And in this island the increase is not to be attributed solely to natural causes as there was a net importation of 1,035 in addition to other slaves who were captured and apprenticed.[82] Conversely, manumissions and exportations did not have any significant impact on the decrease. In Dominica where exportation was most prevalent, this factor accounted for 2,975 slaves. With regard to manumissions, between 1808 and 1825 slaves so freed in St.

Vincent totalled 788[83], in Dominica 1,188 and in Grenada 843. The available evidence indicates that the most satisfactory explanation for the decrease is to be found in an excess of deaths over births.

The cause of this high death rate and consequent general failure of the slave population to maintain itself merits close examination. The literature on the subject is extensive. Morrisey while placing great emphasis on the impact of the brutal lifestyle endured by slaves on the plantations and the inherent dehumanisation, points to a lesser extent to skewed sex ratios and the presence of a large proportion of African slaves of middle age.[84] Ragatz had earlier considered an excess of males over females in the population to be an important factor.[85] Matthew Terry testified before a Parliamentary Committee that the "planters appeared desirous of importing as many males as possible".[86] Male preferencing at this time did not give way to female preferencing if it ever did at all, as is contended for the rest of the Caribbean after 1750.[87] The Governor of Grenada reported in 1788 that the planters in that island generally imported two males for each female.[88] Indeed, of a total of 13,101 slaves imported between 1784 and 1788, 7,974 or about three-fifths were male.[89] In the latter year there were 14,438 males composed to 10,182 females in the slave population.[90] However, the first decade of the nineteenth century witnessed a demographic shift in the sex ratios as indicated in the following tables:

Slave population in Grenada[91]

Year	Male	Female
1812	14,352	14,439
1813	14,026	14,156
1814	13,674	14,005
1815	13,484	13,786
1816	13,451	13,783
1817	13,510	14,188
1818	13,328	14,087
1819	13,155	13,905
1820	13,022	13,878
1823	12,258	13,052
1825	12,037	12,840

Slave population in Dominica, Tobago, and St Vincent[92]

	1823		1825	
	Male	Female	Male	Female
Dominica	7,200	7,850	8,940	9,832
Tobago	6,565	7,106	6,446	7,053
St. Vincent			11,706	12,112

From a comparative Caribbean perspective the slave populations of the British Windward Islands did not achieve female majorities until the advent of the nineteenth century – unlike Barbados and the Leeward Islands which had attained this status in the sixteenth and eighteenth centuries respectively.[93] It must be borne in mind, however, that the latter were older colonies. The eventuality, albeit late in comparison, nevertheless raised serious doubts about the contention that an excess of males over females had any significant impact on the failure of the slave population to maintain itself.

Both Houses of the Legislature of Grenada and Mr. Spooner, agent for the island, added their voices to the debate on this issue. The latter attributed blame to "the premature and promiscuous commerce of the sexes, indiscriminate prostitution of women in the younger part of their lives, their total barrenness brought on by debauchery, frequent abortion (and) immoderate use of rum", while the former stressed "the little attention paid to the cultivation of religion and morality among the slaves".[94] According to this line of reasoning, the fault was to be found in the lifestyle of the slaves and certain practices associated therewith. However, with regard to abortion, it is important to bear in mind the observation that Mr. Spooner, like other Europeans, probably overstated efforts by the slaves to prevent childbearing.[95]

On this question, a factor of crucial importance was the expense involved in rearing young children. In 1788 Mr. Laing of Dominica asserted that "children are a heavy expense until they are eight or ten years old", as the charges for food, clothing and medical assistance were about £12 per annum. Children at this age usually worked as grass pickers and stock feeders, occupations which did not give the master an effective return on his investment. "Until twelve years of age," concluded Mr. Laing, "they do not pay by their labour for the expenses involved in rearing them."[96] Mr. Byam of Grenada seemed to indicate from his remarks on this point that this repayment would not be ensured until children reached the age of 16 at which time they were put to the task of hoeling, although in some instances the age was 15.[97] This tendency among slave owners to calculate human lives in terms of profit and loss impacted upon the failure of the slave population to maintain itself. In fact, Captain Alexander Scott testified before a parliamentary committee in 1791 that the slave owner had calculated that if an imported slave died after four years of productive work on the field it really did not matter, as by then the owner would have had "his pennyworth of him".[98]

Apart from the calculation of costs there was the further reason that the planters lost a portion of the mothers' labour time both before and after delivery. Indeed, during the eighteenth century, they regarded pregnant women and young children as two of the greatest misfortunes they could experience. If we are to believe Mr. John Terry, they would have preferred sucking children to die.[99] It was also alleged that children were so unwanted that "it was no uncommon thing for them to give away a child of two years old, as you would a puppy from a litter".[100]

Because the planters were unwilling to lose too much of the mothers' labour time, pregnant women were kept toiling in the field until close to the expected period of delivery. This situation was not unique to the British Windward Islands. It prevailed in other Caribbean slave economies. Writing on Barbados, Beckles relates the experience of William Dickson who on his arrival in that island in the 1770s was "astonished to see some women far gone in pregnancy toiling in the field, and others whose naked infants lay exposed to the weather sprawling on a goat skin, or in a wooden tray. I have heard with indignation drivers curse both them and their sprawling brats when they were suckling them".[101] About a month after the child was born slave mothers in the British Windward Islands were usually put back to labour in the fields leaving their children "to chance on the part of overseers" or at times actually carrying them on their backs.[102] This was also a feature of plantation life in Barbados where Ligon observed the woman at work with her pickaninny at her back. If the overseer be discreet she is suffered to rest herself a little more than the ordinary but if not she is compelled to do as others do. Times they have of suckling their children in the field and refreshing themselves and good reason for they carry burdens on the back and yet work too.[103]

Slave women on the plantations in the British Windward Islands were not afforded such generosity. Very little time was afforded them to tend to the welfare of their infants while in the field. Captain Hall reported the case of a slave mother who broke the field routine to feed her young child and "was roused from that situation by a severe blow from the cartwhip".[104] Other observers noted that pregnant women were in that matter of punishment treated very little if at all differently from other slaves to the extent that many "deemed it a misfortune to have children".[105] In addition, exposure to the vagaries of the weather, the unhealthy conditions in the field itself, and inadequate nourishment lessened the resistance of the children to diseases "such as small pox, tetanus, yaws and flues",[106] which were prevalent and serious at a time when medical knowledge was not much advanced, and when there were few qualified doctors on the plantation who had to be paid for their services.

The cumulative effect of all these factors was an alarmingly high mortality rate. A Grenada physician and slave owner stated that on the estates that he attended, about one-third of all the children that were born died in the first month and that on his own estates it was even greater.[107] Mr. Byam of that island also admitted that nearly one half of the children that were born died under two years old and that the greater proportion of that half died in the first nine days.[108] From Dominica, Mr. Gregg testified that on his estates of 60 children born in the period 1767-1790 only 22 were alive in the latter year.[109] This would give a survival ratio of one child out of every three that were born. Taking an indiscriminate number of 100 children that died in this island during the course of one year, all under 12 years, Governor Orde estimated that 35 died under the age of 12 months, 42 between the ages of 2 and 4 years, 18 between the ages of 4 and 8, one at 9, two at 10, and one at 11.[110] At the same time, reports from Grenada indicated that not more than one-third of the children that were born reached the age of puberty.[111] A conservative estimate put the mortality rate on the plantations at 3% per annum, a rate comparable with Cuba in the nineteenth century.[112]

This connection between underfeeding and overworking pregnant and lactating mothers and high mortality is also made by Beckles on review of statistical evidence of births and deaths on the Codrington Estates in Barbados between 1715 and 1718, as he writes: "Women watched their children die in quick succession, and buried more than those who lived to become adults. It was spiritually and emotionally crippling for many."[113] If it is true as Morrisey asserts that slave women in the Caribbean wanted fewer children than those in the antebellum south,[114] and there are bits of evidence for the Windward Islands which may be so interpreted, the reasons therefore are to be found in the harsh conditions of slavery itself. Any such decision would have been a perfectly rational one in all the circumstances. In this regard, it was not only the slave owners who regarded the presence of pregnant women and infant children in their charge as a misfortune. Many slave women too "deemed it a misfortune to have children".[115] This is not to suggest, however, that slavery in the antebellum south was in any way less harsh than in the British Windward Islands.

At the end of 1813 the Governor of Tobago, lamenting the decrease of the slave population commented that the picture would change if "regulations for the comfort and security of those in a state of slavery were provided".[116] And yet very little was done even though the planters continued to complain about a shortage of labour and a decrease in production as a result of a diminished and diminishing slave population.[117]

The responsibility therefore clearly rested with the planters. Before 1807 they placed too much dependence on the trade partly because it supplied them with the numbers they wanted and at the times they were wanted. And these numbers were quite considerable. For example, between 1784 and 1791, St. Vincent received a maximum net import of 1,620 new recruits a year,[118] and between 1788 and 1804 Grenada and Dominica received 926 and 647 respectively.[119] During these years the planters were improving and extending their cultivation, and if it is possible to argue that these heavy numbers could not be supplied by breeding then one could excuse them for dependence on the trade, if they could be excused at all. But after 1807 when the trade was no longer open serious efforts ought to have been made to facilitate breeding in their own self-interest.

However, the problem facing the planters at this time was much more than a labour shortage. Rather, the maintenance of the slave system was becoming more and more expensive at a time when prices for their staples were falling and the economy could not bear this expense without great strain. But in spite of this, the planters were unwilling to give up slavery for some other mode of production arguing, as the Tobago Council and Assembly put it, "that without the compulsory performance of service for a master, the West Indies... must cease to exist",[120] and that a wage system could not work.

When, for instance, in 1823 the home government suggested to the planters as an ameliorative measure that they allow the slaves to work on their own one week out of every three for wages, the general reaction was that this was impractical and impolitic. Opinion in Grenada was that the system "would introduce such a system of idleness and its baneful consequences... as would produce insubordination, greatly increase the necessity of punishment, and generally tend to endanger the peace and tranquility of the colony".[121] Another objection was raised because coupled with the suggestion of paying wages was the proposal that a system of task work be implemented on the estates. In defense of the planter interest Governor Brisbane of St. Vincent thought this to be impractical: "The planters," he wrote, "are manufacturers as well as cultivators of the soil – sugar boiling, distilling, and the cultivation, must go hand in hand at one and the same time so that to point out task work to be done is quite impossible."[122] Indeed, what the planter wanted was a regular and constant supply of labour, immediately under his supervision which he could direct and manipulate as he chose.

This becomes clear when we examine the actual routine on the sugar plantations where the planters kept their slaves preoccupied for the entire year. The land was holed, planted and manured between September and January and the crop was reaped between January and June of the following year.[123] Between the cycles of holeing and reaping, the slaves were kept employed in grass picking, making manure for the next crop, repairing the roads and cleaning the provision grounds.[124] Sometimes two crops were harvested in one year, and this was done in Dominica by dividing the land into two and sometimes three sections which were alternately planted and harvested. When the land was cut in three, one-third was planted with young canes, one-third in ratoons, and the last third given to the slaves as gardens for the cynical reason of improving it for planting in the next year.[125]

On the plantations most planters operated on the principle of dividing their slaves into two gangs according to their health and strength. The 'great gang' consisted of the most able-bodied slaves who did holeing, and the 'small gang' of those between the ages of 10 and 15 who were generally put to lighter tasks such as weeding the canes and gathering grass. Included in this group were invalids and pregnant women.[126] On some estates the small gang was further subdivided into the 'weeding gang', and the 'grass gang'.[127] The slaves began their chores at day break and continued until nine o'clock at which time they were given half an hour for breakfast. They then resumed work until noon when they were allotted two hours for meals and rest.[128] However, for those slaves sent to pick grass at this time it was hardly a lunch or relaxation period. At resumption they worked until six and sometimes later. In crop time the hours of work were even longer as manufacturing continued all through the night.[129] The planters relied on the potential threat and in some cases the actual use of physical punishment to ensure that these gruelling tasks were carried out. Mr. Ninian Jeffreys, a captain in the Royal Navy, describes the plantation routine in Tobago thus:

> I observed the negroes at work in the field, with one or two white men looking after them, and a black man or two called a driver, keeping the whip constantly cracking above their heads while at work, and sometimes lashing them with it which I thought a very oppressive situation, sometimes a white man whipping them.[130]

Whereas slave artisans such as sugar technicians who were skilled received fairly good treatment, the majority of the slaves who worked in the field were subjected to a rigid authoritarian control designed to enforce their subordination to their owners. In 1788 it was asserted that the possession of a slave gave the master "an arbitrary power of administering every sort of correction, however inhuman, not immediately affecting the life or limb". [131] Such powers gave unscrupulous owners wide latitude to commit acts of cruelty as happened in Dominica in 1817 where a master after inflicting 39 lashes on a slave applied a composition of country pepper, lime juice, salt and water to the lacerated parts of the skin.[132] What made these atrocities worse is that the provisions in the slave codes designed to prevent them were laxly if at all enforced. As Mr. Robinson of Dominica said in 1789: "It would... be in a great degree impracticable to put in force laws to protect plantation negroes. If the master be a magistrate he may or he may not enforce them, if he be not he is not under the eye of any."[133]

Cases of ill treatment and abuse as the one just cited can in a sense be regarded as inevitable consequences of the vices inherent in the slave system. Indeed, the majority of the planters seem to have believed that the slave was not a human being and so was unable to feel the effects of hard work, pain and suffering. For instance, Mr. Byam of Grenada admitted that the slaves who worked at the fire places during the manufacture of sugar were "exposed to a great deal of heat", but he went on to point out that "the negroes bear [it] without suffering".[134] Also, Mrs. Carmichael, after describing the yearly routine of the slaves in St. Vincent, came to the conclusion that it was easy and that "*to overwork a negro slave is impossible*".[135]

The slave was definitely regarded as an inferior being and was looked upon with disdain. Reverend Charles Peters had not been long in Dominica before he noted that "contempt of the negro race... may with justice be considered an inveterate disease contaminating alike the moral and intellectual principles of our colonists". He further pointed out that the treatment meted out to slaves in that island was "incomparably less adapted to the condition of human nature... than is the agricultural system which prevails in Great Britain to that of domesticated animals".[136] Indeed, this contempt was shared by the free coloureds as well who were themselves the decendants of slaves. As Peters put it: "To be a slave is *here* in the general estimation of *free men*, to have forfeited all title to human sympathy and kindness, and to be degraded, with the faculties of a man, far below the condition of a brute."[137]

This general lack of sympathy and kindness was reflected in the meagre allowances of food and clothing and medical facilities provided the slaves despite the fact that the whole economy depended on their labour. In these vital areas, the masters provided the barest possible minimum. In Dominica, for instance (which was typical of the other islands in this regard), adult slaves were given as food a weekly allowance of five quarts of Indian Corn and six herrings.[138] For clothing each male received annually one pennistone jacket, a hat, and three yards of osnaburghs to make trousers. Each female received a pennistone wrapper, a coat and three yards of osnaburghs, with children receiving half the amounts specified for adults in these two areas.[139] Clearly it was impossible for the slaves to exist on such meagre allowances unless supplemented from other sources.

This was facilitated by land set aside for food growing even though the quantity and quality of such land was limited by the concentration placed on sugar cultivation. If we are to believe the St. Vincent Legislature, at the end of the period of this study the provision grounds were "in extent generally bounded only by the power of the negro to cultivate".[140] The available evidence indicates, however, that this was an exaggerated claim even though more land was put in food as American supplies became more and more difficult to obtain.[141] However, despite their limitations these land allotments did provide some opportunity for the slave to achieve some sort of economic independence. They were thereby enabled to earn a cash income which could be used to purchase clothing and food, and depending on thrift, purchase their freedom. This income was derived from the sale of poultry, pigs, livestock, vegetables, grass and charcoal produced on these grounds. In the 1820s slaves in St. Vincent received 14/- for a roasting pig, 4/6 for a fowl, 12/6 for a pair of ducks,[142] and profits from these enterprises were said to average one dollar a week.[143] Archibald Campbell reported that it was "very common in the Ceded Islands, to see negroes dressed in white dimity jackets and breaches and fine Holland shirts and the women in muslims", articles which "they purchase themselves".[144]

In addition to the allowances of food and clothing, the master provided the slaves with housing and medical assistance. The houses in the Windward Islands were in general constructed of wattle and daub and thatched with cane leaves, but it was said that "the carpenters, coopers and some other principal negroes on the estate usually contrive to make themselves wooden houses".[145] The typical slave house as described for Dominica was 25 feet long, 14 feet wide, with an earthen floor, and divided into a hall and two chambers.[146] In all the islands provision was made for the service of a doctor and most estates had a hospital or 'hot house' for the reception of the sick. In Grenada, the doctor charged a minimum fee of 10/- for each slave he attended and extra fees for inoculations and surgical operations.[147]

There was, however, a group of privileged slaves who enjoyed on the whole a standard of living much higher than the ordinary field slave. These slaves had greater opportunities for earning a cash income and they were mainly headmen on the estates, artisans, and tradesmen and domestics working in the towns. Towards the end of the eighteenth century carpenters in Dominica earned a salary of £6.12 per annum, coopers £5, and domestics 3/6 per day.[148] Many slave masters also sent their slaves to work as porters and boatmen from which both parties benefited. In some cases the slave hired a boat from the master, paying in return a weekly sum out of the profits of the trade.[149] Towards the end of the eighteenth century, these boat-men and porters were said to be charging such "exorbitant prices for their services" that it became necessary for the Legislature to promul-gate a regulatory scale of fees. Slaves employed as boatmen could charge 15/- if their boat was chartered for a whole day provided two men only were transported, but 27/- if the number was four. Fees for carrying packets and parcels ranged from 3/9 for a whole day's work, 1/6 for half a day, 9d for any time exceeding half an hour, and 4½d for quarter of an hour.[150] These rates were increased by about 50% by subsequent legislation passed in 1816.[151]

Even though the domestics were not as well paid as such 'profe-ssionals', they were still much better off than the common field slaves .In some instances they profited from allowances granted by their employers. Whereas in St. Vincent field slaves were given the barest minimum of subsistence, Mrs. Carmichael noted that "all servants have stockings and a long cloth coat, that is given them by their mas-ters".[152] Some servants were even better off than others in this respect, but she remarked that "the majority ... even of the lowest rank dress better than common field negroes". Whereas the houses of the field slaves had earthen floors, those of domestics were of board.[153] Indeed, this contrast in the standard of living albeit exaggerated was not noticed by Mrs. Carmichael alone. Mr. Ninian Jeffreys had not been long in Tobago and Grenada before he noticed that "the domestic slaves are generally... well fed and in consequence saucy and impertinent", while on the other hand, "plantation slaves are a poor depressed part of the human species".[154]

Most of these slaves were almost wholly dependent on their masters for subsistence, which though scantily provided was nevertheless terribly expensive. In 1788, for instance, it was reported that "every negro in the Ceded Islands cost from £4 to £5 sterling to feed, clothe and maintain himself in sickness and health".[155] When to this was added the cost of the land allotted for provision growing the cost worked out to be £12 sterling a year for adults and about £8 for children.[156] Again, when we take into account the cost of ineffective labour – that is aged, infirm and incapacitated slaves – and also the fact that children did not do as much profitable work as adults, the costs must have been higher. During the first two decades of the nineteenth century, the position got worse as the restrictions on American trade sent the cost of food skyrocketing. In St. Vincent for instance, salt fish which cost 15/- per cwt. in 1774 rose to 40/- in 1784 and 82/6 in 1807. Another staple item, Indian corn, rose from 4/6 to 16/6 by the end of the eighteenth century.[157] The price of other plantation supplies also rose significantly but, as we have seen, the price of everything the planter sold depreciated rapidly.[158]

This combination of rising costs and falling prices which made the sugar industry unprofitable could not fail to have serious effects on the slave population, and it increased the reluctance of the plantocracy to initiate ameliorative policies. In 1823 it was said that because of the increasing economic difficulties being experienced by the Grenada planter, he had been forced to "retrench expenses to save him and his family from ruin".[159] Indeed, the effects of this retrenchment of expenditure were severe. In 1813 the slaves on Plaisance Estate in that island complained that they had received no clothing for 15 months and were thus left exposed to the inclemency of the weather which took a toll of 39 lives, especially as no medical facilities were provided.[160] From Dominica, Governor Maxwell reported that: "Many of the planters from embarrassed circumstances [are] unable to purchase supplies of provisions which were extremely scarce and dear. Due to this, their slaves were exposed to the inclemency of the weather and forced to make a scanty meal of the wild and unripe herbs which caused sickness and a lamentable number of deaths."[161]

So at a time when the humanitarians in England were advocating that the planters provide their slaves with adequate food, the low rate of profit and in some cases the absence of profit in the sugar industry prevented the planters from doing so if they wanted to. At a time too when the humanitarians were concerned about the decrease of the slave population and were asking the planters to take steps to rectify this situation, their inability to provide, adequate food, clothing and medical assistance contributed to an increase in slave mortality. Also at a time when they were insisting that the slave's daily routine on the plantations should be mitigated, the planters faced with a decline in production from exhausted soils were concentrating on increasing output without the use of labour saving devices. Again at a time when the humanitarians were arguing that slave families should not be separated when sold for debt, the economic difficulties of the planters resulted in an increase in the number of slaves sold for debt with no attention paid to this condition.[162] In short, all the efforts of the humanitarians to improve the economic, social and moral well-being of the slaves were frustrated, partly because of the economic difficulties that confronted the planters.

The planters in the British Windward Islands knew very well that their economy was beset with many problems. As solutions, however, they looked only to external factors affecting the sugar industry. For example, they asked for a relaxation of the restrictions on trade with the United States, a reduction of the high war duty of 30/- on sugar, the imposition of preferential rates against East Indian sugar, and they even suggested that Britain use diplomacy to secure the abolition of the slave trade to foreign tropical colonial competitors.[163] As far as they were concerned, nothing was wrong with their own internal organisation.

But there were basic fundamental problems in the internal economic organization which, if the planters were willing to admit and tackle effectively, would have provided much better solutions than the lowering of duties or the imposition of preferential rates against East Indian sugar, for example. Adam Smith had earlier pointed out that free labour was much more economical than slave labour,[164] but despite this the planters continued to operate a sugar industry which called for large amounts of slaves who were for the most part unskilled, and whose purchase and maintenance chronically contributed to the high cost of production which made the industry uneconomic. As if this was not enough, they refused to supplement slave labour with mechanical innovations such as the plough since, as has been suggested, keeping the slaves constantly at hard work was seen as a mechanism of social control. On the whole, free labour was generally seen as leading to the ruin of the West Indies. But these were not the only reasons why the planters were determined not to give up slavery. As Professor Goveia points out for the Leewards, slavery originally introduced to solve the labour problem became eventually "far more than a means of supplying agricultural labour for the plantations".[165] It became a way of life, a social institution, the basis of a social order which it became necessary to maintain despite the absence of any economic justification.

In the Windward Islands the whole economy in the town and country became dependent on slavery. Also, families in the islands collected hordes of domestic slaves as symbols of prestige. According to Mrs. Carmichael, a "moderate family" who would have lived comfortably in an English city with three maid servants and a handyman, required in St. Vincent at least ten grown up servants and five young people or a minimum of fifteen.[166] In 1811 Tobago had a total of 1,464 domestics working for a population of 583 freemen. Governor Young who made this calculation thought he underestimated the number.[167] The possession of a gang of slaves was also seen as a means of social as well as economic improvement to many whites and free coloureds. Mrs. Carmichael asserted that there were many slaves whose masters had no property at all, and that "many respectable families are wholly dependent upon the annual hire of a gang of slaves".[168] Indeed, the number of slaves employed in non-agricultural pursuits is striking. As early as 1788 for example 12,000 out of a total population of 28,000 slaves in Grenada were not employed in the field. Rather, they were domestics, mechanics, sailors, fishermen and porters.[169]

The existence of such large numbers of slaves engaged in occupations outside the plantation did in fact have great economic and social consequences. At the establishment of the plantation system in the British Windward Islands, artisans and mechanics, for instance, were all white. But these were gradually displaced by slaves. When questioned as to the degree of participation of whites in these trades in 1788, Archibald Campbell replied: "White tradesmen... seldom work themselves – there are negro tradesmen of every description on the estates whom the white tradesmen direct... the negroes lay out the work – the white tradesmen do the light and nice jobs themselves and seldom do the heavy or fatiguing work."[170] In agriculture the whites were to be found mainly in managerial and supervisory positions, and the net effect of all this was the creation of a proprietary class of whites controlling the labour of a large number of slaves.

Ironically, the whites also used slave labour as a means of maintaining themselves in power against revolts by the slaves themselves and against attacks from foreign powers. In all the islands slaves were used to reinforce and supplement the strength of the militias. During the French Revolutionary wars at the end of the eighteenth century, slaves were armed for the defence under the authority of island legislatures.[171] During the revolt in Grenada in 1795 a corps of 300 slaves fought on the side of the whites against the rebels.[172] At this time, too, the Loyal Dominica Regiment composed entirely of slaves was instrumental in repelling an invasion from the French Islands[173] and in 1814 it played a part in suppressing the Maroons who had been a headache to the plantocracy for 30 years.[174] Indeed, at the end of the period of this study, Negro slavery had become the basis of the social order of the four insular communities comprising the British Windward Islands.

CHAPTER 6

*L*aw as a weapon of state coercion: The Black system of jurisprudence

> Law is a coercive order... The norms which form a legal order must be norms stipulating a coercive act; i.e. a sanction. The evil applied to the violator of the order when the sanction is socially organised consists in a deprivation of possessions – life, health, freedom or property. As the possessions are taken from him against his will, this sanction has the character of a measure of coercion... A social order that seeks to bring about the desired behaviour of individuals by the enactment of such measures of coercion is called a coercive order.
>
> – Hans Kelsen, *General Theory of Law and State* (1946)

In the report of the Committee of the Privy Council which investigated the Slave Trade and the condition of slaves in the British West Indies in 1788, Mr. Reeves, the law clerk of the committee, commented:

> The leading idea in the Negro system of jurisprudence is that which was first in the minds of those most interested in its formation; namely that negroes were property, and a species of property that needed a rigorous and vigilant regulation. The numerous laws passed in the different islands immediately upon their first settlement and for a considerable time after with all their multifarious provisions had uniformly this for their object. To secure the rights of owners and maintain the subordination of negroes seemed to have occupied their attention and

excited the solicitude of the different legislatures; what regarded the interest of the negroes themselves appeared not to have sufficiently attracted their notice.[1]

An examination of the Slave Laws in force in the British Windward Islands indicates that they were no exception to this generalisation. At the institution of slavery and the plantation system in the mid eighteenth century, the ideas, assumptions and techniques for keeping the slave in total subordination had been already formulated, put into operation and elaborated upon in Barbados, Jamaica and the Leeward Islands where slavery had been long established.[2] It seems as if the planters in the Windward Islands profited from this experience since the laws they passed in the 1760s, have a striking resemblance both in their provisions and purpose to those enacted almost a century before in the older settled islands.

In every one of the Windward Islands all slaves were declared real estate of inheritance and widows were dowable of them as of lands and tenements. If the owner's goods were insufficient to discharge his debts, his slaves could be sold for this purpose.[3] But in some of the islands, in order to prevent the estates from being ruined by slaves so sold, it was provided that in such cases the executor could pay the debts from his own pocket and inventory the slaves who would remain as security for the sum advanced at 6% interest.[4]

The laws of the islands also recognised the owner's right to his property in the slave and protected this right from violation by others. Any person violently taking another's slave could be convicted for robbery. If the slave was detained for a period longer than twenty-four hours, the offender was liable to pay the owner damages at the rate of 12/- per day for a field slave and 24/- for a tradesman. A person carrying another's slave off the islands was declared a felon.[5] And even when a slave was condemned to death for any offence except running away, he was appraised by two freeholders and his owner paid £30 compensation.[6]

The experience of the Windward Islands amply illustrates the extent to which police provisions formed the backbone of the slave laws. Since, as Professor Goveia points out, slaves were not mere property but also human beings capable of offering resistance, it became necessary to regulate slave behaviour in the interest of public order and social stability.[7] And in the Windward Islands slave activities such as thefts, running away, maroonage, arson and rebellion posed serious threats to social stability. The preambles of the Slave Laws make it unmistakably clear that the laws were specifically designed to deal with these problems.

In passing its Act of 1768, for example, the Legislature of Tobago declared that the slaves were of a "barbarous, wild and savage nature" and so were totally unfit to be governed by the laws of England. It was therefore necessary to enact "such laws as may restrain the disorders and disturbances to which they are naturally prone and inclined and for keeping them under due subordination and subjection".[8] The Dominica Legislature cited in 1773 the "great insolences, outrages, thefts, and robberies" for which an increasing number of runaways was responsible, as the main reason for the passage of its Act.[9] The Grenada Legislature also gave as the reason for the passage of its act the fact that a large body of runaways had "armed and assembled themselves in gangs to oppose their masters and any that go in pursuit of them". In addition they frequently committed "murders, thefts and robberies... to the great terror and manifest hazard of the lives and properties" of the resident whites.[10] Again in 1767 the Legislature of St. Vincent passed an elaborate code aimed mainly at runaways, subjecting ring leaders to the death penalty.[11]

An examination of the provisions of this Act sheds some light on the heavy and concentrated emphasis that was placed on police measures for the government of slaves in the Windward Islands. For instance, all slaves were expressly forbidden to leave their respective plantations without tickets from their owners signifying that they could do so.[12] Violations of this law were punishable by a public whipping.[13] They were also forbidden to beat drums or empty casks[14] or to carry firearms off the plantations without permission of the master.[15] A slave guilty of "imprudently striking" or opposing a white person was to be publicly whipped, and if the white was in any way hurt, wounded or disfigured, the slave was liable to have his nose slit or any member cut off, or to be sentenced to death at the discretion of two magistrates.[16]

All Justices of the Peace and Constables were authorised to disperse all "unusual concourses" of slaves and take up all those found with clubs or other offensive weapons, playing dice, or drinking in public houses. Retailers of strong liquor were also forbidden by law to sell any to the slaves.[17] For routine checks on their activities, negro houses were to be searched at least once a fortnight for "runaway negroes, clubs, wooden swords and other mischievous weapons". Owners of slaves who refused to permit this search were liable to a fine of £10.[18] Also slaves convicted of setting fire to dwelling houses, canes and cocoa plantations were sentenced to death.[19]

These police regulations were supplemented and reinforced by provisions of an economic nature. Laws were passed to restrict the employment of slaves in certain occupations and to prevent them from planting and marketing certain types of crops. In St. Vincent for example, slaves were forbidden by law to plant sugar canes, cotton, coffee or ginger. Such goods found in their possession were treated as stolen and they were to be punished accordingly.[20] Also it was declared a misdemeanour for any one to barter, truck or receive from a slave "any sugar, cotton, rum, molasses, ginger, cocoa, coffee or other goods or merchandise (except it be logs of wood, firewood, fresh fish and dunghill fowls, goats, hogs and vegetables of any sort)" without the knowledge and consent of his master signified by a note in writing specifying the nature and quantity of the goods, or unless he was accompanied by a white person. Persons convicted for the purchase of such articles contrary to law were liable to a fine of £20 or double the value of the goods purchased.[21]

In 1767, the Legislature of Grenada passed an Act designed to prevent slaves from hawking and peddling goods from house to house, except provisions, and prescribing a public whipping for infractions.[22] But it appears that this law was evaded. For in 1784 the Legislature complained that the practice of permitting slaves to sell produce had been found "to be productive of great mischief by tempting them to rob their masters and neighbours". To prevent this, it was enacted that all slaves found selling sugar, rum, coffee, cocoa, cotton, molasses or indigo within six days of the publication of the Act would be punished severely at the discretion of one justice. If the offence was committed with the connivance of the slave's owner, he too was liable to punishment in the form of a fine of not less than £10 and not more than £50.[23]

The clerk of the market was authorised to take up any slaves found without a ticket and commit them to the cage. He was also supposed to notify the slave's owner, and any slave not claimed in four days after notice was given, was to be put in prison. A similar type of treatment was prescribed for slaves coming from the country-side without tickets and found on the streets after eight o'clock at nights.[24]

Economic laws of this type were essential in the eyes of the legislators, to prevent the slaves from stealing. The slaves were probably induced to steal because of a need to supplement the meagre pittance given by their masters. But the whites also feared that if the slaves were allowed to engage in the process of exchange without the imposition of restrictions they would become too independent. Indeed, this was totally incompatible with the basis of the slave system – the continued dependence of the slave upon the master for most of the necessities of life and the consequent subjugation and subordination in the society. It was also hoped that such regulations, supplemented by others restricting employment, would have assisted them in controlling the problem of runaways by making them incapable of sustaining themselves without the aid of their masters.

This problem of runaway slaves was common to all the islands and all the Legislatures passed laws for their pursuit, suppression and capture. These laws changed to meet new circumstances and sometimes the tactics employed were different in each island. Whereas in Tobago for instance, reliance was placed mainly on police and economic regulations, in Dominica, in addition to these, it became necessary to admit the evidence of slaves against whites in the Courts, contrary to law, and custom in other parts of the British West Indies.

Under the Dominica Act of 1773, a runaway was defined as a slave who resided on the island for one year and was absent from the master's service for three months in that year. All such were to suffer death as felons.[25] Slaves found off the plantations without tickets were liable to be apprehended by any white or free person. On delivery to the owner the apprehender was entitled to a fee of 16/6, if the slave was taken up two miles from the plantation. If the distance was greater he was to receive 15/- and 1/- for each extra mile.[26] The ringleader of slaves of the age of twelve who ran away in gangs of ten or more was subjected to the death penalty and any persons who killed in pursuit a slave who had been absent from the master's service for a period of three months, was also rewarded.[27]

The concealment of runaways was also punishable under the Act. For a slave, the punishment was a public whipping on the bare breech with any number of stripes not exceeding 50. Free persons were liable to fines of £10, £20 and £50 for the first, second and third offences respectively. In addition a free person so offending was subject to prosecution by the slave's owner for illegal detention of his property and if convicted was liable to pay damages at the rate of 24/- a day.[28]

As in the other islands, provision was made for persons possessing warrants to break open the doors of negro houses. But in Grenada for instance, the person so authorised had to get permission from the slave's master or attorney or the search could not be made.[29] But here the person possessing the warrant could proceed without notice and anyone who attempted to hinder him was liable to a fine.[30]

All Justices of the Peace were authorised to grant permission to any white or free person to search the woods for runaways. Such persons were directed to pursue and capture all slaves that appeared to them or they suspected to be runaways. Also on such expeditions it was perfectly legal for them "to use and employ muskets, cutlasses, and other weapons.... and to fire upon, kill or wound any slave... who shall resist or refuse to surrender".[31]

The Commander-in-Chief or the President of the Council was empowered at any time to order a detachment of free negroes, free mulattoes and other persons of colour to go in pursuit of runaways on pain of fines, to which Marshalls and Constables were also subjected for failure or neglect in their duties.[32]

However, this Act and others passed in the 1780s[33] did not seem to have the desired effects, and in the last decade of the eighteenth century, more stringent measures were adopted, including tight economic regulations and the admittance of slave evidence against whites because of an apparent lack of cooperation by segments of the free population.

In 1798 for instance, the Legislature passed an Act complaining that: "slaves absent themselves from the service of their masters and mistresses upon very slight occasions, and are afterwards employed or harbored by evil-minded white persons and free persons of color... whereby such runaways are countenanced and encouraged in continuing absent from duty".[34]

As a deterrent, white persons so offending were subject to fines of £25 and £50 for the first and second offences respectively. For the third offence the penalty was the pillory and imprisonment for one month. The offender moreover was liable to be sued by the owner for damages at the rate of 12/- per day, besides the full cost of the suit. White or free persons employing slaves without the written permission of or tickets from their owners were also subjected to heavy fines.[35]

The Legislature also criticised the practice of persons who concealed slaves guilty of crimes "so that they cannot be apprehended and brought to justice". The onus was put on owners to bring to the courts slaves accused of such offences on pain of a minimum fine of £20.[36] And the Act as a whole was bolstered by the admittance of slave evidence in the courts against whites in certain cases. In introducing this revolutionary measure, the legislature deplored the practice of "many evil disposed persons" who supplied runaway slaves with ammunition and food, by which means they were "enabled to continue in a state of rebellion". These persons persisted in this "wicked practice", it was alleged because they knew quite well that they could not be convicted, since slave evidence was declared inadmissible against whites in the Courts.[37]

As a deterrent, therefore, slave evidence was declared admissible in the Courts against whites accused of concealing slaves or selling to them weapons, firearms and provisions, so long as the accused was not the master. But before the person could be convicted, two slaves had to be examined apart, and out of the hearing of each other, and both had to "clearly and consistently with each other, depose to the same fact, act or circumstance". In addition the case had to be tried within one year of the commission of the offence.[38]

Despite the fact that the slave could not testify against the master or in cases of personal abuse the admission of slave evidence against whites in certain cases in Dominica was a revolutionary event. For all the other islands in the British West Indies refused at this time to give serious consideration to the principle. This provision however, in combination with others described, indicate the extent to which the lives of all classes in the community had to be regulated to maintain the subordination of the slaves and the stability of the society. Indeed, it might seem a bit ironic that the whites, in order to maintain subordination had been forced to give the slave some civil rights, but it was also very practical since the system operated on the basis that the end justified the means. The end was total control and subordination of the slaves and when this was threatened by the behaviour of some sectors of the free population, measures had to be taken to ensure effective compliance Indeed, the whites as well as free coloureds became victims of the Slave Laws, which the whites had initially created.

Throughout the period, except when they posed a problem of public order, it is difficult to resist the conclusion that the slaves were regarded as human beings. For as regards food, clothing, treatment in sickness and old age and protection from arbitrary and inhumane treatment from others, the slave was almost totally neglected. Where the laws made provisions for food and clothing for example, the quantities that they were entitled to receive were in most cases unspecified. Where the law was specific the quantities were exceedingly small. And in most cases it seems as if the intention of the law was to regulate the behaviour of the slave in the interest of public order.

For instance under the Tobago Slave Act of 1768 which was typical of the other islands in this respect, it was provided that all owners of plantations already settled or of which any part had been cleared for two years were to have at all times one acre of ground "well planted with provisions" for every five slaves and a fine of £10 was imposed for neglect. In addition, owners of plantations that had not been cleared who neglected to feed their slaves 'properly' were subject to a fine of 10/- for each slave not so fed. Two freeholders were also appointed to inspect the provision grounds annually and if in their opinion they did not provide adequate subsistence, the master could be summoned before a Justice of the Peace. But if he gave a satisfactory reason he was not penalised.

This clause was indeed vicious because it meant that unscrupulous planters could refuse to provide their slaves with adequate sustenance and probably get off with impunity. What was worse it seemed to be a regulatory clause for the control of runaways. For it was prefaced by the assertion "so that slaves may have no pretence for absenting themselves from the service of their owners or renters, from the scarcity of provisions in the respective plantations".[39]

In some of the laws vague reference was made to clothing and in the case of Grenada it was not mentioned at all, an indication that the plantocracy probably regarded it as unimportant. The St. Vincent law required owners to provide their male slaves once a year with "one pair of drawers and a shirt or close bodied frock" and females with "a petticoat and a shirt, or close bodied frock".[40] And in Dominica, masters were to provide their slaves with "good and sufficient clothing" once a year.[41]

Provisions governing manumissions and holidays seemed to be as in the case of food also regulatory. In Dominica for instance it was stipulated that no person could manumit a slave without first paying into the treasury a sum of £50 from which the manumitted slave would receive an annuity for his support.[42] But in making this provision, the Legislature deplored the practice of persons who manumitted slaves "without making a proper provision for their maintenance and support, which negroes and slaves so manumitted instead of supporting themselves by honest labor and industry, have through idleness and other vice been greatly injurious to the inhabitants of this island".[43]

It seems therefore as if this clause was part intended to prevent manumitted slaves from being a nuisance to the society. In the British West Indies old age was regarded as a liability on the plantations and some unscrupulous masters resorted to the practice of manumitting slaves when they had become infirm and no longer able to bear the hardships of servitude. This practice filled the islands with wandering slaves who not only were an annoyance and a burden on the public for their maintenance, but also resorted to theft.[44] The Dominica Act was part designed to prevent these public inconveniences.

The early laws with the exception of that of Grenada prescribed holidays for the slaves. But here again the intent of these laws was also regulatory. In St. Vincent for example the slaves were allowed Christmas day, the two days following, "and no more days". Owners giving less or more were subject to a fine of £50.[45] Dominica prescribed Christmas day, the day after, Good Friday and August 15 in every year. But in making this provision the Legislature cited "the many inconveniences" such as drinking and thefts, caused by the number of holidays previously given.[46]

The remaining provisions of these early codes were unduly harsh. In Tobago for instance, a slave could be sentenced to death for 'imagining' the death of a white person,[47] and Dominica prescribed the same penalty for insult to a white person.[48] Yet on the other hand a white could murder a slave and get off without a severe penalty. The Dominica Act stipulated a fine of from £100 to £300 or three years imprisonment as the penalty for a white who murdered his slaves,[49] but no penalties at all were prescribed in the Grenada and St. Vincent Codes. Indeed, it seems as if the Legislatures did not regard the wilful killing of the slave as an act of murder which merited the death penalty.

In all the islands, provisions were also made for the trial of slaves for infractions of the slave codes, and these were unique. In most of the islands one or two Justices of the Peace were sufficient for a trial[50] and it was not until 1788 that at Dominica the Justices were increased to three and a jury of six freeholders was added.[51] This irregular mode of trial was copied from precedents at Barbados in 1668 when it was asserted that such offenders "being brutish slaves deserve not from the baseness of their condition to be tried by the legal trial of twelve men of their peers or neighbours, which truly neither can be rightfully done as the subjects of England are".[52]

After discussing the Slave Laws in force in the British West Indies during the eighteenth century, Professor Goveia concluded: "Early English Slave Law almost totally neglects the slave as a subject for religious instruction as a member of a family, or as a member of society possessing some rights however inferior. In so far as the slave is allowed personality before the law, he is regarded chiefly, almost solely, as a potential criminal".[53] The Windward Islands Slave Laws were no exception to this broad generalisation.

Even when the humanitarians were extremely vociferous in their criticism of slavery in the last two decades of the eighteenth century, and when the planters in response to this criticism were pressured to pass new slave laws, the ideas and assumptions behind the old slave codes were not abandoned. In 1788 and 1789 two new codes were passed in Dominica and Grenada.[54] We will focus on the provisions of the Grenada Act as an illustration of the extreme reluctance of the planters to initiate serious reforms in the Slave Codes. The fact that

Tobago and Grenada completely refused to implement any changes in their old slave codes is also quite instructive.

The Grenada Act attempted to restrain arbitrary punishment on the plantations. It was declared unlawful for managers, overseers, or other free persons to inflict any mode of punishment other than imprisonment in "a proper and wholesome place of confinement" and a maximum of 39 lashes, in the absence of the proprietor. If the offence deserved greater punishment the slave was to be tried by two Justices who were empowered to inflict punishment not extending to life or limb. Persons who inflicted modes of punishment other than those prescribed were subject to prosecution at the Court of Grand Sessions and if convicted the penalty was fine or imprisonment.[55]

Provision was made for religious instruction. Towards this end, officiating clergymen of the Church of England were required to visit estates owned by Protestants once every three months in the first year and once every six months thereafter. They were further authorized to baptise and marry all slaves free of charge and Roman Catholic priests were required to do the same on plantations owned by persons of their faith. Clergymen who refused to perform these duties and all persons who attempted to obstruct them were subject to a fine of £20.[56]

The Act also made provisions designed to prevent married female slaves from being violated at the hands of owners and managers. It specifically stated that such persons were not to "debauch and have carnal knowledge of such slave during her marriage". For non-compliance, masters were to be fined £165, Attorneys, half their yearly salary, and transient visitors £50.[57]

With regard to manumission it was provided that owners were not to discard their slaves on account of old age, sickness or infirmity. Such slaves were to be provided with adequate food, clothing, lodging and medical assistance and a fine of £100 was imposed for neglect. Further no manumission was to be accepted as valid unless it was endorsed with a certificate stating that the slave was not likely to become burdensome to the public.[58]

The Act also specified the quantity of clothing each slave was entitled to receive. Male slaves above the age of fifteen were allowed annually a hat, jacket, shirt and trousers, and a blanket. For females the allowance was "a hat, jacket, shift, pettycoat and a blanket" and masters were subject to a fine of £20 for neglect.[59] But it is difficult to regard this provision as ameliorative. The quantity was exceedingly small, and probably not more than he received earlier.

The Act also regulated the hours of work. Evidence of contemporary observers indicates that it was the practice of unscrupulous masters to work their slaves after sunset in the fields.[60] It was stipulated that except in the manufacture of produce that required night or extra labour, the slaves were not to be sent in the field before day break, nor at breakfast, dining, nor after sunset except for the purpose of carrying a bundle or two of grass.[61] But the law did not go far enough since it meant that slaves could still be sent grass picking at rest periods, and it also failed to regulate the hours of work at crop time. This indeed was a time when slaves were forced to work "all night or as long as they can keep awake or stand on their legs".[62]

Finally, to see that the provisions of the Act were enforced it was provided that the Justices were to appoint at each quarter sessions, three persons who were freeholders or owned at least thirty slaves, or their Attorneys, to act as Guardians of Slaves in each parish. Three such persons were also to be appointed for the town of St. George.

The Guardians were required to take an oath of office to do their duties faithfully. All or any two of them were required to visit the estates under their respective jurisdictions once every six months and at all other times when any complaint necessitated their presence. They were to inquire into slave complaints, inspect the provision grounds, and see to the clothing and treatment of slaves in general. Managers, overseers, the medical personnel in the hospital, and all other persons in a position to give information about the food, clothing and treatment of slaves were subject to examination on oath by the guardian and a fine of £50 was imposed for non compliance. When any provisions of the Act were violated the Guardians were authorised to sue and prosecute the offenders. Guardians after serving for a period of one year could stand for re-election three years later and they too could be fined if they refused to carry out their duties.[63]

Only the novel features of this Act have been described here. The remaining provisions were economic and police clauses as in the old slave code of 1773 which need not be repeated here. The main weakness, defects and the working of this Act will be discussed later in this chapter, but to place this Act and that of Dominica in proper perspective we need to keep in mind the fact that at the time they were passed, the agitation against the Slave Trade was growing steadily in England and was a well known feature in the islands. It was a time when the Society of West Indian Merchants and Planters, a lobby for the planter class in the metropolis had feared that the humanitarians might succeed in their objective of getting the Trade abolished if ameliorative policies were not implemented and so they were urging the planters to comply.

The important point is that it was this outside pressure which was mainly responsible for the passage of the legislation in Grenada and Dominica. In fact Henry Hew Dalrymple, a resident of Grenada testified before a Parliamentary Committee in 1790 that the Legislature passed the Act because members were advised in a letter from the colonial agent that "unless they made laws for the protection of the slaves the British Parliament would".[64] Indeed not only would this have raised the irritating question of the right of the British Parliament to legislate in the internal affairs of the colonies, but there was also the fear that the Slave Trade might probably be cut off, a measure which the humanitarians were advocating. But the Legislature was still hesitant to pass an ameliorative code since it was feared that the slaves might interpret it to mean that their masters had less authority over them. However, after some discussion, the Act was finally passed because the members came to a general consensus that its provisions would be "of little consequence", since it would be "made by themselves against themselves", and "carried into execution by themselves.[65]

It should be clear therefore that the realities of the situation placed some of the legislatures into a position where they felt it necessary to do something or face the feared consequences. So they made laws granting the slave a little protection in theory. But it is also clear that they were perfectly well aware that the protective parts of the law would be laxly if at all enforced. Indeed the conception of the slave as a kind of property that had to be kept in rigorous subordination seems to have been the deciding factor in this situation.

Throughout the period the legislatures generally refused to admit the evidence of slaves against whites in the Courts. The only partial relaxation of this policy as we have seen was in Dominica where slave evidence was admitted against whites except the master, and only for the specific purpose of aiding the conviction of those accused of aiding runaways. This general non-acceptance of slave evidence meant as Chief Justice Ottley of St. Vincent pointed out, that slaves were liable "to suffer much abuse and ill-treatment from, an oppressive governor or master without any legal remedy or protection".[66] Cases of abuse only reached the Courts through the interposition of the master since the slave could not file an action and even when this happened, in most cases the law of evidence worked to the disadvantage of the slave. In Tobago for instance, a white man stabbed a slave in the presence of another slave. The slave died on the spot and through the interposition of his owner, the white man was brought to trial. But at the hearing he was acquitted since the testimony of the slave who had witnessed the incident was declared inadmissible.[67]

However, in 1774 a white, Bacchus Preston, was convicted for stabbing a female slave to death in Grenada. At the hearing, a motion in arrest of judgement was made on the grounds that since the party killed was a slave, the perpetrator of the crime ought not to suffer the death penalty. But this objection was over-ruled and the murderer executed.[68]

It does not appear, however that Bacchus Preston was executed solely for the murder of the slave. Henry Hew Dalrymple who was in Grenada at the time discussed the case with the Chief Justice and was told that if Preston was of "good character", or had friends or money to pay for the slave he had murdered, he would not have been brought to trial. On the contrary he was a bailiff, who performed his duties with assiduity and rigour, and behaved in a fashion that made himself "particularly obnoxious" to the inhabitants of St. George.[69]

This evidence leads one to suspect that Preston was executed partly because he was disliked by the community for other reasons. For the available evidence indicates that in general the murder or maltreatment of a slave hardly aroused public animosity among the whites. When for example, a Tobagonian planter broke a slave's leg with an iron bar for running away, not only did he receive no punishment but it was also "not public opinion that any ought to be inflicted for he was equally well received in society after this action as before".[70]

The difficulty or rather the almost total impossibility of effecting successful prosecutions against masters for acts of cruelty was realised by a few white observers. For instance Chief Justice Ottley of St. Vincent, commented that the non-admittance of slave evidence created a situation in which white men were put "in a manner beyond the reach of law". But he himself seemed reluctant to argue for the implementation of the revolutionary measure of the admittance of slave evidence as a remedy, arguing that it was in any case unwise because of "the state of ignorance in which the slaves are at present".[71]

Professor Goveia in her study on the Leeward Islands claims that at the end of the eighteenth century, opinion there was not hostile to amelioration. She further suggests that this might have been so because the slaves on a whole had generally acquiesced in their subordination and this meant that the planters could afford to treat them with less severity.[72] However, we find that at this time, the planters in the Windward Islands were terribly hostile to any suggestions of amelioration. This difference needs examination.

A clue to a probable explanation for this difference in attitude might be found in the differing historical experiences of the two groups of islands at this time. The most important single factor common to both groups at this time and indeed to the West Indies as a whole was the overspill of the French Revolution and its ideas of liberty, equality and fraternity. Indeed, these notions challenged the basic assumptions of the slave society and the whites being panic-stricken took measures to prevent their introduction and realisation. But this still leaves unanswered, why the whites in the Leewards, were more paranoid than those in the Windwards. The answer seems to lie in the fact that the whites in the Windwards had much more to fear than their counterparts in the Leewards.

At this time there were only two efforts at revolts in the Leewards, one at St. Kitts in 1788 and the other in the Virgins in 1790.[73] On the other hand, in the Windwards, there were serious revolutionary disturbances. In Grenada in 1795 there was a revolt which lasted for more than a year which involved a few whites, free people of color and thousands of slaves. In this same year, St.Vincent went up in flames with the Black Caribs fighting the British with slaves. In 1790, there was a slave revolt in Dominica, and in 1795 the island was invaded by French whites from Guadeloupe who were in correspondence with the Maroons. This group had earlier posed a serious threat to social stability and were to invade the settled plantations two years later. The slaves in Tobago at this time appeared to be quiet but in 1801, an insurrectionary plot to murder all the whites in the island was discovered.[74]

It seems therefore that in this situation the whites could not afford to think in terms of amelioration. What preoccupied their attention was self preservation since the translation of the principles of the French Revolution into action threatened to destroy their society. Self-preservation meant the use of counter force and it seems to have increased the necessity to keep the slaves under tighter control. It is this experience which was much different from the Leewards that seems to explain the general hostility of the Legislatures to the implementation of ameliorative reforms suggested in 1797.

In 1797 the West Indians in England who were stoutly defending the slave trade and slavery, introduced into the House of Commons a resolution recommending a policy of amelioration by the Legislatures in the sugar islands. This was indeed a political move designed to mitigate humanitarian criticism of the slave trade and slavery and the Legislatures were asked to pass the necessary legislation. They were told among other things to take steps to remove the causes which prevented natural increase of the slave population taking into consideration the possibility that the slave trade might be ended, to improve the morals of the slaves and most importantly to ensure that they be given "the certain, immediate and active protection of the law".[75]

The reactions of the Legislatures to these suggestions were almost generally negative. Indeed, except what might be regarded as a seeming willingness in the case of Grenada to give at least a tacit acquiescence in the principle of legislative amelioration, the proposals were ignored by the legislatures. The Secretary of State, disturbed by this action or rather lack of action circulated the legislatures with proposals as guidelines for action. He suggested that premiums should be granted to mothers for rearing children, that mothers of six should be exempted from all hard labour, that slaves should be encouraged to marry and that missionaries be employed for religious instruction. Finally, since in his opinion it might be more easy to convert younger slaves to Christianity than older ones, he suggested the imposition of a tax on all slaves imported above the age of 25.[76]

Indeed, even these fairly mild suggestions for reform were too much for the majority of the Legislatures. The Legislature of Tobago favoured the introduction of missionaries from the Society for the Propagation of the Gospel in Foreign Parts, a law to prevent young children from being carried in the field, which was "too general a practice," the imposition of the tax on slaves above the age of 25 and the appointment of two or three persons, to act as Guardians as had been the case in Grenada.[77]

The above propositions were actually written into a new Slave Law of 175 clauses in 1800 and indeed if that law had been passed and its provisions enforced, the slave would have been afforded some protection. But after some debate it was decided to table the bill for a year, the members "thinking it very unwise the bringing it forward at this particular juncture". "The late accounts from Jamaica with other reasons" it was argued "induced the Legislature to come to the above resolution".[78] Neither "the other reasons" nor the late accounts from Jamaica were spelled out. In the latter case it might have been the rebellion or the threat of it and the general slave turbulence in the island around this time.[79] Whatever the reason however the proposed Slave Law was abandoned and the old Code of 1768 remained in force until its repeal in 1821.

St. Vincent's reaction was even worse. Indeed that island's conduct with regard to amelioration is highly notorious. In 1788 despite pressure from absentee interests, the Legislature refused to revise its Slave Code as Dominica and Grenada had done even though the provisions of these codes were laxly enforced. These same interests again reminded the Legislature at this time that it was "indispensably necessary" to implement the reforms, and despite a promise that it was willing "to most readily adopt", the reforms,[80] nothing was done. It is true that the death penalty for the murder of a slave was written into law in 1801[81] but the old Slave Law of 1767 remained in force until its repeal in 1821.

The Secretary of State was annoyed when he did not receive any response from Dominica on the subject matter almost two years after the despatch of the original circular.[82] When a response finally arrived it was not only a negative but also an angry one. Any discussion of amelioration at that time it was argued, would have been "highly dangerous", and followed by "fatal consequences" because of the proximity to the French islands, and "our still having among us many who cherish the baneful notions of universal emancipation, liberty and equality". A revolt which broke out in 1790 "soon after the situation of the slaves had become the object of attention and discussion of the legislature" was cited as a further reason. These reasons aside however, the Slave Law passed in 1788 was "in every respect... fully adequate" to achieve the aims of the resolution and no further law was necessary. For that Act had "fully answered" everything pertaining to amelioration, "as far as the circumstances of the colony render them practicable".[83]

Such a response indicated that to the planter class considerations of self-preservation were clearly more important than amelioration. It can be argued however that this need for self preservation was probably the result of their own failure, to implement meaningful ameliorative policies.

The only fruit of the Secretary of State's Circular in the Windward Islands was the Grenada Slave Act of 1797. The Legislature's initial reaction to the Circular however, that under the existing Act of 1788 the slave was "thoroughly protected" and "secured in every benefit of the laws"[84] was similar to the position advocated by Dominica. In the new code of 1797 all that the Legislature did was to re-enact the majority of the old clauses, and make minor improvements in others, of the Act of 1788, the essential elements of which remained intact.

Under this Act, punishment by masters and overseers was restricted as under the Act of 1788. But the slave was given little more protection at least in theory. Persons who mutilated slaves were liable to prosecution as if the offence was committed against a free person and if convicted they were subject to a maximum fine of £500 and one year in prison. The owner could also bring an action against the offender for damages and if he happened to be the master, the Guardians were entitled either to declare the slave a free person with no obligation to work again for his former master, or sell him to some other person of "humane repute". If the slave was freed however he was entitled to receive an annuity of £10 per year for his support to be paid from the fine imposed on the offending owner.[85]

Upon every plantation there was to be erected within four months of the publication of the Act "a good and sufficient hospital", in proportion to the number of slaves thereon. Medical records were to be kept of the names of slaves admitted, the dates of admission, and the nature and complaints of the diseases. Owners were also required once a year to report on oath an account of births and deaths and a fine of £20 was imposed for neglect.[86]

In an effort to increase the population it was provided that mothers of six children should be exempted from all labor and the owners of such slaves from all taxes.[87] Owners were also forbidden to manumit infirm slaves and no slave was to be freed without his master first paying a deposit of £100 from which the freed slave would receive an annuity of £10 in two half-yearly instalments.[88]

The cardinal weakness of the Act of 1797 as well as that of 1788 as ameliorative measures, was that they both lacked teeth. For the specification that the Guardians were to be freeholders, men who owned at least 30 slaves, or their attorneys, meant that the enforcement of the Acts was left completely in the hands of the slave holding class or men with interests in slave holding. It is indeed difficult to envisage how these men assuming they were well meaning could have fulfilled their dual and conflicting roles. How, for instance, could an attorney or manager say that the food and clothing provided was insufficient knowing without any doubt that if his employer found out what he said he might lose his job? Or how could a slave owner have prosecuted his fellow-man for maltreatment knowing without any doubt not only that he himself might be equally guilty, but also that he might be prosecuted for a similar offence by the accused or someone else at the expiration of his term of office? Indications are that acting impartially would have been against the interest of the Guardians, and the general failure of the Act to appoint independent persons or Guardians who could afford to be more impartial, rendered the Act itself worthless.

As early as 1812 President Adye, writing about the working of this Act, noted that "few instances have occurred of their (the guardians) having acted further than the taking of the oath prescribed by it", and that it was "in most respects a dead letter".[89] Six years later these sentiments were supported by Governor Riall who in addition attributed the reason for lack of success in part to the fact that most

Guardians regarded the job as unpleasant, that their inquiries were often "futile and nugatory", because they also feared victimisation, and prosecutions could not be effected because of the general refusal to admit slave evidence.[90] In 1823, Sir Fortunatus Dwarris was told that "most of the Guardians evade taking the oath as they do not like to meddle with their neighbours", and they generally refused to visit the provision grounds to see that proper food and clothing was administered.[91]

The Guardians usually acted after they were ordered to do so by the Governor on his receipt of complaints from the slaves rather than on their own initiative. In September 1821 they were sent to investigate a complaint about clothing and reported that only a part of the yearly allowance had been granted. The women had received only enough cloth to make an apron each, and such failures of the planters to meet their obligations generally went unpunished.

In 1823 only 52 prosecutions for non-compliance were made since the Act was passed, and while redress was granted in a few instances the majority of the charges were said to be groundless. This is not surprising in view of the fact that the Act refused to admit the evidence of slaves against whites. In addition the juries were reported to be strongly prejudiced in favour of whites in such cases.[92]

The conduct of the juries in this respect in Grenada was equally notorious in Dominica. In that island despite the fact that the Act of 1788 limited punishments to whipping and confinement, masters continued to inflict other horrid types of punishments on their slaves. In 1817 Governor Maxwell, the only spokesman for the slaves, reported "many instances... in which iron collars and chains have been added to their sufferings after a severe whipping", and he began a one-man humanitarian crusade to bring such offenders to justice and prevent such acts in future.[93]

Through his initiative cases were brought to court. These were thrown out because the slave could not testify, even though despite this lack of evidence, it was still the opinion of the Grand Jury that the slaves merited the punishment in most of the cases.[94] That jury also described the Governor's actions as "an improper interference... between master and slave, which has caused considerable agitation and discontent among the negroes and if preserved in is likely to lead to the most ruinous consequences".[95] Under such circumstances, ameliorative policies were bound to fail.

During the first two decades of the nineteenth century, therefore, there was no marked change in the attitude of the Legislatures towards amelioration. The humanitarians had hoped that the cutting off of the slave trade in 1807 would have impressed on the planters the necessity to improve the well-being of their slaves, but this was not achieved partly because of a heavy emphasis placed on force in all dealings with the slaves.

In 1821 the Legislatures of St. Vincent and Dominica passed two new slave codes repealing the ones enacted in the eighteenth century, but the bulk of the legislation still consisted of economic and police provisions for social control. In St. Vincent for instance such provisions made up 72 of the 83 clauses of the Act.[96] The only ameliorative provision was to be found in the Dominica Act which allowed the admittance of slave evidence against whites in the courts on the lines advocated by the Act of 1798 for the suppression of runaways.[97]

Under these two Acts passed just before the final humanitarian thrust the slave was hardly much better protected than he was formerly. But this was not too surprising. For in passing these Acts, the legislatures expressed the view that the laws could be revised only "as far as may be consistent with due order and subordination".[98] This concern influenced to a large extent their reaction to new ameliorative reforms suggested in 1823.

In 1823 the British government proposed a series of reforms which were to be enforced by Orders in Council in the crown colonies of Trinidad, St. Lucia and British Guiana, and through local enactments in those colonies that had representative institutions. The reforms included the abolition of the Sunday market so that this day would be reserved for religious observances, and the provision of another day for the slaves to market their produce; the abolition of the whip; prohibition of flogging for female slaves; compulsory manumission of field and domestic slaves; the admittance of slave evidence; the establishment of savings banks for slaves; and the freeing of female children born after 1823.[99]

The planters regarded the majority of the proposals as objectionable and they generally unanimously refused to adopt them, especially those dealing with the abolition of the whip and the freeing of children.

The consensus of opinion among the Tobago planters was that they "would rather wait the event of interference of Government than bind themselves to the observance of such enactments as would evidently be contrary to their interest". The proposal to free all female slaves born after 1823 was seen as a first step towards total emancipation and consequently "utter ruin to the proprietors or their heirs".[100]

Opposition from St. Vincent was even more angry and intense. Arguing that their property in slaves was a bona fide vested right, the planters went on to state that it was "idle and absurd to suppose they will either willingly consent to any innovation of this sacred principle, or be themselves instrumental to any alienation of those rights".[101]

On the question of the abolition of the Sunday markets and the institution of some other day, they argued that this would have the effect of diminishing by one fifth or one sixth the amount of labour exacted, and that "the proprietor cannot afford this sacrifice". No proprietor in England they claimed would voluntarily consent to a proposal designed to diminish his revenue by 15 or 20% and yet this was what the West Indian proprietor was called upon to do.[102]

The whip, they declared was carried by the driver merely as a symbol of his authority, and it was vitally necessary to have it around since "the time is still far distant, when it would be either prudent or safe to hint to this class of persons that they are no longer amenable to corporal punishment".[103]

In conclusion they argued that they were not responsible for the existence of the institution of slavery. Rather it developed "under the fostering care and protecting hand of the nation"; and they also regarded as "manifestly unjust any propositions which positively or virtually tend to unsettle or depreciate the property of the master". Whenever these were made, they argued, "the colonists will not contumaciously, but they will firmly and unceasingly, oppose them no matter in what quarter they originate or by whose authority they are supported".[104]

The initial reaction of the Legislature of Dominica was the despatch of a circular to the other legislatures in the British West Indies asking them to unite in a general protest against the measures.[105]

However a special committee was subsequently appointed to consider the question and a report was drafted. That report ended by saying that the condition of the slave:

> has much improved, and is daily improving, that their wants and comforts in health and sickness are carefully attended to that punishments are proportioned to offences and have greatly decreased, that they enjoy the benefits of religious instruction possess the means of acquiring property and freedom, and your committee feel no hesitation in saying that the generality of the negroes are happy and contented and, will so remain if their minds are not excited by the delusive hopes of emancipation.[106]

The general tenor of this report was that the slave was well treated and so there was no need to introduce further ameliorative measures, a position which the legislature had earlier stated in reaction to the ameliorative proposals of 1797. But the Slave Code of 1821, a comprehensive mass of economic and police provisions, was still in force, and this code was indeed typical of those in the other islands which had rejected the suggested reforms. After discussing the Slave Laws in the Leeward Islands at the end of the eighteenth century, Professor Goveia concluded that: "The elements of force and fear were still the indispensable basis of slavery, and most of the whites were determined to maintain them in face of all pressure for change."[107] This is equally true of the Windward Islands in 1823.

CHAPTER 7

Law, social engineering, stratification and the free coloured

If power is taken as the basis of right as Hobbs... do, then right,law... are merely the symptom the expression of other relations upon which state power rests... These actual relations are in no way created by state power, on the contrary they are the power creating it... The individuals who rule in these conditions beside having to constitute their power in the form of the state have to give their will which is determined by the definite considerations a universal expression as the will of the state, as law, an expression whose content is always determined by the relations of this class as the civil and criminal law demonstrates in the clearest possible way.

– Marx and Engels, *The German Ideology* (1845)

GROUP STATUS AND ROLE

In 1823 the total population of the British Windward Islands was approximately 88,000 persons. Of these 244 whites, and 13,671 slaves lived in Tobago. The remainder of the population lived in Dominica, St. Vincent, Grenada and the Grenadines. In these islands there were about 3,000 whites and 61,000 slaves, and the total free coloured population was roughly 10,000 persons.[1]

The majority of the free population was concentrated in the parishes with towns, whereas the majority of the slaves were scattered on the plantations throughout the rural areas even though there were slaves engaged in occupations in the towns.

Some detailed population figures given for Grenada in 1820 indicate that in the two parishes with towns, the proportion of slaves to free persons varied from 3 to 1 to 11 to 1, the parish with the larger town having the smaller ratio, and the parish with the smaller town having a greater proportion of slaves to free persons. On average, the proportion of slaves to free persons in these urban parishes was about 7 to 1. In the five rural parishes, on the other hand, the proportions varied from 10 to 1 to 20 to 1, and the average for these parishes as a whole was roughly 17 to 1.[2]

The relationships between the groups of whites, free persons of colour and slaves were determined largely by colour, class and legal status in a particular brand of social engineering hammered out by the white elite which controlled the legal system and used it to the utmost in the desire to maintain racial dominance and superiority The whites were the most prominent and influential group to whom the other two were subordinated. The class of free persons of colour, which included a majority of persons of mixed blood, was made up of manumitted slaves and their descendants and these too were a very important class occupying a marginal position between the whites and the slaves. The large mass of black slaves held the lowest status of all, and were the most deprived and depressed class in the society.

There were, however, differences within each group as well as between separate groups in the community. For instance, there were differences of wealth, privilege and status in the white group and even though the whites were the entrenched ruling class, there were some whites who were denied effective participation in the political system either because of their lack of property or their religious beliefs.

One of the most important distinctions within the white group lay in the degree of participation in local politics allowed the English-born subjects and the French-born subjects who were Roman Catholics and resided in St. Vincent, Dominica and Grenada. The narrow limits set on political participation by this latter group including the right to vote were regarded by the British born Protestants as externally imposed and unwarranted impositions and in Grenada these rights were in 1786 taken away with the consent of the home government.[3] In the other islands the French subjects were allowed to vote only[4] and it was not until 1831 that the restrictions were removed.[5] It is important to note, however, that the existence of these restrictions did not lead to any real serious explosion between the English whites and the French whites, who shared in the economic and social dominance in other respects. For both groups were despite their grouses solidified and unified in the basic necessity to preserve the social order from feared disruption by the deprived and depressed slave population. As the French inhabitants expressed it in a petition in 1766:

> a colony whose cultivation depends on the number, labour and submission of negroes, calls for such absolute influence in the hands of every freeholder in order to maintain them in proper discipline and respect, and renders any unnatural and unnecessary subordination and inequality among whites, that approaches them to the level of their slaves as dangerous as it is odious.[6]

As in Jamaica[7] and other British slave colonies in the Caribbean the free people of colour and slaves were denied any participation at all in the political system and as a result it became essentially a monopoly of British-born subjects who were initially the wealthiest planters and merchants, doctors, lawyers and professional men. They filled the councils and assemblies, the courts of judicature, officered the militias and filled most other public offices in the islands.

UPWARD MOBILITY AND SHIFTS
IN THE RULING CLASS

But the character of the white ruling class changed significantly especially during the nineteenth century because of the existence of the chronic plague of absenteeism. The governors had been instructed by their commissions to nominate the most wealthy planters to the Councils, and there was a minimum qualification of fifty acres of land for election to the Assembly.[8] But as the rich planters retired abroad these qualifications had to be either ignored or abandoned. As early as 1804, only five of the twelve Council members in Tobago were resident on the island, and it was impossible to find persons who had the property qualifications. As a result, lesser whites without property who had earlier been relegated to tasks such as a jury service had to be appointed.[9]

The island of Grenada, faced with a declining white population, abolished its property qualification for election to the Assembly in a new Act passed in 1812.[10] Five years later it was reported that "many of the members of the Assembly were become members thereof who are merely the agents or managers of estates belonging to proprietors resident in Great Britain, and not possessing any freehold estate of their own".[11] At the same time the Dominica Assembly consisted of five proprietors only, eight merchants, four attorneys of estates, and a surgeon. Apart from the proprietors, only two or three of the other members held the required 50 acres which were not even in cultivation.[12]

A NEW CLASS

This general decline in the white population resulted in the admission of a new class of whites, particularly managers and overseers, who had been previously excluded from the ruling group. But while the absenteeism of the planter class contributed significantly to this situation, upward mobility among the white population had been for a long time characteristic of the slave society of the British Windward Islands.

This upward mobility was facilitated to a large extent by the institution of negro slavery itself. Generally speaking, the whites on a whole did little or no manual work. This was in stark contrast to the situation in the seventeenth century when irrespective of gender they constituted the bulk of the labour force under the indentureship system. As Beckles writes:

> prior to the proliferation of the sugar plantation and the revolutionary absorption of enslaved Africans propertyless white women constituted a significant element within the ganged labour force of the sugar estates. These women were recruited from the British Isles... transported to the colonies and engaged as bonded labourers... many were defencless persons convicts vagrants political prisoners.[13]

However in the period under review in agriculture, for example, there were no white labourers, since the lowest starting point for a white was the supervisory position of book-keeper or overseer. And white domestic servants were hardly employed in the towns or in the countryside since there were enough slaves to do that kind of work.

The white artisans and artificers also did little manual work. The majority had ceased to be labourers and had actually become the owners, employers and supervisors of labour.[14] Indeed, at the end of the period of this study, the whites were predominantly a proprietary, professional and managerial group, controlling the labour of large numbers of slaves in almost every aspect of the economy.

The experience of overseers and managers provide an indication of how the whites used the institution of negro slavery to better their economic and social position. The overseers as a class were not paid very attractive salaries and their perquisites were not as great as those received by managers.[15] But despite this, many overseers became managers, and many managers became proprietors of estates. In speaking of white overseers in the British Windward Islands, Archibald Campbell noted that "they are often sons of gentlemen from this country, Scotland, and Ireland who go out... as overseers, and by their good conduct, after having experienced the management of slaves, and manufacturing the produce of the grounds they become managers".[16]

After the overseer had served his apprenticeship and risen to the position of manager, his salary was still not large.[17] But despite this, his economic opportunities were increased especially if the owner of the estate was an absentee. Archibald Campbell noted in 1788 that the salaries paid to managers, along with "the provisions and stock, and other allowances given, which they can raise on the estate, is sufficient to enable them to live comfortably and happily and to save the greater part of their wages". And what was saved was generally reinvested in slaves. Most of the managers were accustomed to "lay out what they save of their salary in purchasing slaves" which they hired out to supplement their income.[18] And speaking about Tobago, Sir William Young also noted that many managers "had commenced a purchase of slaves profiting from the hire of those they possessed to purchase others until they gained a sufficient knowledge of island agriculture to settle a plantation of their own".[19]

As the managers acquired wealth, they like other whites of humble origins were able to move up the social ladder. By the end of the second decade of the nineteenth century this process was accelerated as it was becoming more and more necessary to admit as many whites as possible to the ruling group.[20]

THE PROBLEM OF SOCIAL CONTROL

It is apparent that in view of the decline in the white population the necessity for racial solidarity eventually triumphed over distinctions of class and status. Even though the restrictions placed on the participation of the French naturalised subjects in the political system were not removed until 1831, as early as 1791, the Dominica Council voted for their total abrogation.[21] This at least demonstrated a determination on the part of sections of the ruling class to solidify its ranks by conceding political rights to the most important group of whites kept out of the political system.

It was this necessity for racial solidarity which in part explains the eagerness of the whites to help the more unfortunate of their group. During the American Revolutionary War, a committee of absentee proprietors from Dominica made representations to the home authorities for the removal to the island of the inhabitants of East Florida who had remained loyal to the king. In making the case for resettlement, they expressed concern at the treatment meted out to the Loyalists and saw Dominica as a place where "those unhappy sufferers" would be provided with "a comfortable asylum". But more importantly, their removal to Dominica was seen "as a measure likely to contribute greatly to the strength of the colony".[22]

By the middle of 1785, about 500 loyalists had arrived in the island and they were given grants of Crown Lands in the interior to cultivate as well as a fifteen-year exemption from all taxes.[23] The Governor, fearing that the French naturalised subjects might defect in the event of a war with France keenly welcomed them as a valuable addition[24] but it can be suggested that the fear of upheaval by the slaves and maroons was perhaps a major factor influencing this decision. As a matter of fact, the Maroons had their camps on some of these Crown lands in the interior and during the eighteenth century the authorities

contemplated establishing settlements in these parts, even of free negroes and free mulattoes in an attempt to force them to come into the
open.[25] Indeed such considerations reflect the ever increasing concern of the white population with the overriding problem of social
control in the slave plantation society. This preoccupation with the
question of social control influenced the behaviour of the whites towards the free coloureds as well.

GROWTH RATE AMONG THE FREE COLOURED

The free coloureds constituted 11.4% of the total population of the
British Windward Islands in 1823. In terms of percentages in the total
population in the individual islands these ranged from as low as 4.0%
in Tobago to as high as 11.25% in Grenada.[26] As in Jamaica[27] their
numbers increased rapidly throughout the period and in Dominica
for instance the increase was more than seven-fold in the period 1788
to 1823.[28] This was in marked contrast to the negative growth of the
slave and white population which tended to decrease in almost equal
proportions.

   This point is borne out by population statistics for Tobago which
are typical of the other islands. Here the free people of colour increased from 2% of the population in 1790 to 4.9% in 1823, an increase
of 2.9%. In the same period the whites decreased from 3.5% of the
total population to 1.6% – a decrease of 2.2% and the slaves from
94.5% to 93.5% – a decrease of 1%.[29] This demographic increase in the
free coloured population made the problem of social control more
urgent for the ruling class.

   This rapid growth rate was made possible by three principal
means – natural reproduction, voluntary manumission, and paid
manumission (self purchase). A fourth source of less significance lay
in those Africans who after 1807 were either smuggled into the islands or were the cargoes of Spanish slavers which contravened the
Act of Abolition and were captured and condemned in Vice Admiralty Courts. Most of these Africans were immediately freed while a
few were kept for a time in semi-servile conditions similar to the
Cuban Emancipados[30] and called Apprentices. The 1823 returns

listed 37 of these in Dominica, 10 in Tobago and 1 for Grenada,[31] while that of 1817 listed 60 for St. Vincent.[32]

NATURAL REPRODUCTION

The principal means of increase, however, at least in the initial stages, was natural reproduction in formal and informal relationships between white men and women of African descent. Almost every writer on plantation society past as well as present has commented on the prevalence of these relationships. James Walker, writing in 1818 in a work dedicated to the planters of Tobago and Antigua, was severely critical of the system of concubinage which became "established as a virtue".[33] Heuman attributes the practice in Jamaica to a shortage of white women and "an unwritten rule that young planters arriving in the island remain single".[34] Thomas Attwood pointed out that its origins lay in "a European aversion to matrimony" arising out of the fact that the white men tended to see themselves in voluntary exile for a few years during which time they hoped to make a quick fortune and return home.[35]

But even though there was some truth in this argument, the hard facts of the matter were that white men greatly outnumbered white women in plantation society whereas the opposite was generally the case among the free coloured population, and that of slaves, after the first decade of the nineteenth century. In Tobago, for example, of a total white population of 541 in 1790, 492 were men and only 49 were women. On the other hand, of a total free coloured population of 303, 198 were women and 105 were men.[36] So whereas white men outnumbered white women by as much as 10 to 1, free coloured women outnumbered free coloured men by nearly 2 to 1.

This general disproportion in the male/female ratio in the free coloured population was partly due to the tendency for females to be manumitted in greater numbers than males. The manumission statistics for Tobago for the years 1808 to 1821, which are typical of the other islands, indicate that of a total of 290 manumissions over 80% of these were females.[37] This trend was evident in Jamaica as well. Of 4,011 slaves manumitted between 1817 and 1829, 2,511 or approximately 64% were female.[38] In a slave society dominated in all aspects by a small group of whites the then prevailing power relation enabled white men to make up for the deficiency of white women as sexual partners, by exploitation of females in the free coloured and slave populations.

The available evidence indicates, however, that some of these relationships were far from casual or transient and that in some instances white fathers maintained and saw to the well-being of children born out of such unions even though as one observer pointed out for St. Vincent, these children were not "received on a footing of equality" with white members of the family.[39] Thomas Attwood, writing of Dominica in the eighteenth century commented that white men, rather than marry, were generally willing "to content themselves with mulatto or negro women who bring them plenty children, the maintenance of whom with their own extravagance soon dissipate their savings".[40] From Barbados, Beckles relates the story of Ms Fenwick, an English school teacher and slave holder who nevertheless saw slavery as not being conducive to the proper cultivation of white manhood primarily because of the corrupting influences of black women in white households. "The white men could not resist them and fathered children with them."[41] Fenwick's compatriot Mrs. Carmichael would have concurred as she castigated coloured women in St. Vincent for encouraging relationships with white men "in the hope of making a good bargain... that is a good legal settlement", and as soon as this was achieved the women would "glory in the tie".[42]

In addition to these formal relationships there were others less formal or casual, which also contributed to the birth rate, in the form of prostitution as in many New World slave societies.[43] Archibald Campbell described recently manumitted male slaves in Grenada as what would be called in modern terminology "pimps" who lived "idle upon the gains of negro wenches".[44] Thomas Attwood also pointed to the prevalence of prostitution in Dominica by his cynical comment that "colored women would often submit to the embraces of white men for money and clothes", and in another instance that "colored mothers would often dispose of their virgin daughters for a moderate sum".[45]

The persistence of the practice of prostitution was also of concern to President Ottley of St. Vincent at the end of the eighteenth century.

It was to this he attributed the phenomenal increase in the free coloured population in a space of 24 years so that they outnumbered the whites by as much as 20 to 1. The plantation system in the British Windward Islands was established at a time when the migration of white women to the islands had virtually ceased, thereby aggravating the problem of sexual imbalance in the white community which like the slave community was unable to reproduce itself naturally, albeit for different reasons. This had serious implications for social control and social stability at a time when it was alleged that the free coloured population in St. Vincent was in correspondence with that of Antigua and Martinique about a general plan to better their condition in their respective slave societies. This led the President to suggest that female convicts who would otherwise have been sent to Botany Bay should be transported to the island and other parts of the West Indies to act as mates for the white men. Even if some of these were prostitutes, he argued, the important point was that they would "propagate a race of white children who will be born friends of the government while every mulatto may be considered an enemy in embryo".

> If this system of importation be pursued the colored and black females who in the present state of our manners is far from looking upon prostitution as a disgrace pride themselves upon the preference shown them by white men would find themselves under the necessity of discontinuing these loose habits and would probably marry with the males of their own respective rank, situation and color.[46]

MANUMISSION

Most of the children born as a result of these contacts were either free at the time of their birth or voluntary freed by their white fathers. This practice prevailed in Jamaica as well. As Heuman writes "the liberality of many white fathers added to the population of freedmen. Whites often manumitted their black or brown mistresses and their illegitimate children sometimes at birth".[47] In Brazil a father who refused so to do was generally looked upon with disdain.[48] Similarly, in St. Vincent: "Those children who are the illegitimate offspring of white men are with few exceptions free... when they are not so the father is most justly detested and held up as a character anything but respectable".[49]

But even if these coloured children were not voluntarily manumitted by their white fathers, they along with some black slaves formed a tiny privileged slave elite, which because of the nature of its occupations had greater economic opportunities to purchase freedom than the common field slaves. This is not to say, however, that it was a relatively simple affair to purchase one's freedom even when one had money. The available evidence indicates that masters were generally reluctant to manumit slaves during the eighteenth century at such a critical time in the development of the plantations when they were complaining about a shortage of field hands.[50]

The situation might have been even worse in the nineteenth century after the abolition of the Slave Trade in 1807. Again, during the eighteenth century masters resorted to the inhumane practice of manumitting aged, incapacitated and infirm slaves rather than maintain them since they were of no productive use to the estate. These ex-slaves wandered about the towns and countryside and were a burden on the public for their maintenance. Partly in order to shift the expense of maintenance back to where it rightly belonged the legislatures passed laws stipulating that no slave be manumitted until a certain sum was deposited in the Treasury from which the manumitted slave would receive an annuity for support.[51] The Governor of Dominica regarded this provision as one of the main obstacles to manumission in that island.[52]

LAW AS A TOOL OF SOCIAL ENGINEERING

In Political and Social Activity

Not only did the legislatures discourage manumissions but they also passed legislation which might be interpreted as a ploy to deprive legally manumitted slaves of their freedom. In 1767 for instance, Grenada passed an Act entitled "An Act to prevent the further sudden increase of free negroes and mulattoes" by which such persons could be sold as slaves if they were unable to produce their manumission deeds, or get two white freeholders to testify that they were free at the time of birth.[53] The free people of colour in Jamaica also had to provide proof of their freedom. They were required to register in a parish and appear before a magistrate for proper certification thereof. The freedman regarded such requests as degrading.[54] A similar law was in force in Dominica and was one of the targets of attack by the free coloureds in their fight for recognition in 1822. As they complained, the effect of that Act was that: "the coloured man is made to hold his liberty if liberty it can be called by the most precarious tenure and it frequently happens that he who cannot prove his freedom, by clear legal evidence, is by a presumption founded on the colour of his face, reduced from freedom to slavery".[55]

The existence of such pieces of legislation inhibited but did not prevent manumissions. Unfortunately, no manumission statistics have been unearthed for the eighteenth century. Those for the nineteenth century however indicate that between 1808 and 1823, 311 manumissions were effected in St. Vincent, 865 in Grenada, and 946 in Dominica. However, these statistics do not always indicate the mode of manumission that is whether by gift or purchase, and the amounts that were actually paid in the latter case. But of 117 manumissions effected in Dominica between 1812 and 1823, four of these were by purchase, totalling £268.4[56] or £67.1 on average. And opportunities did exist for a minority of slaves to acquire this sum, particularly the coloured and black slave elite.[57] Gilbert Franklyn testified before the Investigating Committee on the Slave Trade that Jeffrey, a slave carpenter he once owned, purchased his wife's freedom for 80 pounds. Jeffrey also owned two houses in Scarborough the capital of Tobago and his total assets were valued at about 600 pounds sterling.[58] However, the acquisition of freedom and property did not guarantee acceptance if at all into white society and moreso on a basis of equality.

In every one of the British Windward Islands the free people of colour were not allowed to hold "even the lowest public situation" of any kind, neither were they permitted to vote in elections. They were not eligible to sit as jurors in the courts[59] and in Dominica their evidence was declared inadmissible against whites in criminal cases that carried the death penalty.[60]

Even in places of worship the laws discriminated against people of colour. As in Jamaica[61] separate seating was allocated for whites and coloureds in the Anglican Church. When a Vestry Act was passed in St. Vincent in 1820, the act specifically stated that the pews in the lower part of the church be rented to white persons only.[62] The free people of colour in Tobago complained in 1822 that "even in church, prejudice is carried so far as to oblige us to sit apart while paying equal rents for the pews".[63] Indeed, a missionary stationed in this island asserted that even he in his religious capacity had to be "very cautious of intercourse with them [the coloured people] as even sitting on the same seat with them would be enough to ratify his dismissal from all European Society".[64] The free people of colour in Dominica also complained of "this painful and mortifying distinction which even in the House of God is the fruit of monstrous prejudice" and wondered if "the public worship of the Almighty is a duty which... they are not to perform under a feeling that they are all the offspring of one gracious parent".[65]

The prevalence of discriminatory practices are again reflected in punishments prescribed for whites and free coloured persons for the commission of similar offences. As in Brazil,[66] there was one set of laws and punishments for whites, and another for free coloured persons. A Dominica Act of 1775 for instance prescribed a fine of £5 for all persons who assaulted slaves and stole from them produce purchased for their masters. If unable to pay the fine, the offender if he were white, was sentenced to three days imprisonment whereas if he were coloured, the term was six days.[67] Again, under the game laws of that island, whites convicted of shooting in the prohibited period were fined £10, whereas free persons of colour were fined £5 and sent to jail for a month. Lastly, whites convicted of poisoning the rivers were subjected to a six month prison term, whereas for free persons of colour the term was one year.[68] In St. Vincent, a free person of colour convicted of striking a white was to be whipped and imprisoned for one month, whereas, a white striking a free person was merely bound over.[69] It has not been possible to ascertain the extent to which all these laws were enforced. Even allowing for some possible divergence between the law and practice, bits of evidence which have been unearthed indicate that justice for the free coloured was arbitrarily administered and unduly harsh.

In 1818, for instance, it was reported that a group of inebriated whites stormed uninvited into a party staged by a group of free coloured persons in Roseau, the capital of Dominica, and started throwing chairs and tables around. According to this report, the free coloureds retaliated, and "bloodshed occurred on both sides". One of the white offenders left the scene and summoned the military which went to the homes of two of the free coloured men who had been at the party and threw their belongings outside. In subsequent court proceedings one of the white instigators of the trouble was fined £15 and allowed to go at large despite a court order that he remain in custody until he paid the fine, whereas four free coloured men were given prison sentences ranging from one to three months and bound over for a year in the sum of £50 each to keep the peace. The Governor had to intervene to get the punishment meted out to the free coloured men remitted but efforts by him to secure the arrest of the convicted white were to no avail. In fact, the Marshall told him bluntly that he would not issue a warrant for the arrest of the offender, since it was never his practice "to commit any person to prison for a trifling fine if he considered him responsible".[70]

The laws themselves actually threatened the freedom of movement and social activities of the free persons of colour. In Grenada for instance, after a fire had destroyed the capital in 1775, the legislature acting on a suspicion that the free coloureds were implicated, passed a law requiring them to carry a lighted lantern on the streets between the hours of 9 p.m. and 5 a.m. on pain of arrest.[71] Later on, a bell was set up in the market place and was rung five minutes before 9 p.m. and five minutes before 5 a.m. as a reminder. It was also stipulated that no coloured person was to hold a meeting or dance in the town without prior consultation with two Justices of the Peace who if they agreed were to fix the hour at which it should terminate and this was set at 12 p.m. In addition free people of colour found gambling at night could be sent to prison for a maximum of 15 days.[72]

The free coloureds in Trinidad were subject to similar humiliating disabilities and consequently voiced similar complaints and concerns even though they "seemed among the least disadvantaged of the Caribbean".[73]

In the Military
According to Herbert Klein, the Militia in Brazil, provided an important avenue of social mobility for free coloured men. In support of this contention, he cited an instance in which a coloured man actually

rose to be commander of a group of white militia troops.[74] But no such opportunities existed for free coloured males serving in the Militia in the British Windward Islands even though for some of them it was an honour to be a part of that body.[75] In all the Militia Acts that were passed, the free coloureds, as in the Leewards,[76] were disqualified from holding commissions and were generally relegated to minor operations such as the services of the artillery and forts, and such other tasks as the whites preferred not to perform. When, for instance a Militia was organised in St. Vincent in 1776 at a time when relations with the Black Caribs were deteriorating and the whites did not want to risk their lives in patrolling the border of the territory they inhabited, it was specifically stated that only free negroes and mulattoes be sent to these parts and also on expeditions to apprehend runaway slaves.[77] From Trinidad Professor Campbell recounts a somewhat similar practice. He cites the case of Dr. John Baptiste Philips, a medical practitioner from a family of wealthy slaveowners who suffered the humiliation of having to serve in the militia as a private and by being sent to the interior to hunt runaway slaves.[78] Again, when in 1767 the legislature of Grenada passed a Militia Act and the free people of colour were required to serve in it, it was specifically stated that they should be separated from the whites in rank and occupation "by a just distinction of inferiority". It was further specified that their names should be called last in the muster rolls, that they should be positioned on the left when halted and march in the rear when the post of honour was in the front, and in the front when the post of honour was in the back, and that they be relegated to the under-services of the artillery and forts, acting as pioneers on all occasions.[79]

In later years, segregated companies of free coloured militia were formed in all the islands. But even these companies provided little mobility for the coloured man since as in Jamaica[80] the commanding personnel were all white.[81] In St. Vincent a concession was granted in 1806 when three coloured regiments were headed by coloured non-commissioned officers.[82] But the coloured man had no hope of becoming a commissioned officer. The free people of colour in Tobago complained in 1822 that "many now in the coloured militia have been serving upward of many years and are still in the ranks, while every day they witness whites arriving and placed over them".[83]

In Economic Activity

Even though the free coloured as a class participated in the economic life of the islands to the extent that they were allowed to do so, they were still, as Franklin Knight has pointed out for Cuba,[84] regarded as lazy, idle and dishonest. Governor Robinson described the free people of colour in Tobago as being "poor, idle, and dissipated in the extreme and... the least worthy part of our community",[85] and Governor Matthew remarked that those in Grenada were "so given to idleness that they will not attempt to earn more than will barely keep them from starving".[86] According to Archibald Campbell even those slaves who were recently manumitted, instead of trying to make the best of their new situation, became worthless. The women he accused of receiving stolen goods from slaves, and the men of living "idle upon the gains of negro wenches: I never knew a free negro in any of the islands work in the field for any wages. Their general idea of liberty seems to be not to be obliged to work".[87]

Knight also points out that it was not so much that the free people of colour in Cuba did not want work, but rather that they were not encouraged to work.[88] The situation was probably worse in the British Windward Islands. Here discriminatory legislation debarred free persons of colour from engaging in certain occupations. In some instances that same legislation set narrow limits on the scope and size of free coloured owned enterprises. And in others, it dictated the racial composition of the labour force, regardless of whether the owner of the enterprise was coloured or white.

In Dominica, for instance, the free people of colour were prohibited by law from owning taverns and liquor stores, restaurants and lodging houses. When in 1784, the Legislature passed an Act granting licenses for these enterprises that Act specifically stated that no free person of colour was entitled to a license.[89] Pushed out of the enterprises in Dominica, in St. Vincent, employment for the free coloureds in certain occupations was severely restricted and limited because of penalties enforced on white persons and even persons of their own class for their failure to employ whites in certain positions of trust. An Act of 1820 for instance stipulated that all merchants, practitioners of law and medicine, all persons holding public office, and all other persons who received an annual salary of £2,000 must employ one white person, "thus depriving all persons of colour from filling any respectable situation".[90] Free persons of colour who owned boats employed in the coasting trade were also required by law to employ one white man on pain of a fine of £150.[91]

The situation was even worse in agriculture. Since the free coloureds as a class were generally reluctant to labour in the fields, and since they generally tended to reside in the towns,[92] the only other available positions open on the estate if they were not owners, were the supervisory ones such as managers, bookkeepers and overseers. But these were closed to them since they were reserved for whites.

In fact consistent with the practice in Jamaica[93] and elsewhere in the Caribbean each island passed Deficiency Laws compelling owners of plantations to employ a certain number of able-bodied men in proportion to the number of slaves they owned and these men had to be white. Even when a free coloured owned a plantation he was compelled under the Deficiency Laws to employ white men. Under a Tobago Act of 1804, for instance, each owner or renter of slaves was required to employ one white man for every 50 slaves on pain of a fine of £50.[94] Not only did this Act limit the number of free coloured persons who could be employed on an estate owned by free coloured persons, but it subjected them to this discriminatory tax until 1819, in which year it was repealed, for the further reason that whites generally regarded it as degrading to work with coloured owners. As Governor Robinson said in 1819:

> it has been proved by the experience of many years that white men would not remain with mulatto planters and in few instances where they had acknowledged themselves to be perfectly content with their situation their white brethren would laugh them out of them, so that the owners of such estates had no remedy and were compelled to pay the penalties in spite of their utmost endeavours to obtain white men.[95]

The participation of free coloureds in agriculture as plantation owners was also in some cases limited unlike the situation in Trinidad where there was "no limit set on the amount of land or slaves they could own".[96] In St. Vincent for instance the free coloured landholder, as in Antigua[97] was declared ineligible to own more than eight acres of land. If he happened to own more than this amount he was given a period of six months in which to sell the surplus and if it was not disposed of in that time, it was forfeited.[98]

The free people of colour in Tobago boasted in 1822 that they owned a "great number of slaves and several valuable sugar estates". Those in Dominica and Grenada made a similar boast.[99] That the free coloureds owned slaves and plantations is undoubtedly true but the available evidence indicates that these claims were exaggerated, and probably deliberately, since they were directed at public opinion in England at a time when the free coloureds were soliciting support in their struggle for full equality with whites.

In no territory in the Windward Islands for which statistics are available did property holding by the free coloured attain the heights that prevailed in the Naparimas in Trinidad where they owned 35% of the estates and 30.1% of the slaves.[100] A comparison with Dominica where statistics indicate significant property holding by the free coloureds is instructive.

In Dominica, for instance, the free coloureds as a class owned 3,548 slaves in 1820 which represented roughly one-fourth of the total slave population. Plantations operated by free coloureds were also in this year responsible for one-fifth of the sugar and coffee produced in the island.[101] This indicates that the free coloureds as a class were playing a vital economic role but when the statistics are broken down we find that the majority of the slaves were owned, and the majority of produce grown, by a small free coloured elite who were members of the Committee of Correspondence formed in 1820 to present the case for full political and social rights.[102]

The 3,548 slaves for instance were owned by a total of 309 individuals out of a total free coloured population of 3,000. This indicates that roughly one out of every ten free coloured persons was a slave owner. And of the total, five had holdings of 100 or more, five of 50 or more, four between 40 and 50, three between 30 and 40, and 40 between 12 and 20. All the others had holdings of less than 20 and of these some had as little as one, three and eight slaves. Of the sugar produced, one estate owner was responsible for 500 cwt., another for 232, and another for 143. The same applied in the case of coffee.[103]

It was still possible however for those free coloureds who could not become large planters to establish themselves as small holders. In 1788 for instance Governor Matthew of Grenada remarked that freed slaves who were not mechanics were "fond of becoming planters of small pieces of land in coffee and cotton". [104] Since this class was generally reluctant to labour with its hands, it is possible that those persons who owned less than 20 slaves may have deployed them in this field of endeavour.

OCCUPATIONS AND POPULATION DISTRIBUTION

With regard to the occupations of the free coloureds outside of agriculture, reliance has to be placed largely on travel accounts and contemporary histories. Tobago, however, is a notable exception. A report prepared in 1811 which gives detailed listings of the occupations of the free sector of the population is quite informative and corresponds closely with accounts given of the occupations of the free coloureds in the other islands by contemporary writers. In 1811, that island had a total free coloured population of 350 of whom 92 were men, 153 were women and 105 were listed as children. The total white population numbered 550 of whom 501 were men, 49 were women, and 35 were children.[105] We can assume therefore that the total free coloured labour force was 245 and that of the whites 550.

In the professional group which comprised government officials, clergymen, lawyers and doctors and numbered 48 persons, these persons were all white. In agriculture which employed 275 persons, 254 of these were white and 21 were coloured. And of the whites, 220 were managers and overseers, 27 were planters and 7 were servants. Of the free coloureds, on the other hand, 10 were managers and overseers, only one was listed as a planter and 10 were servants. In the commercial group which listed 35 persons, 12 of whom were merchants, no free coloured person was engaged in this occupation. Of the remaining 23 persons who were storekeepers and shopkeepers, only one was a coloured person. Of 70 persons employed as clerks, only four were free coloured persons.[106]

These occupations absorbed a total of 402 European males and 15 free coloured males. Of the remaining 91 Europeans, 52 were artisans, 14 were fishermen, 5 were tailors, 19 were auctioneers, and the rest worked as shoemakers, printers, butchers and bakers. Of the remaining 76 free coloured males there were 48 artisans, 6 fishermen, two bakers, two butchers, two saddlers, one silversmith, one barber and two tailors. White females apparently did not work.[107] But the

153 free coloured females were employed primarily as hucksters "travelling constantly their circles around appropriate districts of the plantations" and accounted for one-third of the retail trade.[108]

The occupations of the free people of colour in the other islands were quite similar. In Dominica, Dr. Bermingham was the only free coloured person engaged in the medical profession. In fact a European writing about this island in 1828 asserted that Europeans "generally engross a large share of the mercantile transactions, as well as the management of estates" and there are "few of the professions or trades in which the number of Europeans is not considerable". Of the free people of colour he noted that two-thirds of the males were employed as master coopers, carpenters and blacksmiths while the rest were mainly tailors and shoemakers. The women were generally employed as house servants, seamstresses, maids, washer-women and hucksters.[109]

Of the 60 apprenticed Africans in St. Vincent in 1811, the majority of the males were employed as carpenters, coopers, masons and tailors, and the women as domestics.[110] In fact, Mrs. Carmichael noted that most of the males in the free coloured populations were employed as tradesmen while a few were accountants, clerks in merchant stores, copying clerks to lawyers and owners of retail shops. Those women who were not domestics were engaged in the sale of dry goods, preserves, and pickles which they bought and retailed "at a considerable percentage".[111] Free coloured men and women in Jamaica were for the most part employed in similar occupations.[112]

Most writers on the free coloureds in slave societies have pointed to the fact that they were a predominantly urban people.[113] In Jamaica for instance at the end of the eighteenth century nearly half of the freedmen lived in Kingston or Spanish Town.[114] To this generalisation however Professor Campbell has isolated Trinidad as a notable exception as in 1811, 52.9% of the free coloured population lived in the countryside. By 1825 this figure had increased to 65.2%.[115] The British Windward Islands, however, conformed to the general pattern of urban residence. This was partly due to the nature of the occupations of the free coloured class since the towns provided more opportunities for the employment of free labour than the rural areas which were dominated by the large sugar plantations. Some detailed population figures given for the British Windward Islands, indicate quite clearly, that the free coloured population was concentrated mainly in the parishes with towns, and that the parish with the largest town usually had the greatest concentration.

In 1811 for instance, St. Vincent had seven distinct settlements of population, three of which may be classified as towns. Of these towns, two were located in the parish of St. George, and these were Kingstown, the capital, and Calliaqua the second important town. The other settlement that may be classified as a town was Barrouallie in the parish of St. Patrick. Other centres of population such as Layou and Buccament in the parish of St. Andrew, and Chateaubelair in the parish of St. David were nothing more than small villages. Of a total free coloured population of 1,406, only 72 resided in Charlotte the largest parish which contained no town, but the finest and most extensive sugar estates in the island. The parishes of St. Andrew and St. David had free coloured populations of 60 and 78 souls respectively while the town of Barrouaille in the parish of St. Patrick had a total of 169 free coloured residents or more than these two parishes combined. The largest concentration of free coloured residents was to be found in the parish of St. George, which contained the capital and the second principal town. This parish alone contained 1,627 free coloured persons or roughly 73% of the total free coloured population of the island.[116]

This urban concentration of the free coloureds was in marked contrast to that of the slaves which was predominantly rural. Coupled with the restrictions on the movement of slaves outside the plantation it tended to physically isolate both groups from each other. But in any case the very nature of slavery itself engendered a deeper and far more significant isolation. Indeed, despite one or two instance of inter-marriage between slaves and free coloured persons,[117] and despite the fact that both groups fought on the same side in a revolt in Grenada in 1795 in which whites were also involved,[118] the relationships between the free coloureds and the slaves were for the most part characterised by hostility and antipathy.

FREE COLOUREDS SEEK NEW ALLIANCES

This was largely due to the fact that the free coloureds in their aspirations and interests generally sought alliances and identified with the whites, while sedulously avoiding any such relationships with the slaves. As Cox correctly points out the free coloureds in Grenada "made no pretense whatever of allying with slaves, in fact they vehemently denied having a similarity of interests with them".[119] He also observed that the free coloureds in making the case for an improvement in their own socio-legal status did not advocate drastic social change.[120] In fact even a superficial reading of the petitions put forward by the free coloured elite for the removal of disabilities makes it unmistakably clear that their aims were directed towards sharing political, social and economic power with the whites, while totally denying the same to the slaves. They saw themselves as having common interests with the whites, especially the white elite, basing their claims for recognition in part on their "education", "wealth" and "respectability".[121] Writing about Barbados, Jerome Handler and Arnold Sio commented that this elite "viewed itself as an extension of the local bourgeoisie".[122] This remark is applicable to the free coloured elite in the British Windward Islands and their counterparts in Jamaica.[123]

It must not be forgotten for one moment that this elite which undoubtedly set the standards for other members of the free coloured group accepted the system of slavery and were themselves slave owners. When in 1800, official authorities in St. Vincent discovered some secret correspondence between the free coloureds of that island, Martinique and Guadeloupe in which they put forward a plan for equality with whites, it was noted that some of the letters contained "proposals for monopolising a considerable portion of the Slave Trade".[124] Writing about the free people of colour in St. Vincent, Mrs. Carmichael noted:

> The first thing they are anxious to possess is a slave, and they certainly keep their slave to his duty under a very different discipline from that practised by white people; and to be sold to a coloured owner, is considered by a negro to be an extreme misfortune.[125]

With regard to this stereotype of the free coloured as a brutal slave master Professor Campbell has sounded a note of caution. However, while it is possible to regard such a view emanating from white contemporary writers and other apologists as self serving in the interest of maintaining racial superiority,[126] the same cannot be said of those whites such as Reverend Peters of Dominica who although reformist had no real axe to grind.

He observed that: "The first thing to which every free person of colour aiming at independence here naturally directs his thoughts is the possession of a slave", and he went on to point out that "people of colour are of all proprietors of slaves by far the most rigorous and cruel".[127] In 1822, the free people of colour in Tobago in a petition for the abolition of disabilities complained that their retention denied them the respect to which they were entitled from the slave population.[128] And in Grenada, the free people of colour in similar vein remarked that in a country where the slave population greatly outnumbered the free, it would be "prudent policy to extinguish as much as possible all feelings of jealousy that may exist between the free classes", since both had a vested interest in maintaining the security of island from "foreign as well as internal enemies".[129] Indeed, the common origins of the free coloureds and slaves embittered rather than strengthened relations between them. As Reverend Peters remarked:

> It matters but little difference either in the sentiments or the behaviour of these persons, whether they be free by birth, or by enfranchisement; the mode of education is to both the same; they both imbibe, from their infancy a similar contempt of that degraded race to which (priding themselves on diversity of colour) they would fain disown all affinity whatever.[130]

Another European who lived in this island also observed: "The coloured people are rather jealous of the domination of the whites; and the slaves hold the coloured people in contempt – between the two latter there is no union".[131] It should not be surprising therefore that in most slave revolts in the British Windward Islands, the free coloureds were seen as enemies rather than as potential allies. When for instance, a slave revolt was planned in Tobago at Christmas 1801, the conspirators had "sworn to the total extermination of all the white and coloured people".[132]

RULING CLASS UNCOMPROMISING

But as much as the free coloureds as a class generally despised the slaves, and as much as they gravitated towards assimilation into the society of the whites with whom they had common interests since they were also slave and plantation owners, and even though they used this common interest as the French naturalised subjects had done earlier on as an argument for the concession of full political and hence social rights,[133] the whites were not willing to make such concessions because of their overriding preoccupation with the problem of social control in the slave society. This becomes abundantly clear when we examine the response of the absentee proprietors of Dominica to a petition from the free coloured inhabitants in which they advocated that they be granted full political rights.

The ground of the argument they declared, "is an abstract right, which if admitted, would destroy the distinction which the policy of our ancestors and the experience of ages has deemed necessary for protection". Because the ascendancy of the whites over the blacks, they argued, "is known to arise from their acknowledging a superiority, more than from the command of a physical force, and if destroyed by the admission of people of colour in the Legislature or on the Bench, the feelings of respect which the blacks entertain for the white population would rapidly diminish". And further, if the rights and privileges were granted as an abstract right, "a free black would be considered equally as eligible as a free man of colour to hold either a judicial or legislative situation, and all respect for the white population being destroyed, insurrection and ruin would ensue".[134] And finally, if the political system was to be altered:

> by an association with a class, against whom the blacks entertain the strongest feelings of jealousy and dislike and the elective franchise granted as now prayed for, the number of free coloured population exceeding three-fold that of the white; and the facilities of obtaining qualifications from the abandonment of landed property being greater in Dominica than in any other island the House of Assembly would soon

be entirely composed of people of colour with whom the white population could not act.[135]

These objections also reflect the race and class nature of the society. The whites who were the entrenched ruling class saw the admission of the free coloured to political rights as the first step in a gradual process by which they could lose control of the political and social life of the islands. The maintenance of this control depended to a large extent upon an accommodation by the other groups to the white superiority/coloured and black inferiority calculus. When this was challenged they trembled for their safety since they felt that they could never be secure unless they alone were the ruling class. One is tempted to conclude that the whites were more concerned about the feared effects that such concessions might have upon the behaviour of the slave population and social stability, rather than with the legitimacy of the demands. It can be suggested that they might have taken a more sympathetic attitude towards the petition had they not been so preoccupied with the problem of controlling the slave population.

In the slave society of the British Windward Islands, the slaves were at the bottom of the social ladder. But not all slaves were treated in the same manner, and there was a slave elite that resided mainly in the towns and engaged in occupations outside the slave plantation.[136] Indications are that a great proportion of these slaves were of mixed blood and it can be suggested that it was probably because of their colour that they were given the opportunities to pursue occupations which were less laborious and servile and more rewarding than the common field slaves.

For instance speaking of St. Vincent, Mrs. Carmichael noted that coloured slaves were generally employed as "tradesmen, some domestics, while others are hired out either as servants or for carrying goods about the country for sale." Very few of these slaves, she pointed out, were "employed in the field as many of them considered it too mean an employment".[137] In this aspect they shared the general outlook of the free coloured class and this was further reflected in their behaviour towards the black slave population. Mrs. Carmichael pointed out that they regarded it as a downright insult to be addressed even by a white without prefixes such as 'Miss' or 'Sir', and that they were "so tenacious of their rank, that they must always have a negro about to assist them in whatever they are about".[138]

THE CONDITION OF THE FIELD SLAVE

The field slaves who were the backbone of the whole economy in the British Windward Islands lived in extremely wretched and miserable conditions compared to the free coloured class and the privileged slaves of mixed blood. Indeed, no other group of slaves was subject to such a state of degradation and misery. On the plantation they were forced to work for long hours under the discipline of the whip. Because they had fewer opportunities for earning a substantial cash income than those slaves working in the towns, they became heavily dependent on their owners for most of the basic necessities of life. But because of the need to keep profit margins as high as possible, and also because of the low rate of and, in some instances, the absence of profit in the sugar industry, the quantities of food, clothing and other necessities made available to them were exceedingly small. In contrast to the drivers and other 'principal negroes' on the estates, the field slaves lived on the barest margin of subsistence and enjoyed the lowest standard of living.

The inevitable results were ill health and a high death rate. Diseases such as small pox, leprosy, scurvy, yaws, tetanus, worms, and mal d'estomac caused from eating dirt were common among the slaves, and accounted for fatalities.[139] In addition, as the Grenada Legislature noted, "continued labour... will in these climes at least, wear out the firmest fibre, in a much shorter time than it does in Europe".[140] As a class then, the field slaves were unhealthy and lived for shorter periods than the domestics and artisans who enjoyed a better standard of living. As the Governor of Grenada remarked, "their lives in comparison of free coloureds, or white people who live better and labour less are of course of short duration".[141] In addition, infant mortality was terribly high, with the result that the slave population failed to maintain itself.

To check this tendency it was necessary to remove the causes. But this the planters were unwilling to do. For example, in assigning reasons for the low birth rate they pointed to such things as "the premature and promiscuous intercourse of the sexes", prostitution, immorality, and the infrequency of stable monogamous unions. This last, one clergyman attributed to "their present imperfect state of civilization",[142] but in so doing he was merely attacking the symptoms without more It is suggested here that the root causes for the unpopularity of marriage among the slaves are to be found in the system of slavery itself. But this few planters were willing to even consider. For in the West Africa from whence the majority of the slaves were imported[143] the established form of marriage was polygamy and adultery was severely punished. As the Governor of Tobago pointed out in 1811, the position of the man in the household, was something like that of a despot. But on the slave plantations in the West Indies, the African was denied the kind of command he was accustomed to, since the women were the property of the master, and could be violated at his will. According to Governor Young, he could not even "check infidelity or be assured of his offspring". As a result, the African in the West Indies "revolted at a settled connection so little conformable to the customs of his nation and his rights over his women". It is to this that he attributed the fact that the slaves in Tobago "rarely settled in families, and indulged in promiscuous intercourse, little favourable to population".[144]

The plantation slaves were in a world of their own almost totally isolated from the rest of the community. Their contacts with the free people of colour were limited partly because these tended to concentrate in the towns. And for this reason, contacts with most whites were limited too. The detailed population figures for Dominica in 1813, indicate that in the parish of St. George which contained the capital, there was a total of 582 white persons, and in the parish of St. John which contained the other town Plymouth, there were 79 white persons. This made a total of 661 whites living in the parishes with towns. The total white population of the island was 1,261 persons. There were then only 600 whites living in the eight rural parishes.[145]

Not only were contacts between the slaves and the free people of colour and whites limited, so too were contacts between slaves of different parishes and even those of neighbouring plantations in the same parish. For the control of these large numbers of slaves was always a problem for the whites. Because of their insecurity they tended, not without some justification to view slave meetings as occasions for plotting rebellion and so these were, under the slave laws which were part of the mechanism of control, as far as possible discouraged. As a result, for most of their existence, the slaves remained trapped by the boundaries of the plantation.

SOME ASPECTS OF SLAVE CULTURE

Despite the rigours of slavery the slaves were able to maintain and practice their own cultural forms involving a set of common beliefs and customs which had their origins in African cultural traditions. At the establishment of the plantation system in the British Windward Islands in the mid-eighteenth century that area of the West African coast between Senegambia in the North West and Angola in the South East had become the main supplier of slaves to the British West Indies. The available evidence suggests that most of the slaves in the British Windward Islands came from this region. According to Sir William Young during his visit to St. Vincent when on tour of the West Indies in 1792, three ships arrived with slaves from the Guinea Coast. The first landed a cargo of 300 from Bassa, the second 210 from Wydah, and the third 370 Eboes.[146] When Mrs Carmichael conversed with Africans in St. Vincent during the 1820s some told her they were Mandingoes and others Eboes.[147] In his reports on the progress of the settlement of Tobago in the early 1770s Sir William Young always listed separately a group of slaves whom he designated 'Koromantee Men'.[148] He was obviously referring to the Koromantyns who came from the coastal kingdoms of the Gold Coast.

But in spite of their diversity of origin, the slaves in the British Windward Islands as in the other British West Indies retained elements of a broad general African culture. More specifically in her study on the Leeward Islands, Elsa Goveia[149] has shown the presence of the African tradition in aspects of the slaves' cultural life such as music, dancing, dress, and religious beliefs and Orlando Patterson[150] and later Edward Braithwaite[151] made similar findings for Jamaica The customs, ways and habits of the slaves in the Windward Islands were quite similar to those of the Jamaican slaves and those from the Leeward Islands and, by extension, the slaves in the wider Caribbean.

Traces of African survivals in the customs of the slaves are to be seen in the burial of the dead and customs connected with it. Attwood describing a funeral ceremony in Dominica noted that the coffin of the deceased was filled with "pipe and tobacco" and other things which he was fond of in his lifetime such as food and drink, "because of a superstition that the deceased must eat and drink with them".[152] The slaves generally returned to the graveside once a year after the interment to pay their respects. At the graveside, libations were offered. Offerings consisted of "meat, whole kids, pigs or fowls with broth, liquors etc.", which were laid around the grave in dishes. Then one slave who was designated leader of the proceedings would take up pieces of this meat and then throw them onto the grave, calling out at the same time the name of the deceased, saying as follows: "Here is a piece of such a thing for you to eat, why did you leave your father, mother, wife, children and friends?" A portion of rum was thereafter sprinkled on the grave, with the leader saying in the same manner: "Here is a little rum to comfort your heart, goodbye to you, God bless you."[153]

The slaves gathered around the graveside would also participate in rum drinking and the ceremony was concluded here by singing and dancing. They then dispersed to their homes, met again, and continued celebrating until morning. This rite was described as "a piece of superstition which all negroes are addicted to and which if they were to neglect doing they firmly believe they would be punished by the spirits of the deceased persons".[154]

Some indication of the nature that the ceremony took after the slaves left the graveside is given in the following extract of a letter quoted from the diary of a Methodist Missionary who was stationed in Tobago:

> The principal reason assigned for this [the congregation at his preaching was much smaller than usual] was, that a negro dance had been given the preceding evening at Hope Estate, where the negroes had remained carousing during nearly the whole night. On inquiring as to the manner and cause of this dance, I found that it was purely African; and that it was performed as a rite, in behalf of an unbaptised slave, who had been dead nearly twelve months. On these occasions, the relatives of the deceased often go to a considerable expense in providing a feast, and invite a number of their friends to partake with them. A fowl, which they select with some caution, and which their superstition dictates

must be either a black or white one, is prepared in a peculiar manner, as being intended entirely for the benefit of the dead. Previous to their sitting down to feast themselves, this fowl is, with a good deal of ceremony, thrown out at the door of the hut, and with a quantity of rum and water, it being supposed that their departed friends must needs want to drink as well as eat.

All this being done under the cover of night, the negro easily bring his superstitious mind to conclude that what he throws away in the dark is actually devoured by the hungry ghost of his long lost relative. This momentous rite being thus duly performed, and the craving appetite of their invisible guest perfectly satisfied, they immediately turn their attention to eating and drinking; after which, when the maddening fumes of liquor begin to ascend they "rise up to play" and spend the night in performing their wild barbarous dances to the savage din of the African tom-tom.[155]

This custom of offering libations at the grave of the deceased, and holding annual ceremonies on behalf of the said deceased at which fowls are sacrificed, is extant and documented with respect to Carriacou in the Grenadines.[156] However probably because these aspects of the slave's cultural life were incomprehensible to Europeans, and probably because they conflicted with European beliefs and practices, the reaction of white observers varied from outright hostility to mockery. This might very well be the explanation for the comment of the Tobago missionary that such ceremonies were "rude" and heathenish", and "scenes of nocturnal riot and confusion",[157] and Attwood's remark that the Dominica custom was "truly laughable to white people who see it".[158]

The slaves were regarded by the white ruling class as being uncivilised and "heathen". The Established Church and the Christian missionaries working in the islands were therefore used as agents for "civilising" and "christianising" them. Indeed the missionaries in particular made devoted and unstinting efforts to do this with some apparent success,[159] but at the end of the day the slaves in general retained or maintained their own religious beliefs and practices. According to the Europeans, the slaves held a variety of religious beliefs of their own. Mrs. Carmichael noted that several Africans whom she conversed with in St. Vincent told her that in their native country, "they went every fourth day to church to say prayers to one very great Massa, whom the great God sent down into the world a long time back to teach people to be good. The great Massa never come to

Africa [sic], but he stop in a country far off from them where the sun rise".[160]

The agent for Grenada also stated in 1788 that the slaves in that island as their relatives in Africa, acknowledged the existence of two supreme beings. They believed, he continued, that there was "one God for white; another for black men". But they also believed that the first was "a being of more beneficent nature than the last who delights in doing mischief, and is the author of most of the calamities they experience in life".[161] Attwood, after witnessing the funeral rites ceremony in Dominica, concluded that it was "a plain indication that the negroes have some notion of the immortality of the soul",[162] and similarly, a Methodist Missionary in Tobago asserted that "the Africans have evidently some belief in the doctrine of transmigration of souls."[163] In fact, it was to this belief that he attributed the failure of the slaves to accept the tenets of Christianity, especially baptism. He observed that many of the slaves refused to be baptised, "from the consideration that their being made Christians would prevent them from returning to their native country... They imagine that on returning to their native country they shall be born in other bodies and live again as men and women".[164]

The slaves in the British Windward Islands believed in and practised obeah which was a multifaceted custom embodying a religious element. The agent for Grenada noted in 1788 that the obeah practitioners were usually natives of Africa. Belief in obeah, he argued, was strongest among the newly imported Africans who "have great faith in it, and practice its charms for the protection of their persons and provision grounds, hogs, poultry etc. and often imagine that they are obeahed or bewitched".[165] The practice of obeah involved the preparation of phialls and spells which were designed not only to protect the possessor and property as the agent pointed out, but also to inflict harm on enemies, as well as the herbal treatment of diseases. In St. Vincent, Mrs. Carmichael, observed that as a defense to obeah it was customary for slaves to "have bottles hung round and about their houses and in their grounds, full of some sort of infusion which they prepare to prevent the obeah from infecting them, they also wear an amulet or some such thing, as a charm for the same purpose".[166]

Attwood regarded obeah men and women on the plantations in Dominica as extremely dangerous. He pointed out that they were thoroughly familiar with the quality of many poisonous herbs which grew in the island and these they prepared and gave to slaves as charms to be administered upon their victims. Even many white people were killed in this manner by drinking mixtures prepared by them not knowing them to be poisonous, because they were told that the effect would be that their slaves would become obedient and faithful servants.[167] However, other white contemporaries spoke in glowing terms about the medical aspect of their profession. The agent for Grenada noted that, "from their skill in simples, and the virtues of plants, they sometimes operate extraordinary cures in diseases which have baffled the skill of its practitioners and more especially in foul sores and ulcers. I have myself made use of their skill for the last with great success".[168]

But to most white observers, Obeah was nothing more than a belief in witchcraft and its practitioners were regarded as a group of evil people. Indeed, they failed to see what was the functional role of the obeah man in a slave society. In Africa the Obeah man or woman was regarded as a doctor, philosopher and priest,[169] and it is apparent that similar roles were retained and maintained on the slave plantations in the Caribbean. The agent for Grenada observed that they believed they were commissioned with special powers from the "God for black men", to guide the lives of the rest of the population:

> Obeah Men avail themselves of these notions and delude weak people into the belief that this malevolent being communicates his intention to them, instructs them what is to be done to avert injury that may be inflicted on the persons or property of their country men and if they neglect to perform, or treat with contempt they are told will draw on them his vengeance.[170] The impressions made on people's minds are so great that they obey the mandates of Obeah Men, perform rites and ceremonies, consult them on all occasions, [and] are governed by the directions.[171]

Attwood also noted that the obeah men in Dominica had a "commanding influence" over the rest of the slaves and that even those who professed Christianity still would have recourse "to their superstitious confidence in powers of the dead, of the sun and moon, even of sticks, stones and earth from graves hung in bottles in their gardens".[172]

Music and dance featured prominently in the cultural life of the slaves. Dancing as Edward Brathwaite points out was their characteristic form of social and artistic expression and was both secular and religious.[173] We have already noted the prevalence of music and dancing in the performance of ceremonial rites to the deceased. But the slaves also danced merely for the purpose of recreation, social entertainment and relief.

According to Mrs. Carmichael, after crop season was over "a great band" of her slaves came to her house in town accompanied by the estate's fiddler and dancing immediately began in an outhouse. This was probably designed to express relief from the long hard months of holeing the land, planting, nurturing, reaping and processing the canes. Dances were also held on Sundays in most parts of the island more particularly in the country and at some of these more than 200 slaves would attend. This activity was also very prevalent at Christmas when it was customary for some proprietors to have a grand ball to which the slaves would be invited.[174]

The music played at the dances was depending on their nature, either European or African or a variety of both. At a Christmas ball held on Sir William Young's Calliaqua estate in St. Vincent in 1792, he recollected hearing the slaves play "two or three African tunes". He was particularly impressed by a group of 12 female dancers whose performance was "curious and most lascivious... with much grace as well as action of the last plenty in truth".[175] Mrs. Carmichael noted that native Africans in St. Vincent were accustomed to "dance their own African dances to the drum".[176]

A variety of musical instruments were used at these dances, some European, some African. Slaves were very expert in the use of European type instruments such as the fiddle. For instance, Sir William Young asserted that at his Christmas Ball: "Our music consisted of two excellent fiddles, Johnny and Fisher from my Pembroke estates."[177] African instruments consisted of the tambourin, the African balaso, "an instrument composed of pieces of hard wood of different diameters, laid on a row over a sort of box: they beat on one or the other to strike out a good musical tune" and triangles.[178] But of all the musical instruments, the drum was probably the most popular and most important. At most dances held by slaves, exclusively for slaves, whether for serious ceremonial purposes or for pure relaxation and entertainment, it appears that the music centred around the drum. And even those creole slaves who played the fiddle at public dances "of an evening among themselves… will sing, dance, and beat the drum".[179]

The slaves exhibited and displayed a remarkable degree of kindness and hospitality in the face of great adversity. When questioned by the Investigating Committee on Slavery and the Slave Trade in 1790, about the "temper and dispositions of the Africans", Charles Berns Wadstrom, a Swede who visited West Africa, replied: "They were very honest and hospitable, and I had not the least fear in passing often days and nights quite alone with them; and they shewed me all civility and kindness without my ever being deceived by them."[180] When questioned further about the strength of their "natural and social affections" as compared with those of other people, he replied: "According to my observations on this sort of people, I am quite convinced that they have them in a much stronger and higher degree than any of the Europeans that I have had opportunity to examine."[181]

Africans arriving in the West Indies brought these traits with them. According to Archibald Campbell, the slaves in the Windward Islands were "fond of giving entertainments to their friends and country men". He admitted seeing slaves "give feasts when they have had every variety of wines [and food] well spiced with country peppers". On these occasions women wore the African turban or improvisations of African headgear made from handkerchiefs "folded tastefully above their heads". If necessary slaves would borrow their masters plate and linen to entertain their friends.[182] They would engage in lively chatter in the Creole language, a combination of English, or French as was partly the case in Grenada and Dominica, with their traditional African speech patterns or "negro dialect".[183]

The foregoing aspects of the cultural life of the slaves influenced by Africa and the plantation stood out boldly in stark contrast to that of the whites which was greatly shaped by their European background. The whites spoke English or French as their official language, had their own European type music and dancing, and accepted Christianity as the official religion The culture of the whites was officially regarded as "superior"and that of the Africans as "inferior". However, a few coloured slaves and the free people of colour as a whole tried to disassociate themselves completely from the African elements of their culture.[184] For instance, Mrs. Carmichael noted with a degree of sarcasm that the language of the coloured people in St. Vincent was "much more intelligible than the negroes" even though the "lower classes" spoke mostly "negro dialect". The "higher classes" were able to "express themselves much better although generally ungrammatically", and they all had "the strong nasal pronounciation and creole drawl, which was prevalent among the whites as well. She also noted that the coloured women were accustomed to "dress more shewily and far more expensively" than European ladies, and that they had an "insatiable passion" for dresses, jewels, silk umbrellas, "tight kid shoes and silk stockings".[185]

In this regard the outlook of the free coloured in the British Windward Islands mirrored that of their counterparts in Jamaica where Heuman observed that... "coloureds... emphasised their affinity with whites in a variety of ways... they sought to imitate European fashion often in an exaggerated form. Brown women frequently dressed in the latest and loudest English clothes, to outdo their white competitors".[186] Like the whites who revelled in conspicuous consumption and ostentation, the coloured men were reported to be "very fond of good living and to indulge a great deal in this way". They would "entertain each other frequently with great splendour and ceremony" and have "frequent public balls to which many of the white unmarried men go by invitation".[187] Free coloured men in Jamaica also held their own balls and dinners which although being lavish and expensive undertakings,[188] were as in the British Windward Islands a sad reflection of their racial, cultural and social inferiority in the slave societies.

At the end of the period of this study the economic, political, and social inferiority of the free people of colour and of the slaves which had been earlier established was being maintained by force, habit and custom. But the social system was being challenged. When in 1822 the free people of colour protested about their degradation, this in itself endangered the basis of white rule in the islands. At this time too, the economic basis of their power was also almost eroded as sugar cultivation became more and more uneconomic. Almost at precisely this time the whole social order was under attack from the humanitarians who called for reforms in the slave system. The slaves themselves influenced in part by this criticism began to demonstrate in unmistakable terms that they were prepared to challenge the system. As a result of the interaction of these forces there was a complete overturn of the traditional system of relationships on which the society survived, shortly after the end of the period covered by this study.

CHAPTER *8*

Religion as an agent of social control and social stability

Slavery authorised by God, permitted by Jesus Christ, sanctioned by the apostles, maintained by good men of all ages is still existing in a portion of our beloved country...
> – Mary H. Eastman, *Aunt Phillis's Cabin; or, Southern life as it is*
> – quoted in Stanley Elkins, *Slavery* (1959)

The Mosaic Law declares every slave holder a thief. Paul the apostle classes them among the vilest criminals.... To tolerate slavery or to join in its practice is an insufferable crime which tarnishes every other good quality. For whosoever shall keep the law and yet offend in one point he is guilty of all.
> – George Bourn, *Picture of Slavery in the United States of America*
> – quoted in Stanley Elkins, *Slavery* (1959)

*I*t was not until the last decade of the eighteenth century that any serious attempts were made to convert the slaves in the British Windward Islands to Christianity. The pioneers in these attempts were missionary societies having no connection with the established Church, particularly the Methodists. Indeed, the record of the Anglican Church with regard to conversion in the British Windward Islands was as notorious as in other parts of the British West Indies. Between 1769 and 1792 the Bishop of London had granted licenses to

19 clergymen to preach in the British Windward Islands.[1] But at the end of the period of this study Grenada had only three clergymen of the Established Church, St. Vincent two, and Dominica and Tobago one apiece.[2]

But these clergymen ministered largely to the white population. Dr. Coke who pioneered the work of the Methodist missions in the West Indies observed that even though Grenada had an establishment of five clergymen in 1784 "the white inhabitants have been almost the sole objects of their attention". He continued: "The benighted African has in general been disregarded and considered in relation to futurity as an outcast from the works of God."[3]

The regular clergy were supported financially by fees for officiating at ceremonies such as baptisms, marriages and burials, by vestry allowances, and grants from the island legislatures which displayed a remarkable reluctance and at times unwillingness to make any provision at all, and is indicative of the attitude of the planter class to religious instruction during the eighteenth century. It was not until 1798 for instance, that the Legislature of Dominica passed an Act to provide a salary for a minister.[4]

Even when the legislatures made provisions, the amounts granted were, according to one clergyman, "trifling" and totally inadequate.[5] This led to a situation in which some positions were not filled, and incumbents generally were of the inferior sort. To alleviate this situation it became politic at times to reduce the number of livings. For instance, up to 1808 there were four livings in Grenada and one in its dependency Carriacou and emoluments of the five totalled £2,000 at a salary of £400 each on average. These were subsequently reduced to three at an average salary of £660 each in an effort to attract ministers.[6]

The slaves were allowed to attend the Established Church if they so desired and some were baptised at the request of their masters. But this was as far as the regular clergy went. They did nothing more to promote their conversion and it was the Roman Catholic priests who took the initiative before the advent of the missionaries.

These Roman Catholic priests were active in St. Vincent, Grenada and Dominica which had fairly large populations of French naturalised subjects. As early as 1789 Dominica had four Roman Catholic priests,[7] Grenada had five[8] and even in St. Vincent where the French population was comparatively small there were two priests.[9] These clergymen, unlike those of the Established Church, did not minister only to the white population, and well might the Governor of Dominica boast in 1811 that "more religious exists among the French than the English negroes".[10] The inference need not be drawn, however, that within the context of New World slavery the French were more attentive to the religious needs of their slaves than the English.

The workload carried by the few scattered and underpaid clergymen of the Established Church must have been undoubtedly heavy. But this in itself should not absolve them from their failure to perform their religious duties. Of more importance in this regard is the fact that most of the clergymen lacked a true sense of vocation and saw their offices mainly as stepping stones to positions of power, privilege and profit in the colonial society. Indeed, with few exceptions the character of the clergymen in the British Windward Islands was truly deplorable.

Like the planter class, some of the clergymen of the Established Church were absentees. In Dominica, for instance, a rector who was appointed for the parish of Roseau took up residence in England, leaving his duties to be performed by a deputy who was frequently off the island because he also had another ecclesiastical appointment in England.[11]

The Revd John Audain of Dominica was more interested in smuggling goods from the French islands of Martinique and Guadeloupe than ministering to the inhabitants. In 1808 the Lieutenant Governor reported that the interference of the Bishop of London was necessary to induce him to return to his duties – "he having been absent from the island without leave either from my predecessor or myself for nearly twelve months, during which time he has openly and notoriously been engaged in mercantile pursuits".[12] And if we are to believe Timothy Kelly, a sign placed on the door of the place of worship one Sunday during the regime of Mr. Audian's successor, read as follows: "No service this day, the parson being too drunk and not out of bed yet."[13]

Although it is clear from the foregoing that some of the clergymen lacked a true sense of vocation for religious duties, it must be pointed out that their behaviour was typical of that of the whites to whom they ministered. In slave society of the British Windward Islands hardly anybody went to Church.

According to William Doyle, the largest congregation he saw in Dominica numbered 25. This he argued was exceptional, as generally only 12, 8 or as little as 6 attended. He pointed out that in Grenada "scarcely anybody goes to church at all", and there was so much irreligion that the whites did not even want a minister among them. This disregard for the Church was in his opinion responsible for what he described as "a general depravity of manners and brutishness of behavior" in the entire British West Indies.[14]

In one sense, however, it might be wrong to blame the Established Church for its failure to promote the conversion of the slaves since, during the eighteenth century, this was not seen as wise policy. According to Dr. Coke, some of its representatives in the West Indies were not only indifferent but perhaps opposed to missionary activity among the slaves because they believed that "it would render them worse servants by inspiring them with higher notions than it was prudent to entertain and consequently with a spirit of independence".[15] This assessment seems acceptable, for the clergy like the white ruling class with whom they identified generally accepted the system of slavery and saw nothing wrong with it.

To this generalization, however, Revd Charles Peters of Dominica was the notable exception. In two sermons preached in the cathedral at Roseau on Good Friday and Easter Day 1800, he chided the planters for brutality towards their slaves and called for reforms in the system of slavery itself. Indeed, contrary to the prevailing view of the planter class which regarded the slave as a human being only in those aspects of his behaviour which threatened social stability, Peters 'believed' or 'was of the opinion' that in all aspects of his existence the slave was a human being like everybody else. And finally stressing the point that the inhumane treatment of the slaves was inconsistent with the teachings of Christ, he called for an end of all atrocities.[16]

Reverend Peters earned the reproach of the entire community because of the sentiments he expressed in his sermons. At a meeting of the Council on April 15, 1800 the sermons were described "as being of a nature and tendency the most alarming and dangerous and as such to threaten the subversion and destruction of the colony". The members voted unanimously to summon Peters before the Council Board with his sermons so that they could be thoroughly inspected.[17]

Reverend Peters appeared before the Council as requested and after vindicating his conduct, he tendered his resignation after less than two years' service in the island. One local newspaper, in hailing his departure, urged the necessity for "the utmost vigilance" in the future, to exclude "such ungrateful and dangerous wretches".[18] Another described him as "a diminutive wolf in sheep's clothing" and suggested that he should "exchange his grown for the party-coloured trappings of the French Republicans".[19]

That this was the reaction of the white ruling class is, however, not too surprising, for Peters was a 'radical', a 'revolutionary' in slave society. It should be noted, however, that Peters did not attack the institution of slavery per se, and that he did not advocate emancipation even though he was in favour of the abolition of the slave trade – a sentiment he did not express in his sermons.[20] All he asked for was reforms in the system. But in doing so, he attacked one of the central myths used by the whites to justify their inhuman treatment of the slaves – the myth of negro inferiority – by pointing to the equality of men. This the planter class could not accept and indeed, from their standpoint Reverend Peters was truly a subversive and dangerous man to have in the island.

Reverend Peters held a unique place among all the religious figures who worked in the British Windward Islands during the period of this study. This stems from the fact that he was the only one to get up in public and speak on behalf of the depressed slave population. All the representatives of the missionary societies sedulously avoided making any pronouncements on reform in the institution of slavery. They were all instructed to confine their activities to the religious conversion of the slaves without at all interfering in their social situation. In so far as they refused to call for reforms in the institution of slavery, they obeyed the instruction of non interference. But in one sense they did interfere even though it was to the benefit of the planter class. For as we shall see, in their teachings they stressed the virtues of obedience, submission, humility and respect for authority and seemed to have convinced many of their hearers who accommodated themselves to their inferior position in the society. In so doing they made an invaluable contribution to social stability.

The missionary societies involved in the task of conversion were the Methodists, the Moravians and the London Missionary Society. The work of the last two, however, was confined to Tobago and only for short periods. In 1810 the Society for the Conversion and Religious Instruction and Education of the Negro Slaves in the British West Indies sent a missionary to St. Vincent but he died soon after his arrival.[21] The Methodists then were the only society that remained active in most of the islands from the last two decades of the eighteenth century throughout the entire period of this study. It should be noted, however, that they did not establish a mission in Tobago until 1820.

The Moravians established a mission in Tobago in 1789. This mission, like other Moravian missions in the West Indies was dependent on a slave plantation for its support[22] and its existence was due largely to the initiative of Mr. Hamilton, a resident planter who solicited contributions from his fellowmen. It needs to be emphasised, however that the motives of Mr. Hamilton and his subscribers were far from being purely religious. It is true that they expressed "the utmost concern" about "the deplorable state of ignorance and heathenism in which the negroes of this island have been for a length of time". But they also stressed the practical advantages they hoped to gain from the establishment of such a mission. It would be beneficial, they argued, to have the Moravian brethren in the island since the experience of their 60 years work among the 'heathen' had clearly demonstrated not only that "many had been brought to knowledge of the gospel, but by obedience to its divine precepts, have become more contented and happy in their situation and more faithful to their masters, more regular and virtuous in their lives and conversation and consequently more loyal subjects and useful members of society".[23] Clearly, then, the promoters hoped to reap such benefits from the work on the brethren.

Towards the end of 1798 the brethren decided to send Brother Schirmer and his wife as missionaries to the island. Mr. James Walker, an absentee planter, instructed his attorneys to make an annual subscription to the Mission on his behalf, and also to allow the brethren free access to his slaves.[24] Sir William Young, who was later to become Governor of the island, motivated by the good results he had gained from the work of the Moravians among his slaves in

Antigua, gave the missionaries a personal letter of recommendation to present to his attorney, expressing his approbation of the matter and recommending "on my estate... every hospitality and assistance."[25]

Brother Schirmer and his wife began their labours in the island on January 23, 1799. Preaching on the estates was well attended and during the first year, 9 men and 11 women were baptised. The directors were so pleased with these results that they sent out another missionary, Brother John Church in 1800.[26] At the end of this year, 20 men, 11 women and 3 children were baptised and the congregation numbered 51.[27]

But in the midst of this success, the mission came to a close in 1802. The capture of the island by the French in that year and the uncertainty as to whether it would revert to Britain at the close of hostilities undoubtedly influenced the directors in their decision to suspend the work. However, the principal reason seems to have been the failure of the brethren to secure as had been promised a spot of land for a house and permanent settlement as was typical of their other missions in the West Indies, and the refusal of the planters to continue their subscriptions after the death of Mr. Hamilton, the original promoter of the scheme.[28]

However, before the brethren left Tobago, they did their best to inculcate Moravian principles into the 50 or so slaves they had baptised during their stay. These principles were in keeping with the "Instructions for the Members of the United brethren..." published in 1784.[29]

The missionaries were directed in their dealings with the 'heathen' to preach the fatherhood of God and the martyrdom of Christ so as to appeal to the sympathies of their hearers. When they had succeeded in attracting converts by these means, the next step was an period of instruction to be followed by baptism only if the hearts of their pupils were truly converted.

After baptism there was to be further period of instruction and private prayer until such time as the baptised candidate was in the opinion of the missionary fit for admittance into the congregation. During this second stage a knowledge of the Bible was to be inculcated in the converts since the brethren felt that the more they were acquainted with its tenets the less was the possibility that they might relapse into former ways of life. When finally the candidate was admitted into the congregation this did not mean the end of instruction or supervision since more was expected of these full members than any others. From among them, assistants would be chosen to report all transgressions among members particularly the grave offence of 'backsliding'. When this happened, the convert was either reproved, absolved, or expelled from the congregation.[30]

An examination of the records of the work of the brethren in Tobago indicates quite clearly that they faithfully stuck to the letter of these instructions. When for instance Brother Schirmer visited for the first time a group of slaves "the most of whom had never heard the gospel", he preached to them about "the crucifixion of Jesus... his painful sufferings, bitter death and bloodshedding".[31]

When the brethren accepted candidates in classes for preparation for baptism they exercised strict caution. An examination of the minutes of their conferences at which they decided who was fit for baptism is quite revealing. Not only do they indicate that it took a minimum of one year before the slave was considered fit for the sacrament, but also that the slave could be rejected even after a decision was taken if his demeanour was not satisfactory at the time of the ceremony. For instance, slave Sage of Lowland estate was first proposed at a conference in April 1800 but he was rejected at this and subsequent conferences held in the following year. A decision was finally taken to baptise him in January 1801,[32] but up to March this was still not done, because when he turned up he "appeared to be in a light and trifling mood", and probably intoxicated.[33] The missionaries spelled out clearly their reasons for this caution:

> When conversing about the necessary attention to be paid to those who come among the candidates for baptism it was concluded that unless they duly attend to their meeting for further instruction, and we trace in them a real concern for their salvation; we cannot think of baptising them; for otherwise, instead of having a living congregation of Jesus, we shall have a baptised heathenish congregation which will be worse than having none.[34]

The missionaries also kept a close watch over the private lives of their members and imposed a systematic discipline which included reprobation and in some cases exclusion from the faith for breaches or misconduct. They even attempted to regulate the sexual lives of their converts which, however, is not surprising since in a report submitted to the Privy Council in 1788 concerning the work of the brethren in the West Indies it was clearly stressed that polygamy would not be tolerated. The rules laid down were as follows:

1. That they could not compel a man, who had before his conversion taken more than one wife, to put away one or more of them without their consent.

2. But yet, that they could not appoint such a man to be a helper or servant in the Church.

3. That a man who "believeth in Christ if he marry should take only one wife in marriage, till death do us part".[35]

In 1801 a convert was suspended from the congregation for breaking the last of these rules.[36]

Count Zinzindeorf, the Moravian missionary pioneer whose ideas and policies exercised a strong influence on the shaping of the early missions, had always insisted that his missionaries should obey the secular government and that they should not interfere in the relationships between the employer and the employed.[37] In the report submitted to the Privy Council in 1788 it was asserted that "if they [the slaves] receive punishment for misdemeanours, though they might seem too severe, the brethren have no business to interfere".[38] This policy was pursued by the Moravian brethren in Tobago. In addition, they preached the virtues of obedience, submission and diligence to their converts and by so doing they made a fairly significant contribution to the maintenance and stability of the slave society.

But perhaps in a sense this might have been the only option open to the brethren given the realities of the situation. The brethren were undoubtedly pious men interested in the conversion of the 'heathen' to Christianity. But they had to depend on a planter class which had ulterior motives, for access to the slaves and financial support. The entire mission in itself was dependent financially on the very institution of slavery. If the brethren had attempted to attack the social order they would have been most likely forced to leave the island, as in the case of Revd Peters of Dominica, and the whole process of conversion would be endangered.

Perhaps, then, in order to further their work of conversion the brethren did their best to conciliate white opinion in the island. For example, at a church service where Mr. Hamilton was praised post-humously for the support he had given to the mission, they exhorted the slaves "to show their thanks and love to the son of their late dear master... who is inclined to take the same share in their prosperity as the late Mr. Hamilton did, by... being dutiful and obedient ne-groes".[39] When again in 1799 Brother Schirmer went to say the last word to a slave who was about to be executed, this was what he said:

> though God is merciful and gracious and forgives repenting sinners, yet he also executes his vengeance against those who persist in sin and commit iniquity with greediness and has authorised the powers he had established in the world, to do the same.[40]

In 1800 rumours spread of a planned slave revolt that was to take place at Christmas. Immediately, the brethren called their slaves to-gether and told them "not to follow bad advice that might be given them". They exhorted them to disclose, instead, any information they might receive of what was intended.[41] The revolt was nipped in the bud, and well might the brethren boast that "none of the negroes of Riseland estate, nor any of those under the care of the brethren were concerned in this conspiracy".[42]

After the Moravians suspended their work in Tobago in 1802, that island remained destitute of missionaries until 1808 when the London Missionary Society sent one of its representatives. This soci-ety, established in 1795 from an agglomeration of nonconformist sects such as the Baptists, Presbyterians, Episcopalians and Inde-pendents, was "a child of the Evangelical revival in England origi-nated by the Whitfields and the Wesleys".[43] At an inaugural meeting held on September 22, 1795 it was stated that "the sole object [of the society] is to spread the knowledge of Christ among heathen and un-enlightened nations".[44] It was decided first of all to concentrate on the South Sea Islands, but as time went on, the West Indies was consid-ered to be a desirable area of penetration.[45]

The mission in Tobago was like that of the Moravians established through the initiative of a group of planters. Mr. Robley one of the largest planters on the island with 1,000 slaves on his estates ap-proached the directors of the Society assuring them that he could so-licit enough contributors to the support of the mission.[46] He further stated that if his request was granted he would like to see the missionary in person since he "must be a man who would conduct himself with propriety and not preach liberty to the negroes".[47]

The proposed missionary, Mr. Elliott, was subsequently interviewed by Mr. Robley who "seemed satisfied with his character",[48] and he arrived in Tobago in June 1808. He took up residence on one of Mr. Robley's estates, and began daily rounds preaching to the slaves on a total of seven as well as in the capital.[49] By 1809, however, the work became too much for one man and the directors sent out another missionary, Mr. Purkis, to assist him.[50]

Shortly after Mr. Purkis' arrival, however, the mission ran into difficulties as he and his colleague began to quarrel about its direction. Mr. Purkis seems to have accepted the view that the slaves were incapable of religious and moral instruction and preferred to preach to the free coloureds whom he considered more intelligent. Even though his colleague believed that the free coloureds ought to be included he could not agree on totally neglecting the slaves.[51]

Apart from this quarrel there were financial problems. Ever since Mr. Elliot's arrival he had repeatedly complained of the heavy expense of the mission, and his colleague Mr. Purkis soon began, too, to complain about this problem.[52] Mr. Elliot had been promised a salary from the Legislature, but this never materialised. He had also been promised support from a Presbyterian Society he had founded but he only received a part in 1809 and this was discontinued in the following year.[53] And even Mr. Robley himself, the original promoter of the scheme, had refused to continue his subscriptions in 1810.[54]

But there was a more serious factor involved in the situation. Elliot wrote to the directors accusing his colleague of "paying his addresses to a coloured woman, who makes no pretensions to religion". This woman, he claimed, was "fond of balls and pursues with eagerness the pleasures and vanities of the world." He also asserted that he had facts to back up his allegation because he had heard from the woman's sister that Purkis was with her "almost every night till a very late hour".[55]

The directors, giving credence to the report, decided that Mr. Purkis' recall was "a measure highly proper and indispensably necessary" and he was ordered to leave the island forthwith.[56] But the mission never recovered from the shock occasioned by this scandal. It was even given prominence in the local newspaper and had the effect of detracting from the feeble support given to the mission.[57] This, coupled with the financial problem led the directors to abandon it in 1812.[58]

But although the mission did not last very long, its missionaries (like the Moravians) had made a contribution to the maintenance and stability of the slave society. Indeed, this was the price that the missionaries were prepared to pay for toleration. Like the Moravians this mission was established at planter initiative, with the condition that the missionaries were not to preach liberty to the slaves. Like the Moravians too, this mission depended on financial support from the planters. Even though each missionary received a fixed stipend from his society, he was also expected "to endeavour to produce on their minds [the planter class] a favourable impression towards the cause in which he is engaged, in order that they may be disposed to support it wholly or in part".[59] To ensure the continuance of this support therefore, the missionaries tried to conciliate white opinion by preaching the virtues of obedience and submission to the slaves.

In fact, the directors of the society had expressed the view that its missionaries "should abstain from all observations on the subject of slavery either in public or in private". When questioned as to his observance of this rule, Mr. Elliot replied as follows: "I not only endeavour to avoid any expression which might be misunderstood in this respect but always endeavour to endear them to each other, and particularly their employers, in fact all who have any authority over them."[60]

In speaking of the good effects of his preaching on an estate he pointed out that "there are no complaints made of... stealing... which used to be almost a continual thing among them". The gospel was thus "conquering and accomplishing with ease what the lacerating whip could not accomplish with all its severity".[61] In fact he noted that the slaves on this estate were very obedient, orderly and industrious. During the Christmas holidays, the slaves spent the time peacefully, rather than in drinking, and contrary to usual practice the manager "had no trouble to get them to work".[62] The directors of the Society were quite pleased with such reports since the results, it was believed, would facilitate the work of conversion and the financial support necessary for the conduct of the mission.[63] This was also true of the Methodists.

The Methodist missions in the West Indies owed their existence primarily to the dedicated efforts of Dr. Thomas Coke, a pious ecclesiastic. Indeed, until his death, he devoted all his energies towards effecting the conversion of "the swarms of uncultivated negroes..." to Christianity.[64] The first Methodist Mission in the British Windward Islands was established at St. Vincent in 1787.[65] From St. Vincent, Dr. Coke made visits to Dominica and Grenada to investigate the feasibility of establishing missions. Towards the end of 1788 he had formed a society in Dominica,[66] and Grenada was penetrated by 1792.[67]

With the exception of Grenada, membership in these societies grew rapidly during the late eighteenth century and the first decade of the nineteenth century. In 1790 for instance, after less than two years' work it was reported that "several hundred" slaves had joined the society in St. Vincent.[68] In 1798 membership in Dominica was 115,[69] but by 1804 this had increased to 1,000, and in this same year that in St. Vincent was 2,100.[70] Only in Grenada where the slaves spoke a French patois, which most missionaries could not understand, was membership comparatively small. In 1804 the society had a membership of 103[71] but this exceeded the 1792 figure by a mere 23.[72]

But all in all, it was an impressive achievement despite setbacks occasioned by not enough workers, by insufficient funds and the death of missionaries from yellow fever – and in particular at Prince Ruperts in Dominica. This area was truly a white man's grave. One missionary who spent eight months in that locale had fever five times, and this factor accounted for a reluctance on the part of missionaries to assume responsibilities there.[73]

But the greatest obstacle to the work of the missionaries up to this time was the hostility of the planter class. This hostility generated from a fear that preaching the gospel to the slaves would instill in them ideas of liberty and equality which were incompatible with their subordination in the society. In Dominica, for example, the planter class deliberately requested the resident missionary to do militia duty on Sunday because they well knew that this would interfere with his preaching.[74] But it was in St. Vincent, where the mission was most progressive, that opposition was most intense. Early in 1791 some whites broke into the chapel in the capital, damaged the benches and other articles, took away a Bible "and hanged it on the gallows where it was found... next morning".[75] At a meeting of Council in June of the following year, the missionaries were accused of preaching subversive doctrines and ordered to stop preaching until they had procured licenses to do so. One missionary who refused to comply was arrested. He was only released after Dr. Coke made representations to the home authorities, immediately after which he left the island.[76]

The reports submitted of the work of the Methodist missions in the West Indies in 1816 indicate that St. Vincent had a membership of 2,940, Dominica 710, and Grenada 173.[77] The decrease in membership in Dominica was due largely to the unhealthy atmosphere prevailing at Prince Ruperts which initially had the largest numbers. In Grenada, numbers continued to be small mainly because of the prevalence of the language barrier between the missionaries and the slaves.[78] Toward the end of 1818 a mission was established at Tobago.[79]

At the end of the period of this study, the total membership of all Methodist societies in the British West Indies consisted of 955 whites and 25,176 slaves under the care of 50 missionaries. Of these, the British Windward Islands had 35 whites and 3,722 slaves under the care of 12 missionaries. St. Vincent, the Methodist station par excellence of the group had a complement of 5 missionaries and a membership of 12 whites and 2,889 slaves. In Dominica, 3 missionaries saw to the spiritual welfare of 8 whites and 430 slaves. In Grenada, 8 whites and 330 slaves were under the care of 3 missionaries, and the infant mission in Tobago had a membership of 4 whites, 46 slaves and a complement of 2 missionaries.[80]

In addition, the missionaries had the children of adults enrolled in mission schools. The Executive Committee for the Management of Missions saw elementary instruction to black children as very important for "enabling them to read the Holy Scriptures, and preparing them to receive greater advantage from the public ordinances of religion".[81] Three schools had been established in St. Vincent with a total of 231 pupils, one in Dominica with an enrollment of 150 and another in Tobago with 90. The children were reported to be progressing satisfactorily in the schools. From Tobago it was said that many were able "to repeat with considerable exactness, the whole of the Catechism, the Apostle's Creed, and the Lord's Prayer".[82]

Had Dr. Coke been alive in 1823 he would have been undoubtedly pleased with this achievement. That energetic ecclesiastic under whose zeal and enthusiasm the missions had been founded, and who for many years had been General Superintendent of the Missions, died in 1814. The work however was carried on under the direction of the Methodist Conference in London and an Executive Committee composed of all resident preachers and two general treasurers.[83] In 1818, the General Wesleyan Methodist Missionary Society was formed. Its object, as was stated in its first report, was "to excite and combine, on a plan more systematic than has heretofore been accomplished" the efforts and exertions of all societies established by Wesley and Dr. Coke. The executive of this society undertook the work of formulating rules, appointing missionaries and raising funds for the support of the missions.[84]

The money collected was in part used to pay the salaries and travelling expense of the missionaries, to upkeep chapels and mission houses, to defray printing expenses and to purchase books and other miscellaneous items.[85] Additional funds were donated by the planters themselves especially during the second decade of the nineteenth century. For instance, Mr. John Ross of Grenada subscribed £100 in 1820 and £132 in 1821.[86] The planters also provided building materials for chapels and mission houses. In 1815 a donation of 500 feet of lumber was made by a planter from St. Vincent. But the slaves were also expected to contribute. In the British Windward Islands, all slaves made a small weekly contribution to the mission and it was believed that this would make them "acquire an interest in it which they would not otherwise feel". Collections were also made in the chapels during Sunday Service.[88]

The Society also exercised strict caution in the method of selection of its missionaries. The missionaries were sent to their stations only "after having undergone strict examinations as to their character and qualifications" by the Committee. Each appointee received a copy of Instructions for his guidance, some of which were general and others more specific to the conduct of the mission in the West Indies. And before he was sent out he had to swear on oath that he would obey the instructions and his continued employment was dependent on the observance of them.[89]

Even the manner of preaching was regulated by the Committee and each missionary was given a specific plan which he was supposed to follow. The missionaries were directed first of all "to instruct the adult negroes, who were entirely ignorant in the elements of religion, by suitable catechisms". Then, "when serious and religious impressions are made upon their minds" they were formed into classes which were met either by the missionary himself or by some experienced person appointed by him who was called a "class leader". Then, "after suitable instruction and trial" they were formed into classes which met weekly and their behaviour was closely scrutinized.[90] The missionaries were also given special instructions relating to polygamy: "As many of the negroes live in a state of polygamy, or in a promiscuous intercourse of the sexes, your particular exertions are to be directed to the discountenancing and correcting these vices, by pointing out their evil both in public, and private, and by maintaining the strictest discipline in Societies.[91]

How far these and subsequent instructions were followed in the West Indies is indicated by letters and reports from missionaries working in the British Windward Islands. A letter from two missionaries in Grenada in 1820 indicated that they preached to the slaves about the fall of man, redemption by Jesus Christ, the blessings of redemption such as justification, regeneration, sanctification and eternal glory, the resurrection of the dead and eternal judgement.[92] In an earlier dispatch they pointed out that they had refused to admit some slaves into the society because of their extreme ignorance. They did however form the more serious into classes of catechumens and made sure that recalcitrant members were disciplined: "We had however, to exclude three members the last quarter for neglect; for no member who is absent from class three times is suffered to remain any longer".[93]

On this question of discipline and sanctions to enforce obedience and conformity, the Methodist mirrored the Moravians. Reporting on the work of the Missions in the British Windward Islands in 1823, the Society cited as an achievement the fact that suspensions and expulsions for deviation from standards of religious conduct was "a discipline which most of them dread more than corporal punishment; and is on that account found a very effective means of moral control". The missionaries were also reported to have made phenomenal success in the eradication of polygamy.[94]

The missionaries also faithfully followed the instructions laid down by the Committee governing their relations with the civil government. These instructions were formulated during the first decade of the nineteenth century, but they were kept secret until 1820 when they were published in an effort to exculpate the Society from the belief that the teaching of its missionaries was in some way responsible for the slave insurrection in Barbados in 1816, as Richard Watson had earlier on tried to do in his book published in 1817.[95]

The first instruction defined clearly the religious nature of the work of the missionaries: "Your particular designation is to endeavor the religious instruction and conversion of the ignorant, pagan, and neglected black and coloured population of the island, or station, to which you may be appointed, and of all others who may be willing to hear you".[96] The missionaries were not to attempt to instruct the slaves without the approval of the planters and such instruction was not to cause them any inconvenience. They were also explicitly told to confine themselves to the religious nature of their work, and were expressly forbidden to interfere in the social situation of the slaves:

> Your only business is to promote the moral and religious improvement of the slaves to whom you may have access, without in the least degree in public or private, interfering with their civil condition. In all persons in the state of slaves, you are diligently and explicitly to enforce the same exhortations which the Apostles of our Lord administered to the slaves of ancient nations...servants be obedient to them that are your masters...[97]

But the Methodist missionaries, like the missionaries of the London Missionary Society, and the Moravians, did not only abstain from interference in civil affairs. Indeed, they knew quite well that the cooperation of the planter class was essential for access to the slaves but also for financial support. The Methodist missionaries, therefore, for the sake of conversion and for the sake of financial support preached to the slaves the virtues of fidelity: industry, submission and respect for authority. In so doing, they made a fairly substantial contribution to the cohesion and stability of the slave society. Indeed, it was this aspect of the teaching of the missionaries which largely accounts for the virtual disappearance of the hostility generated against them during the eighteenth century and their ability to carry on their work during the nineteenth century, relatively free from interruption.[98]

This is not to say, however, that there were no admirable features of the work of the Methodists. For the Methodist missionaries, like the other missionaries in the Windward Islands did what few whites had done under the slave system as they attempted to establish a close personal contact with the slaves in an aspect of their lives which had nothing to do with forced labour on the plantations. They also generally refused to accept the prevailing view that the Christian religion was beyond the intellectual and moral capacity of the slaves, and in the end proved this view to be untenable. Indeed, in describing the work of the missions in the West Indies, the Executive Committee remarked in 1820 that "there is a teachableness in the negro character: a readiness to fall under the influence of a white person who approaches him with affection, concerns himself about his welfare, and offers his instruction".[99]

The Methodist missionaries made an invaluable contribution in the field of elementary education for the slaves by the establishment of mission schools – a task which the planter class had for obvious reasons failed to undertake. From Grenada, for instance, it was reported that many of the slaves who became proficient in reading "did not know a letter before these schools were instituted".[100] Indeed, well might the Committee boast that "the capacity of the negroes to be instructed, once so strenuously denied... has been fully established".[101] The missionaries also employed slaves from the congregation to exhort and supervise their converts, thus enabling them to rise to positions of responsibility and leadership – positions more honourable than those allowed them by the planter class and which were generally associated with coercion and the whip. In Dominica, for instance, it was a class leader who held the society together and kept the work in progress during the long absence of the missionary.[102]

But these praiseworthy aspects of the work of the Methodist missionaries were, from another point of view, outweighed by the contributions they made to social stability. It seems as if this was the price they were prepared to pay for toleration. They were instructed to concern themselves only with the spiritual conversion of the slaves and not with their civil condition, but it is difficult to believe as Professor Goviea points out that they did not grasp the important fact that there was a conflict between the Christian doctrines that they preached and the nature of the social system in which they worked. Rather, as she points out, maybe they were not prepared to resolve this conflict at all, since attempts to do so would have most likely impeded the progress of their work.[103]

In 1820 the Executive Committee adopted the position that the whites, in the West Indies had "a right to be assured as to the character and objects of all persons who appear there as instructors of negroes, or the greatest mischiefs might ensue", and that it was "but just that a sufficient pledge be given to the white inhabitants, that the influence of the missionaries shall be employed only for beneficial purposes".[104] The planter class did in fact reap such benefits. If not, why did the Grenada planters donate £1,200 for a chapel, and one planter pay the expenses of a missionary to instruct the slaves on his estate alone?[105] If not, why did George Rose of Dominica request a travelling mission into the interior parts of the island?[106] Indeed, at a time of increasing economic difficulties, the planters would not have done these things if they were not benefiting substantially from the work of the missionaries.

From St. Vincent in 1816, Mr. Josias Jackson reported that he had "reaped inestimable benefits from their labor [the Methodists] in the very great improvement of the morals of his own negroes". The slaves were reported to be very orderly and industrious and it was said that even the children "work in the field... cheerful as birds in the spring. They have no dread of the whip".[107] From that selfsame island another planter congratulated the Methodist Society for the benefits he received from the teaching of its missionaries:

> Confining myself to my own observations, I hesitate not to declare, that the happiest results have attended the indefatigable exertions of the preachers... the fear of God and his omnipresence hangs over the negroes... and his former propensities to theft, drunkness, and other vices, are thereby greatly corrected... his domestic and social habits have been highly strengthened and improved, and what above all, will be perhaps considered most to the point... his duty to his master, instead of being shaken or seduced, is confirmed upon a much better assurance than ever, upon a principle of obedience inculcated, not by the authority of the driver, but by the scripture.[108]

It should not be surprising therefore that the Executive Committee could boast in 1816 that the slaves taught by the missionaries were "superior to those who are left in their pagan ignorance and vice, in industry, sobriety and faithfulness", and that their price at public auctions "had been greatly advanced by the statement of fact, that they were religious negroes".[109] From Grenada, Mr. Ross who had done much to support the missions also spelled out in 1820 the advantages he had received:

> I am now quite convinced (indeed it is scarcely possible it should be otherwise) that the more the slaves are instructed in religious truths, the better they will and do behave. I have full experience of this in several of the slaves on my own estate, who have been admitted into the Methodist Society; and, in some instances, of those on other estates, who have become most exemplary in attending to their duties, who were formerly very indifferent characters.[110]

In Dominica a spokesman for the planter class stressed the political advantages of the work of the Methodists, arguing that: "It is not in the hand of the religious negroes that the torch and dagger will be found." Internal tranquility, he argued, could only be "effectively promoted... by a faithful promulgation of the gospel".[111] When again in 1820, the decrease of the slave population in Tobago became a matter of concern, an expansion of religious instruction was seen as the most effectual remedy,[112] and Mr. Laing of Dominica took a similar view in advocating an extension of the work of the missionaries in that island.[113]

It should be clear by now that the Methodist missionaries like the other missionaries in the slave society of the British Windward Islands were an invaluable asset to the plantocracy. For example, they had tried to impress on the minds of the slaves the notion that polygamy, a legitimate form of marriage in Africa and a part of their culture, was a sin, and by encouraging stable monogamous unions they were helping to increase the birth rate in the islands. This indeed was of inestimable benefit to the planter class especially after the abolition of the Slave Trade when one of their most frequent complaints was a shortage of field hands.[114] Also at a time when the humanitarians were attacking the social order in the West Indies and advocating ameliorative reforms, the missionaries were doing their best to cement the bond of union between the slave and his master by inculcating a sense of moral obligation which to a certain extent lessened the need for force to maintain his racial and social subordination in the society. Again at the critical period before Emancipation when the planters thought it necessary to increase their productive efficiency, the missionaries were preaching to the slaves the virtues of industry, honesty, faithfulness and obedience. Indeed, at the end of the period of this study, the missionaries had become one of the most important forces contributing to the cohesion and stability of the slave society in the British Windward Islands. In this respect they played a role identical to that of their counterparts in the Antebellum South.[115]

CHAPTER *9*

Slave resistance, marronage-, rebellion, revolt

Saint Augustine says... "There is no law unless it be just." So the validity of law depends upon its justice. But in human affairs a thing is said to be just when it accords aright with the rule of reason; and, as we have already seen, the first rule of reason is the natural law. Thus all humanly enacted laws are in accord with reason to the extent that they derive from the natural law. And if a human law is at variance in any particular with the natural law, it is no longer legal but rather a corruption of law.
— St. Thomas Aquinas, *Summa Theologica* (1273)

So from whatever aspect we regard the question, the right of slavery is null and void, not only as being illegitimate but also because it is absurd and meaningless. The words slave and right contradict each other, and are mutually exclusive. It will always be equally foolish for a man to say to a man or a people: I make with you a convention wholly at your expense and wholly to my advantage; I shall keep it as long as I like and you will keep it a long as I like.
— Jean Jacques Rousseau, *The Social Contract* (1762)

In the slave society of the British Windward Islands during the period of this study a small white ruling class held in subordination a middle class of free people of colour who were predominantly brown, a mixed group of brown and black privileged slaves, and a very large group of agricultural field labourers who were almost all black. Race, colour and class were the most important determinants of status in a society that was held together by the elements of force and fear, the divide and rule policy of the white ruling class, but most importantly by the apparent adjustment of the majority of the slaves to their inferior position in the social order.

The words 'apparent adjustment' have been chosen *ex abundanti cautela* and with full appreciation of the fact that no exercise in semantics will obviate the inherent difficulties in understanding complex human behaviour, moreso given the realities of slavery. In his seminal study of slave rebellion in Barbados, Beckles holding that not all slaves were in fact rebellious asserted that: "The majority seemed to have settled down to their labours with a tragic sense of psychological abandonment broken by their perceived hopeless situation."[1] Professor Goveia had earlier made a somewhat similar finding. She asserted on the basis of cogent evidence that the majority of the slaves in the Leeward Islands accepted their subjugation or acquiesced therein.[2] There are some data on the experience of slave resistance in the British Windward Islands which support this contention. On this theme, Gaspar added the variant that "most slaves were neither strictly nor unambiguously docile nor rebellious". In fact, he suggests that it is possible to delineate a wide range of responses between the poles of abject submission and total resistance at opposite ends of the spectrum.[3] Gaspar's insight is consistent with the earlier characterisation of slave personality types formulated by Blassingame with respect to antebellum slave society. He describes it as the "sambo" and "rebel" phenotype.[4] The slave who on day one exhibited the sambo characteristic would on day two be a rebel. To this we may add a combination of both rebel and sambo on day three and neither on day four. Appearances tended to mask or diverge from realities.

But although the society had succeeded in maintaining a degree of relative stability, there were forces at work that were likely to destroy it. One was the very nature of the economic system itself, which was gradually crumbling under the impact of gross mismanagement, inefficiency and Great Britain's fiscal economic and commercial policies all of which made the sugar industry uneconomic during the period of this study. This gradual erosion of the economic base of the society could not fail to pose a threat to the political power and hence to the social dominance of the white oligarchy which controlled it.

While the sugar economy tottered on the edge of total bankruptcy, the humanitarians began to attack the social system. Initially
they asked for reforms in the slave system and subsequently for its
abolition. These radical demands, like the unprofitability of the economic system, also posed a threat to the power which the local white
oligarchies wielded over the groups in the insular communities in the
Windward Islands.

The social system was also threatened by those slaves who refused to adjust themselves to their inferior position and also by others
who began to question this status. Slaves (male as well as female) participated actively in resistance movements which created instability
and exposed the extent to which the system in itself was vulnerable.
Morrisey has shown that slave women were not passive participants
in the struggle.[5] Bush, in similar vein, is critical of what she perceives
as a tendency in some literature to regard the arena of slave rebellion
protest and revolt as a predominantly male enterprise. She opined
that to many Europeans, female slaves were regarded as more troublesome than male slaves. It was partly for this reason, she asserts,
the planters in Trinidad protested the law of 1823 which banned the
whipping of female slaves.[6] Trinidad was not unique in this respect.
In St Vincent such a law could not be externally imposed but the
island Legislature opposed the measure and refused to enact the legislation on similar grounds. Since "women were the most intemper-
ate and turbulent persons in the gang", punishment was even more
necessary.[7]

All slaves, therefore, irrespective of gender, were involved to
varying degrees in challenges to the system including rebellion. In
some instances the slave exploited external developments such as the
antislavery movement in England and the revolution in France with
its ideology of liberty, fraternity, equality. However, this did not
mean that the slave revolts and other types of resistance in the British
Windward Islands did not have their own independent existence and
ideology. There is merit in Beckles' criticism of a tendency to regard
manifestations of slave ideology and activism as being "mostly cata-
lytic imports". He notes, for example, that CLR James in *The Black Jacobins* "sought perhaps with too much theoretical enthusiasm to link
the slave rebellion in St. Domingue with French revolutionary ideology". He argues further that while it is true that slaves sought allies

with forces external to their struggle, "those forces played no part in the initial acts of rebellion".[8] This insight gains support from the experience of Tobago. In that island the years 1770, 1771, 1772, and 1774 were each marked by violent slave uprisings. In November 1770 slaves were involved in a rebellion which lasted six weeks. In June 1771 the island experienced another of fourteen days' duration. About seven months later, in January1772, there was another servile revolt which lasted eleven days. After a hiatus in 1773 the slaves revolted in March 1774 and held out for a fortnight. This last was said to be the most dangerous, as a total of 80 whites were killed.[9] These were rebellions that predated in long measure the development of the revolutionary ideology in France, which culminated in the storming of the Bastille in 1789.

The resistance movements of slaves and maroons will be analysed and interpreted against a background of increased heightened political consciousness as a result of tensions and contradictions in the slave society. In fine, they strongly indicate a fairly sophisticated level of political protest and organisation among the participants which falls to be analysed within the context and methodology of prevailing political theory. We will not be deterred by detractors who question the relevance of this approach. Professor Gordon Lewis and later Hilary Beckles have already demonstrated the utility of the concept.[10] Furthermore, it is a fact that in the contemporary world individuals and groups are faced from time to time with making decisions directed at effecting changes in institutions and structures which they find unresponsive to their needs. However, strangely enough, it is not fashionable to call into question the use of the term 'political', no matter how loosely employed in these situations, and we see no rational basis for holding that political action is irrelevant to slave activism. Such a view is essentially eurocentric and consistent with the myth of the innate inferiority of the slave.

In a persuasive and authoritative study, Ted Gurr proffers a typology of political violence which is relevant to the phenomena under discussion. He identifies three major forms of political violence.[11] The first, which he describes as *turmoil*, relates to relatively spontaneous unorganised political violence with substantial popular participation, including violent political strikes, riots, political clashes and localised rebellion. Day to day acts of resistance by slaves in the British Windward Islands as detailed hereafter – including petitioning, strikes, marches on government buildings, demands for 'rights of audience' before governors and other persons in authority, demonstrations and other forms of civil disobedience, including what would be termed roadblocks in Jamaica today – would fall somewhere along this continuum. The second, *conspiracy*, involves inter alia, highly organised political violence with limited participation, including political assassination, terrorism, coups and mutinies. The third, *internal war*, is described as highly organised political violence with widespread popular participation designed to overthrow the regime or dissolve the state and accompanied by extensive violence including large scale terrorism and guerrilla wars, civil wars and revolution.[12] Slave rebellions, plots, conspiracies, and marronage would fall within the second and third categories.

The preconditioning factors most likely to precipitate turmoil as well as the other forms of political violence are "the institutions, persons, and policies of rulers which have inspired the wrath of their nominal subjects throughout political life".[13] The nature of the institution of slavery in itself, the reality of oppression of the slaves by the minority ruling class, and the numerous regulations and policy measures designed to maintain that iniquitous social system in the British Windward Islands provided a fertile breeding ground for turmoil and other expressions of political violence. The relevant institutions and policies lead to what is described as a relation "between perceived deprivation and the frustration concept in frustration-anger-aggression theory".[14] This provides a rationale for a more general definition of magnitude of violence and a more precise specification of what it comprises.

The basic frustration-aggression proposition is that "the greater the frustration the greater the quality of aggression against the source of frustration". Intense frustration can motivate men to either intense or short-term attacks on their frustrators. The severity of deprivation affects both the intensity of violence, that is the extent of human and physical damage incurred, and its duration.[15] With regard to popular involvement, the proportion of a population that participates in violence ought to vary with the average intensity of perceived deprivation. Mild deprivation will motivate few to violence; moderate deprivation will push more across the threshold; very intensive deprivation is "likely to galvanise large segments of a political community into action".[16]

To sum up, the primary casual sequence in political violence is first, the development of discontent and secondly, its actualisation in violent action against political objects and actors. Discontent arising from the perception of relative deprivation is the basic instigating condition for participants in political violence. The linked concepts of discontent and deprivation comprise most of the psychological states implicit or explicit in such theoretical notions about the cause of violence as frustration, alienation, drive and goal concepts, exigency and strain. Relative deprivation is defined as "a perceived discrepancy between mass value expectations and their value capabilities". Value expectations relate to the goods and conditions of life to which people believe they are rightly entitled. Value capabilities are the goods and conditions they think they are capable of attaining or maintaining from the social means available to them.[17]

In an earlier study Smelser outlined his 'value added' model of a series of determinants of collective behaviour. This model with slight modifications is also applicable to slave protests and rebellions, which were undoubtedly social movements involving collective action. Smelser sees the behaviour of the participants in a social movement as "a product situation to which a value or probability for social action is added as each of the necessary but insufficient conditions may come to exist".[18] First of all, the situation must be structurally conducive to some form of collective behaviour. Secondly, the situation must be "socially strained". Thirdly, the existence of a "sufficiently generalised belief within the population" that some avenue to the strain is open. Fourthly, "the ultimate action must be mobilised by some precipitating event"; and fifthly, it must be allowed to continue or even be inflamed to higher degrees by inadequately implementing mechanisms of social control.[19]

Lewis McKillan examines social movements within the context of social and cultural transformation and changing values and norms in the society. A social movement is "an ongoing protest... it is always possessed with a sense of mission".[20] The characteristics of social movements which McKillan describes were also present in varying degrees in the several challenges to the slave regime in the period under discussion. These he lists as the existence of shared values, a goal or objective, sustained by an ideology; a "sense of membership, a weeness", involving a distinction between those who are for and who are against; norms; shared understandings as to how the followers should act; definition of outgroups and how to behave towards them; and lastly, however unorganised or unplanned, a structure and a division of labour between leaders and followers and between different classes of each. Like Gurr and Smelser, frustration is seen as the "preconditioning and precipitating factor giving rise to social movements as of all forms of collective behaviour".[21]

J.E. Greene, in similar vein writing on "Contradictory Aspects of Protest and Change in the Caribbean", analyses protest movements in terms of the demands made on those who hold political office. He asserts that protest "essentially evinces challenge to those in authority as it questions the legitimacy of regimes, threatens to erode the legal bases on which power rests, or overthrows them by extra legal methods". Depending on the level of organisation and direction, protest by pressure groups has the potential to create instability within the political system which will eventually force those who hold power to respond to demands.[22]

From the literature on the historiography of slave resistance in the Caribbean, Beckles has extracted a three-dimensional typology. At one end of the spectrum he identifies what is termed day-to-day resistance with objectives designed to undermine the efficiency of the slave system leading to its ultimate demise. At the other end is the incidence of successful rebellion including long-term marronage. In the middle is to be found diverse unsuccessful plots and revolts with reformist and revolutionary objectives.[23] This formulation in some respects shares common ground with Gurr's theory of political violence discussed above. However, while each category is to some extent separate and independent, it can be argued that none is totally mutually exclusive. In some instances there is evidence of significant overlap not only between but within categories. Some if not all of these genres were manifest in the phenomenon of resistance in the British Windward Islands and impacted on the final outcome of black liberation. To this, however, there is an important caveat. While the classification is attractive and indeed workable, it may be unwise to attempt to fit the complex anatomy of slave resistance into a limited number of straightjackets or convenient pigeon-holes. Neither should the categories be regarded as necessarily closed. Further re-search will undoubtedly unearth other variants or modifications as present developments indicate.

The slave also resisted by committing individual acts of violence against white persons. When for instance the obeah men and women administered poisonous mixtures to slave owners with fatal effects they were executing vengeance on those who kept them in bondage. In this regard, Bush notes that female domestic servants "because of their close proximity to whites were able to disguise poison in food and drink with the minimum of personal risk. The poison... often in-duced a slow death which was difficult to detect".[24] But the means were not always as subtle as this. In the British Windward Islands there were many instances of slaves openly murdering their white masters with knives and other weapons. Running away was a more widespread form of resistance. Indeed, the fact that all the slave codes contained many provisions for the pursuit, capture and sup-pression of runaways seems to indicate that the incidence of this form of resistance must have been high. Other mechanisms of resistance included arson, plunder, deliberate sabotage, malingering and re-fusal to work.

But individual acts of violence such as poisoning and murder hardly threatened social stability. The same can generally be said about the act of running away since it was for the most part an indi-vidual and peaceful method of resistance to slavery rather than a col-lective and violent one. As a matter of fact, Gaspar suggests that slave owners over a period of time tended to regard the practice as a normal predictable and inevitable incident of a slave holding or "as an inescapable offshoot of slavery, a nuisance if nothing more".[25] When, however, the escaped slaves established viable self-sufficient communities and used them as basis for collective assaults on the set-tled plantations – assaults involving arson, plunder and murder – the very existence of the plantation system was at stake. Grenada suf-fered from this type of activity until 1771[26] after which Maroon resis-tance apparently ceased to be a major problem. However, of the territories comprising the British Windward Islands, it was in Do-minica that the Maroons posed the most serious threat, in particular in the period 1785-1815.

According to a contemporary work in the field, the Dominica Maroons were originally slaves of Jesuit missionaries resident on the island at the time it became a British possession. With the establishment of British rule, the missionaries sold their lands and slaves to English settlers. It is alleged that these slaves for some reason took a strong dislike to their new masters and deserted the plantations with their wives and children for interior parts of the island where they were joined from time to time by runaway slaves from other estates, whom they sheltered and protected.[27] There they organised themselves into social and political units headed by chiefs, sub-chiefs and captains. From these bases, these 'banditti'[28] demonstrated their hostility to the British presence by making attacks on the plantations, which resulted in destruction of property and loss of life.

The actual number of Maroons cannot be established with any degree of accuracy. One estimate given in 1785 put the number at 300,[29] and when they were defeated in 1814 a total of 578 were reported as having surrendered.[30] Again in 1800 military captains found a camp of 80 houses, each capable of holding from 10 to 12 persons.[31] Craton estimates the population to be at least 800 by mid-1812, situated in nine locations.[32] Whatever their actual numbers, they were certainly a force to be reckoned with.

The scholarship on Maroons indicates that maroon communities had to be almost inaccessible and located in inhospitable, out-of-the-way areas if they were to be viable.[33] The topography of Dominica offered such viability and effectively aided the Maroons in their struggles. As one governor reported in 1785, the mountainous interior which they inhabited abounded with fastnesses, places of concealment and roads that were almost impassable. In addition, there was "a great plenty of ground provisions in all parts" and streams of water on almost every acre.[34] A detachment of troops that penetrated a Maroon camp was surprised to find 300 acres of land "fully stocked with all kinds of provisions" and even sugar cane.[35] The Maroon camps therefore not only provided their inhabitants with a haven almost inaccessible to Europeans but also with commodities necessary for sustenance.

Indeed, throughout the eighteenth century the Dominica Maroons were rated second in organisation, discipline, strength and unity of purpose to their counterparts in Jamaica.[36] Although they commenced operations shortly after the establishment of British rule, it was not until the last two decades of the eighteenth century that they were regarded as extremely dangerous as they took to open raiding on the plantations. In 1785 one governor described them as "an internal enemy of the most alarming kind",[37] and for the next thirty years they truly constituted an "imperium in imperio".[38] It was Maroon policy to always make use of the element of surprise in their attacks. They would suddenly come down from their fastnesses to the plantations, burn, loot and kill any white people they encountered and then retreat behind their almost impregnable hideouts. Such raids were sometimes reprisals for punishment meted out to their colleagues whom plantation owners had recaptured and re-enslaved. For instance, upon the receipt of information that one of their band had been recaptured and disciplined by the governor who owned a sugar estate, a party of 100 fully armed proceeded to this estate at 7 o'clock the following night. They burnt all the buildings to the ground and threw four whites and others they killed into the flames. It was said that they treated the "principal black" on the estate in the same manner and wounded his family (wife and children). They then returned to their homes carrying considerable booty.[39]

The year of this incident, 1785, was the same year that they had reportedly threatened "to destroy every English estate in the island".[40] Bands of Maroons ranging in numbers from 40 to 50 set fire to five estates completely destroying buildings and crops, forcing the whites to retreat to other areas. So serious was the situation that the metropolitan power sent out huge supplies of arms and ammunition for use by the local troops with instructions to the governor to apply for additional reinforcements from the neighbouring islands of St. Vincent and Grenada.[41] But the military expeditions were totally unsuccessful as it was impossible to penetrate far into Maroon territory, especially the stronghold controlled by Pharcelle, who made good use of his knowledge of the terrain.[42] Indeed, as Maroon activities intensified and as British efforts to suppress them became more ineffectual, the colonial political leaders opted for negotiation with leaders of the communities. They sought to win over to their side Pharcelle, reputed to be the strongest Maroon leader, with the hope that he would assist them in suppressing the movement.

Accordingly, on October 15, 1794, the Assembly unanimously voted that the government should hold talks with Pharcelle. Members voted to propose to Pharcelle that he and such others of his party as he should name, would be given their freedom and parcels of Crown land by legislative enactment in return for a pledge of assistance in hunting and capturing runaways and Maroons. Such an accommodation was regarded as vital to the existence of the plantation system on the island .The Council concurred with this opinion and a special committee was appointed to begin negotiations with Pharcelle. On December 9, 1794 an agreement was reached between Pharcelle, the Governor and members of the Council and Assembly. The essence of this agreement was that Pharcelle, his two wives – Martian and Angelique – and 12 of his men would be declared free and granted Crown lands adequate for their present and future subsistence. In return for this, Pharcelle and such of his following as he would select were to hunt the woods for Maroons and other runaways, receiving a monetary compensation for each one brought in. It was further agreed that after the passage of the Act conferring their freedom that Pharcelle and his party would be subjected to military discipline in the same manner as the soldiers in the King's regiments and that he would be under the effective jurisdiction of the Governor who was authorised to appoint a chief of the party in the event of his death, incapacitation or infirmity.[43]

This agreement, however, failed to curb Maroon activity and hence guarantee any degree of stability to the island. Indications are that either Pharcelle was being deliberately deceptive when he put his signature to the text or that he subsequently changed his mind, because he did not fully carry out his part of the bargain. The last decade of the eighteenth century, particularly the period after the treaty, was marked by an intensification of guerrilla-type activity and "very considerable desertion of negroes from the estates"[44] to the camps. Indeed, such activities taxed the resources of the colonists to the limit and the situation was aggravated by the fact that military campaigns yielded little, if any, results. In one attack on a camp, provision grounds were reportedly destroyed, but in an attack on another, a sergeant was killed and when the troops finally arrived inside the settlement they found it deserted. This lack of success was attributed to a suspicion that the Maroons "were perfectly acquainted with our expedition, and were prepared for us".[45]

The captain of another detachment reported a similar occurrence. After a long and tiring match of six hours' duration he found that the Maroons had deserted the camp. "Indeed," he wrote, "we have reason to suspect that they have too many friends in every direction along shore to leave them ignorant of any step taken against them."[46] Such suspicions were not unfounded. The Maroons did in fact have emissaries, spies and informers on the slave plantations, and this was so not only in Dominica but in other parts of the New World where Maroons were to be found. Indications are that they were quite aware of the military expedition in 1797 and adopted the counter-strategy of leaving their camps for the settled plantations at precisely the time when the troops had left these areas in search of their hideouts.

This, indeed, was a time when Maroon activity created a situation in which "trade and cultivation was much retarded and the colonists [were] kept in increasing agitation". Bands of Maroons marched through the country-side, burning, looting and plundering and on one occasion they even advanced as far as the capital, Roseau, demanding the Governor's head.[47] The capture and execution of three of them by local militia troops and the public display of their heads in the market-place as a deterrent to others[48] seemed to incite them to even more attacks. Maroon "outrages were such as to occasion much uneasiness". And the regiments found it more and more difficult to reach strongholds, with increasing casualties from traps such as pikes and stakes set in the vicinity of the camps.[49] In instances where they were able to penetrate they found the areas deserted. After one such expedition, Pharcelle who had served as a guide was jailed for "insolent and highly suspicious conduct", and the political leaders also considered banishing him from the island.[50]

The first decade of the nineteenth century brought no relief to the plantocracy. This period "can aptly be termed the second Maroon War in Dominica' The Maroons were at the time increasing their strength with runaways from the estates at great economic loss to the planters, one of whom put up his estate for sale since he had no slaves to cultivate it. On one estate, Castle Bruce, the entire slave force numbering some 75 deserted to join the Maroons[51] who were reported to be "plundering and murdering white and peaceable coloured inhabitants", with life and property being equally insecure.[52] As the planters began to abandon their estates in large numbers, a hue and cry was raised for tough and firm action. In response to this pressure, troops were mobilised from the neighbouring islands and the Governor issued a proclamation on May 10, 1813 offering the Maroons free and unconditional pardon if they surrendered by the fourth day of June. Those who refused to comply, it stated, if taken by military might, would be treated "with the utmost rigour of military execution, their places of refuge and harbours destroyed, their provision grounds laid waste and the punishment of death inflicted on those who are found in arms".[53] This military force consisted of the local militia, the troops stationed in the island, including an all-black detachment, and a special corps of Rangers.[54] A copy of the proclamation was sent to a Maroon camp by a Maroon who had earlier turned himself in and offered his services to the local authorities. But upon his arrival he was, consistent with Maroon discipline, tried and shot for treason by Chief Quashee. Upon receipt of this information, the Governor offered a reward for Quashee's head, but Quashee in return, offered a reward of two thousand dollars for the Governor's.[55] The Maroons refused to comply with subsequent proclamations urging them to surrender[56] and, as a result, the troops were mobilised against them. At the end of November 1814, 559 of them had surrendered, 195 to the Black Corps, 111 to the other troops, and 153 to managers and constables to the estates. Only eighteen were killed in action. Of those who surrendered, 81 were tried at court-martials, and 13 were hanged. The majority, however, were banished from the island or worked in chains.[57]

Several questions immediately pose themselves. Why were the Maroons who inhabited such inaccessible and out-of-the-way areas and engaged in unconventional types of warfare so easily defeated? And why did the defeat take the form of a surrender? Further, what role did Pharcelle, who had arrived at an accommodation with the authorities in 1794, play in all this? In assessing the defeat Craton stresses the importance of British command of the sea, which facilitated rapid movement of troops throughout Maroon strongholds than was possible by land. However, he seems to regard as being of greater import the effect of two hurricanes in 1813 which "laid waste the mountainous provision grounds without which the maroons could not continue to fight".[58] But this was not the first time that the island experienced severe hurricanes. As we have shown, the year 1787 witnessed three not two hurricanes, also at a time of heightened Maroon attacks and increasing inability on the part of local forces to contain them.

This does not mean that there was no connection whatsoever between the hurricanes of 1813, the consequent effect on food supplies and the capability of the Maroons to wage internal war. But these factors cannot be considered in isolation. It is being suggested here that the burning of provision grounds by colonial troops – the fruits of which the maroons relied on for their sustenance – was of greater impact than the hurricanes which merely aggravated, albeit seriously, a pre-existing situation. And in this scenario the available evidence indicates that Pharcelle, by acting as guide on some campaigns, opened a door to British penetration into Maroon territory, a door which was widened by other Maroons who went over to the Government, and that this contributed to the debacle of 1814.

It was not until the last decade of the eighteenth century that British troops managed to penetrate a Maroon camp and this was done with the assistance of Pharcelle, even though he was arrested afterwards. The camp was vacant but the troops set fire to the provision grounds in an effort to starve the Maroons into surrender.[59] This tactic they pursued in the 1813 campaign as they gained access to other camps with the aid of Maroons. The Maroon who was tried and shot by Chief Quashee had not only turned himself in, but also offered his assistance to the local authorities in the location of hideouts and suppression of the movement, an offer which was of course accepted.[60] As the troops gained access to the hideouts by these means, the Maroons retreated to other areas. But the troops burnt the provision grounds and used the captured areas as bases for similar assaults on other pockets of resistance. By March 1814 this tactic was largely successful and well might the Governor boast that the Maroons had the choice of "either starving in the woods or surrendering".[61] The final success of this stratagem accounts for the fact that only eighteen Maroons were killed in action while the majority surrendered.

The final defeat of the Maroons, however, should not detract from their achievement. As in Jamaica, the Maroons were exceptional for their effective and prolonged resistance to slavery and white control of the island. It is clear that their actions were directed towards the sole aim of destroying the white ruling class and they saw that this could be done by forging an alliance with the plantation slaves who were the most oppressed group in the society. For a period of 30 years they waged internal war, destroyed entire plantations, disrupted commercial activity, and kept the whites in a state of terror and panic.

And despite their defeat they made a contribution to the destruction of the slave system in the island. Craton makes the important point that the victory of the Dominican plantocracy was far from unequivocal as the island never recovered from the shocks occasioned by the Maroon wars.[62] When emancipation came in 1833 it was the result of a combination of forces – humanitarian, social, political and economic. Eric Williams has highlighted the importance of the deterministic impact of economic factors set in motion as early as the second half of the eighteenth century. As the position of the planter class deteriorated economically, so did the political influence they exercised in Parliament and had used to veto policies thought to be antagonistic to their interests, such as slave emancipation. The Act of Emancipation itself was in one sense a political defeat for a planter class that had been weakened economically. It should be clear by now that the activities of the Dominica Maroons contributed to the erosion of the economic base of the planter class in that island and that this in turn helped to destroy them as a political force and therefore make emancipation possible.

While the stability of the society in Dominica was being disturbed by the activities of the Maroons in the 1780s, revolution broke out in France in 1789. This was followed by revolutionary activity among the slaves in the French West Indian Islands, in an attempt to make the ideals of the revolution a reality. The whites in the British Windward Islands regarded the ideas of liberty, equality and fraternity, the slogans of the French Revolution, as extremely dangerous. For they rightly feared that if these were translated into action in their respective societies, the political and social dominance which they exercised might come to an end. All of them therefore took measures to insulate their societies from these egalitarian ideas.

During the revolutionary wars a large number of refugees and their slaves from the French West Indies sought entry to the British Windward Islands and the authorities exercised great caution in admitting them. As the President of Grenada reported in 1792, such precautions were necessary "to prevent them from infecting our slaves who are at present happy and quiet".[63] Later, that island placed a ban on the importation of slaves from the French West Indies, and free people of colour were also denied entry which was given "very sparingly" only to those whites who in the opinion of the governor were not infected with republican principles.[64]

To the whites, the prospect of revolution grew more real after the French government had been forced, apparently by the circumstances of revolution and war, to grant emancipation to the slaves in its colonies in 1794. In this year, the revolutionary agent Victor Hughes was able to recapture Guadeloupe from the British with the aid of the slaves, in the name of freedom, equality and the French Republic. The whites in the Windward Islands trembled even more for their own safety. After the recapture of Guadeloupe, Dominica was said to be in "a most critical and dangerous situation" because a number of French Patriots had landed in the outbays and were "joining with... evil disposed subjects... endeavouring to excite the negroes to rise, promising them freedom and equality".[65] To make matters worse, the authorities intercepted a letter addressed to Pharcelle, the famous Maroon chief. This letter sent by a Frenchman who refused to sign his name for security reasons stated:

> je t'ai fait remettre par la porteur la proclamation des Commissaries delegues par la Republique Francais au isles du vent, qui abolit l'esclavage dans toutes les colonies, avec un cocarde nationale que le consul de Saint Barthelemy m'a remis pour tois, comme un signe de bonheur que la genereuse nation francais vous prepare.[66]

This caused the whites to panic as they believed the island was about to experience violent turmoil. This belief was heightened in November when it was discovered that a large number of Frenchmen and their slaves were furtively entering the island at the numerous bays and creeks on the coast. The local militia, a corps of rangers and a

Figure 8 • Map of the island of Tobago

detachment of slaves were sent out on patrol, but so critical was the situation that martial law had to be formally declared.[67]

The Legislature of Tobago also passed an Act in 1794 designed to further prevent the spread of French principles. That Act deplored the spirit of "anarchy and insubordination" in the French islands which had spread its "baneful influence" among the slaves, and had instilled into them "ideas of liberty and equality totally subversive of all good government". It stipulated that no slaves other than those directly imported from Africa were to be landed until the Governor had obtained "a full and distinct knowledge of their principles and morals" and was satisfied that they could be sold "without prejudice to the tranquility or safety of the colony or danger to the morals or principles of the slaves residing in it". Slaves already in the island were forbidden "to by words, action or otherwise however, endeavour to excite sedition, promote conspiracies, or spread a spirit of revolt, mutiny or disobedience..." on pain of transportation.[68] In addition, the belief was current that Victor Hughes had sent emissaries to the island and 4 suspected agents along with 17 others who refused to take the oath of allegiance were banished. Measures of this sort were regarded as vitally essential if Tobago was to remain a white man's country. For it was argued, "if they [the Republicans] get hold of the negroes they could easily persuade them to join the Republican Standard and then the colony is ruined".[69]

But despite these precautionary measures, revolutionary ideals gained headway in all the islands and attempts were made to make them a reality. In March 1795 Grenada and St. Vincent were experiencing revolutionary disturbances and in June of the same year a threatened revolution in Dominica was put down. Early in the next century, the authorities unearthed a plot to murder all the whites and free coloureds in Tobago. In St. Vincent, the Black Caribs/Kalinago embarked on internal guerrilla war. In Grenada, the revolt was led by a mulatto from Guadeloupe, but in both uprisings slaves were involved.

In Grenada, on the night of March 1795, the revolt began simultaneously in two parts of the island, at Grenville in the East and Gouyave in the West. At about midnight, the leaders Fedon and Besson with about 100 slaves and mulattoes captured the town of Grenville by surprise, murdering all the English-speaking whites, and burning and looting their houses. On the other side of the island, Etienne Ventour and Joachim Phillipe with the assistance of slaves and mulattoes attacked the town of Gouyave and took all the British residents as prisoners.[70] As the insurrection spread, the participation of the slaves became more and more widespread. Towards the end of March, the President reported that: "The negroes are daily joining the insurgents and desolating the estates, all of which have been plundered, and a number in the neighbourhood of the town have been burnt." At the time this report was made, the rebel force consisted of 350 men with muskets, 250 with pikes, and 4,000 slaves.[71] There were further reports of slaves deserting the estates en masse for the rebel camps where they received military training.[72]

Shortly after the outbreak of revolt in Grenada, St. Vincent went up in flames, as the Caribs led an assault against the whites. Relations between these peoples had never been cordial. There were bitter memories on both sides of the war of 1772 and the resultant treaty failed to satisfy both parties, especially the whites, who frequently accused the Caribs of repeatedly violating its terms.[73] By the middle of March, the Caribs under their leaders Chatoyer and Duvalle, whom

Victor Hughes described as an "officier des armies de la republique",[74] had almost devastated the entire island with the aid of runaway slaves whom they sheltered and protected.[75] Then on June 5, the Brigands, a group of Maroon slaves who had already captured St. Lucia from the English, landed in Dominica "where they had so many well wishers and the negroes all disposed to rise in their favor".[76] The attempted rising in Dominica was, however, quickly suppressed. One hundred and four of the conspirators were court-martialled and sent to England for sentence and another 95 were banished from the island.[77] But the rebellions in St. Vincent and Grenada continued much longer. It was not until the end of 1795 that the Carib War was brought to a close after a long and protracted campaign with the assistance of General Abercrombie and his forces. He then proceeded to Grenada and subdued the rebels by July the following year.[78] The participation of the slaves in these revolutionary disturbances clearly demonstrated their will to be free. It also demonstrated that they were not prepared to sit idle and wait for freedom as a dispensation from their masters and that they saw in revolutionary action a means of effecting social change.

During these disturbances in the 1790s, the slaves in Tobago remained relatively quiet. But early in the next century, they too demonstrated that they were prepared to resort to revolutionary action to shake off the shackles of enslavement. In 1802, the President reported that "an insurrection of the Negroes of this island having been intended for the purpose of murdering all the white inhabitants was... discovered two days before Christmas Day, when their diabolical plan was to have been carried into execution".[79] This revolt was well planned, with operations to take place simultaneously in three different parts of the island. The slaves on two estates (Belvedere and Bacolet) were to disarm and kill all whites and set fire to the canes. The slaves on Mr. Robley's estates were to perform a similar operation at the same time. At this time too, the slaves in the capital were to rise after the execution of the Commander of the Armed Forces by two of his servants.

As preparatory measures, the slaves were furtively organised into companies and given military training by appointed officers. On Belvedere estate, Roger, a driver was appointed Governor with full responsibility for the execution of the plan and Thomas, a cooper was nominated Colonel. And in the capital, leadership and strategy was delegated to a council of five chiefs.[80] The design, however, was not carried into execution because one of the slaves told a magistrate of what was intended, thus giving the authorities time to act. Martial law was declared immediately and during its operation two slaves were shot dead and 200 arrested. A court-martial began sittings on December 20 and its proceedings were terminated on January 9 in the following year. Five slaves were found guilty of conspiracy and were executed, while another four were banished from the island.[81] The authorities expressed a certain degree of shock and disbelief in the aftermath of this conspiracy. This was so because as in other slave revolts in the New World, "most of the chiefs were either drivers, tradesmen or principal people on the estates; and they were not only in possession of the comforts but even the luxuries of life".[82]

This indeed was so because these slaves were not subject to the harsh rigours of plantation of life, and were much better off materially than the common field slaves. Some of them were in confidential positions on the estates and were used as agents for enforcing the subordination of the other slaves to their masters. It was hoped that by making these slaves relatively comfortable they would have had an interest in maintaining the system. But unfortunately they did not regard these "comforts" as advantages more "solid and lasting" than those to be derived from what was described as "mistaken ideas of liberty and equality".[83]

This conspiracy represented the last major organised attempt of the slaves in the British Windward Islands to overthrow the social system by force. This attempt, however, like the disturbances of 1795 was preceded by a revolt in Dominica in 1790. The available evidence indicates that in this revolt, the slaves exploited the humanitarian criticism of the slave trade and slavery, which was being conducted in England. On such occasions, the slaves resorted to and accelerated protest action since they generally held the belief that the King had issued orders that they be freed, or their workload lessened, and that their masters were deliberately refusing to carry them out.

The revolt was contained and suppressed in two parishes but the rebels had a larger plan. According to Polinaire, a free mulatto who was tried for his alleged part in this conspiracy, the slaves had planned to take possession of the entire Windward side of the island, by massacring all the whites except a few 'good planters' whom they would permit to remain. Pharcelle, the famous Maroon leader had promised them 300 muskets, and another chief 200 more. Every free person of colour who refused to assist when solicited was to be put to death. Upon every plantation involved, a chief was appointed for directing operations which were to begin with a massacre of whites at supper.[84]

Polinaire further testified that the slaves had planned such action because on the arrival of the Governor from England they had heard that he had been instructed to issue orders to the planter class to the effect that they be allowed three days in each week to work on their own. But the planters not only refused to carry out this instruction when ordered to do so, but treated them harsher than usual.[85] Polinaire's version of the story is corroborated by an article written in a local newspaper by Thomas Antkell, in which he blamed the revolt on "the mistaken humanity of deluded people at home", although he also believed that "the unfortunate disputes in Martinique and the seducing there and then arming mulattoes and slaves" might have been a contributory factor.[86] The Governor, himself, also thought that "the present situation of the foreign and neighbouring islands" had something to do with the outbreak, but he also admitted the influence of the humanitarian agitation in the metropolis.[87]

He pointed out that on January 12 he received reports that "one or two small gangs of negroes had claimed two or three days in the week for themselves" and when this was refused, "some individuals absconded, and others would not go to work". During the next few days, efforts to procure a work resumption proved fruitless. The slaves "persisted in their claim, and in their refusal to work though without going off the estates or attempting any acts of violence". A visit to two estates three days later revealed that the slaves were "generally at work, convinced of their misconduct, and apparently well disposed". But on the night of January 20 the slaves rose in rebellion at 10 o'clock. Fortunately, detachments of the 30th regiment were in the island and with their assistance the revolt was suppressed but the planter class remained concerned about potential threats to their survival. Despite the calm after the storm, it was obvious that "notions and opinions have certainly got root in the minds of the slaves in general, which will melitate [sic] against their ever being such faithful, obedient and contented servants as they were formally".[88]

The society of West Indian Merchants and Planters, in a memorial to Lord Grenville, expressed their indignation at the revolt which they observed "appears to have been founded upon no pretence of ill-treatment, as to food, clothing or other particulars, but to have occurred in pursuit of what they termed their 'rights', which in their interpretation, extend to an exemption from labour four days out of seven". They further expressed their "utmost concern that these doctrines which are novel among negroes, have originated from the new language and proceedings in this country respecting the slave trade; information of which has been disseminated by various channels among Negroes", and warned that such deliberations should immediately cease since the slaves had interpreted them "to favour their own emancipation".[89]

After this revolt, the magistrates were cautioned to keep as secret as possible any discussions concerning amelioration, as a precaution against further unrest, and to communicate any semblance of turbulence to the Commander-in-chief at the earliest opportunity. When, for instance, Wilberforce's motion for abolition was defeated in 1792, the following circular was sent to the magistrates: "No emancipation of the negroes at present... Are your Negroes quiet?"[90] This was not, however, a new policy. When in 1788 the home government sent out the queries on the slave trade and slavery, they were secretly distributed and discussed "to defeat any disturbances among the slaves which possibly may arise, from the knowledge of the subject in agitation".[91]

In the end, however, these precautions proved for the most part to be futile. Not all slaves were illiterate, some slaves were able to read – a process facilitated inter- alia by the Methodist Mission Schools. Notwithstanding the capacity to read, the slaves were cognisant of the social and political milieu and outwitted their masters who erroneously believed them to be stupid. Mrs. Carmichael also noted that several free negroes in St. Vincent read the English newspapers in which the debates on slavery were printed, and by this medium antislavery information was disseminated to the slave population even though "in a most distorted and mangled form".[92]

When, for instance, the question of abolition once again became a subject of Parliamentary debate in 1807, the Governor of Tobago after a return from England, reported that he heard "anecdotes circulated of conversation among the slaves on a supposed emancipation of them in view".[93] The slaves held the belief that he "was invested with secret powers to strike off half their labour and divide their week in three days service to their masters and three at their own disposal". At this time, slaves "traversed the country in large bodies" issuing complaints against their managers. During the next month, he continued, "sixty stout negroes... came to Government House and finding I was gone to Windward sent a deputation of eight... after me twenty-six miles to my house;... soon after my return to Mt. William another large body came to Studley Park". They were told that their complaints would not be listened to "if made by a deputation of more than two or three". These "marches of inquiry" persisted, and the situation was regarded as serious to warrant the summons of a special meeting of the Legislature.[94]

But no sooner was the Legislature in session than "a large and riotous gang" began a march towards Government House. They were, however, prevented from taking the building, but not without putting up opposition in which 42 of them were arrested by the local militia troops. On later examination it was discovered that "this gang had quitted their work, throwing down their hoes together, using the most opprobrious language to their manager and overseer present; and in a meeting clearly pre-concerted quitted the estate".[95]

As the humanitarian campaign against slavery gathered momentum, and as the planters displayed an almost inflexible reluctance to introduce suggested ameliorative reforms, the slaves became increasingly impatient and resorted to further types of action. In 1815, for instance, in order to prevent the illegal importation of slaves into its colonies in contravention of the Act of Abolition, the British government decided to make compulsory the registration of all slaves. All the legislatures objected to the proposed bill on the constitutional point that Parliament had no right to legislate in the internal affairs of the colonies, but more importantly, they expressed fears about the social implications of such a measure. The Dominica response, which was typical of that of the other islands, deplored such interference as potentially inflammatory and extremely dangerous since it was "always considered by the slaves, as if the Government at home meant to support them against their masters, and thus tending to produce among them discontent, mutiny, insubordination and desertion".[96]

Past experience had in fact proved this to be the case. In Barbados, the immediate response of the slaves was a revolt involving some 82 plantations.[97] Soon after the outbreak it was reported that the slaves in St. Vincent were "impressed with an idea of speedy emancipation and have become in many instances careless of subordination".[98] From Grenada, it was also reported that although no insurrection had yet occurred "the minds of the Negroes in the Government appear to be much unsettled and to be impressed with the same". On many estates the slaves quitted their jobs and deserted, escaping the vigilance of the local militia troops.[99] Similar instances of discontent and protest were reported for the other islands.[100]

We have already noted that the planters in the British Windward Islands had unanimously opposed the proposed ameliorative reforms of 1823.[101] Indeed, their behaviour was typical of that of their counterparts in the other British West Indies. In Jamaica and British Guiana, this attitude of the plantocracy coupled with the belief held by the slaves that emancipation had been granted by the King but was being withheld by their owners, triggered revolts. In the British Windward Islands there were also manifestations of discontent, including revolutionary planning.

In St. Vincent at this time Mrs. Carmichael noted that there was a marked change of behaviour among the slaves, and the feeling they generally entertained was that "there is to be no Massas at all, and Massa King George is to buy up all the estate land and give them to live upon".[102] In Dominica the slaves in the parish of St. Andrew refused to work and evidence of a planned revolt was discovered in two other parishes. After examining the causes of this unrest, the Governor concluded that "there remained no doubt that the slave population expected immediate emancipation and had an idea that it was kept from them".[103]

It should be clear by now that at the end of the period of this study the slaves were determined to gain their freedom by any means necessary, including armed struggle, despite the efforts of the planter class to maintain the slave system. This determination which was manifest on the transatlantic passage and continued in varying degrees and expressions from and since the establishment of the plantation system, persisted with ever increasing intensity right up to emancipation. From this perspective, legislative intervention to abolish slavery in 1833 was no more than a face-saving act of desperation designed to stave off the inevitable victory of the slaves in the liberation struggle.

CHAPTER 10

Conclusion: comparative perspectives

The institution of slavery was inevitably mobile.... It had a logic of its own broader than any system of law or custom, tradition or belief. What the law and tradition did was to make the social mobility easy and natural in one place, difficult and slow and painful in another. In Brazil and Spanish America, the Law, the Church and Custom put few impediments in the way of vertical mobility of race and class and in some measure favoured it. In the British, French and United States slave systems the law attempted to fix the pattern and stratify the social classes and the racial groups. But the law failed. The Haitian rebellion, the Civil War in the United States and the abolition of slavery in the British West Indies are all part of the same process.

– Frank Tannenbaum, *Slave and Citizen* (1946)

The acquisition by Great Britain of the four territories comprising the British Windward Islands did have profound effects on their development. In a ten-year period (1763–1773) an economy based on coffee, cocoa, tobacco and spices was transformed into one favouring the monoculture of cane. This transformation, as in the older British West Indies and Cuba in the nineteenth century,[1] was accompanied by the displacement or departure of many whites who could not compete with or were bought out by large sugar planters, and the introduction of large numbers of negro slaves. As a result, the racial composition of the islands was significantly changed and a society based on the twin props of sugar and slavery emerged.[2]

The population of the British Windward Islands at the end of the period of this study[3] consisted of approximately 3,244 whites who were all free, 10,000 free persons of colour, and 74,761 slaves. The vast majority of the slaves lived on the plantations in the rural areas whereas the Whites and free coloured were to be found mainly in the towns. Because of the great disproportion between free whites and black slaves, which in Tobago for instance was as high as 56 to 1 in 1823, the existence of slavery and the plantation system posed a tremendous problem for the society as a whole – a society that was fundamentally based on inequality which, in turn, coincided with distinctions of race and colour.

The white oligarchy which controlled the reins of power consisted of planters, merchants, lawyers, clergymen, and even the managers of absentees. These men held positions on the councils and assemblies, were responsible for the functioning of the courts, officered the militias, served as vestrymen and church wardens, filled all other public offices, and dominated the entire social and economic life of the islands.

Immediately below them, however, was a class of secondary whites consisting mainly of overseers, storekeepers, small shopkeepers, artisans, fishermen and hucksters who were not as financially well-off and hence had less privileges than the white elite. But there were few signs of open hostility between these groups. Both were affiliated by ties of race; both had a vested interest in maintaining the social system and in a class structure which was fairly open; the less privileged had opportunities for gaining admittance if not full acceptance into the elite group: they could vote so long as they acquired the necessary property qualifications, they could acquire political power as their economic well-being improved and, indeed, the institution of negro slavery provided them with a grand opportunity of doing so.

In the British Windward Islands, whites of every rank were able to improve their economic and social position by either purchasing, hiring or supervising the labour of slaves. Again, their opportunities for political enhancement grew, especially during the first two decades of the nineteenth century when because of the decline in numbers of the white population, property qualifications for seats on the

Assembly were either ignored or abandoned in an effort to admit as many whites as possible to the ruling group since this strengthened white control of the political system.

The logical outcome of this policy should have been the extension of full political rights to the French naturalised subjects who were Roman Catholics. But even though this did not happen during the period of this study, they, like all other whites, rich or poor, had a vested interest in maintaining the system and asserted claims to their superiority over the two other classes in the society.

To achieve this, the whites adopted a rigid, consistent and inflexible policy designed to keep the free coloured in an inferior position by denying them political and civil rights and deliberately restricting their opportunities for economic and social improvement. In none of the islands were they allowed to vote or stand as candidates for election or nomination to the councils and assemblies. They were not allowed to hold even the lowest public or parochial office, nor hold commissions in the militia – not even in the segregated companies, composed of persons of their own group. They could not sit as jurors in the courts, their evidence was generally not accepted against whites in capital cases, and even in the Churches they had to sit apart from the whites. Even though some of them owned slaves and plantations, the stigma of their descent from slaves, coupled with white fears of free blacks and eventually slaves themselves demanding participation in the electoral process was seen as sufficient justification for the non-concession of political rights, as seen in the response of the absentee planters of Dominica to free coloured solicitations on this subject.

The plantation slaves held the lowest status of all groups within this society. But between this group and the free coloured class there was an intermediate group of privileged slaves who seem to have been mainly coloured and were generally relegated to more rewarding and prestigious occupations than the common field slaves. These occupations provided them with an opportunity of earning a cash income with which they could purchase their freedom if this had not been obtained as a dispensation from their white fathers. Like the free coloured, this group sedulously avoided agricultural labour and despised the common field slave. Indeed, this latter attitude engendered a counter-reaction from the field slave, and this mutual hostility which was also partly a result of the divide and rule policy of the white ruling class, was one of the forces contributing to the stability of the social system.

The vast majority of the slaves who did agricultural work on the plantations lived in conditions of acute poverty, misery, degradation and oppression. On the plantation the field slave was forced to work for long hours under the threat of the whip. Even though his whole life was geared to economic production for the profit of his master on whom he was almost wholly dependent for his subsistence, unlike his counterpart in the American south, the quantities of food, clothing and other necessities made available to him were terribly small. Frequent whippings, tortures and other atrocities were everyday occurrences on the plantations in the British Windward Islands. Other reasons aside, this callous treatment persisted because the slave was seen as an economic item whose purchase price and maintenance his master recovered after four to seven years productive work in the field, plus a profit even though he might die.

Indeed, the general overall dramatic decline in the slave population after abolition in 1807 is evidence of how even at this time when the planters were complaining about a shortage of labour they still remained callous, indifferent and insensitive to the value of human life. One of the most damning indictments of slavery in the British Windward Islands – the failure of the slave population to maintain itself as it did in the American South – was attributable to the above policy since it influenced the attitude of the planter towards pregnancy, field labour during pregnancy, and child rearing. In this respect, the slave society of the British Windward Islands closely resembled that of Cuba.[4]

The planter class enacted legislation designed to regulate the activities of the slaves in the form of slave codes. Indeed, these codes were one of the most vicious mechanisms of control to be devised and enforced. In all of them we see a heavy concentration on police regulations. So-called humane provisions were almost non-existent. The heavy concentration on police regulations should make it clear that the main intent of the codes was the regulation of the activities of the slaves in the interest of public order and social control.[5]

The treatment meted out to the slaves was indescribably harsh. In order to rationalise this treatment, the whites made use of the myth of negro inferiority. This myth played a functional role in the society, and in retrospect it seems as if a fair proportion of the slaves either believed it or accommodated themselves to their inferior position in the society. For indeed, if this was not the case it seems difficult to see how the whites could have been fairly secure, and could have kept in subordination for so long a group of people who vastly outnumbered them in a society where, unlike the American South,[6] military forces were terribly inadequate and were seen as necessary for protection only as a last resort.

Despite their few admirable achievements particularly in the field of education, the Christian missionaries working in the islands, especially the Methodists, had become an agency of great significance in maintaining the status quo even though their activities were at first viewed with a certain degree of suspicion and hostility. Their sole aim was the conversion of the slave from his 'heathenism' to Christianity. They all saw slavery as a civil question outside the confines of their mission and as one in which they should not interfere. Being heavily dependent on the planter class for access to their slaves and for financial support, they all sought to conciliate white opinion in the islands. Hence they preached to the slave the virtues of industry, fidelity, submission and respect for authority and succeeded in bringing him closer to his master by "a principle of obedience inculcated not by the authority of the driver, but by the Scripture".[7] This was generally characteristic of their work in the other territories comprising the British West Indies.[8]

However, a combination of forces – economic, political and social – operated to undermine the foundations of this society. The planter class in the British Windward Islands, like their counterparts in the rest of the British West Indies, had generally believed that the sugar industry was the only worthwhile form of economic activity and that compulsory labour in the form of slavery was the only means of pursuing it. A fairly recent study by two cliometricians, Engerman and Fogel, on the economics of American negro slavery has argued that slave labour was both efficient and profitable.[9] However, the data used to support the argument of efficiency are open to question and indeed this whole work has encountered serious strictures from Gutman.[10] Profitability and efficiency do not necessarily go hand in hand, and even if the authors were right, slave labour in the British

West Indies situation proved to be profitable at least up to the middle of the eighteenth century even though it was inefficient.

This was because the planters used archaic and outmoded implements of production.[11] They equipped their slaves with simple and crude devices such as the hoe and the bill. They displayed a remarkable distrust for innovation and they refused to profit from the use of mechanical improvements which would have undoubtedly increased efficiency as some of the Cuban planters were to do later on in the nineteenth century.[12]

Again, although the planters used force as a stimulus to labour, even under the threat of the whip the slaves simply idled, sabotaged operations or refused to work.[13] And slaves were costly to purchase, feed, clothe and maintain, especially after the American Revolution when the cost of foodstuff and other plantation necessities skyrocketed at a time when the prices received for tropical staples deteriorated considerably.

The net result was that the plantation enterprise in the British West Indies became more and more unprofitable to Great Britain and opposition mounted against its monopoly of the sugar market and the high prices needed to maintain it.[14] This economic decline was paralleled by a decline in the political importance of the West Indians as a pressure group in England. They found themselves with their backs virtually against the wall when their social order was attacked by the humanitarians who found it morally indefensible, by the free coloureds who were agitating for equal rights, and other interests opposed to slavery.[15]

At the same time that these economic and political changes were taking place the slave society was attacked by radical ideas of social reform. Despite their relative security, the planter class had always feared that their social order might be overthrown from below and indeed this seemed real after 1789 when the ideas of liberty, equality and fraternity – the slogans of the French Revolution – spread to the West Indies. Despite attempts by the local oligarchies in the British Windward Islands to insulate their respective communities from these egalitarian ideas, they gained headway and were translated into revolutionary action. The most critical years were 1795, a few years after the outbreak of revolution in Haiti, when there were disturbances involving slaves in Grenada, St. Vincent and Dominica;

and 1802 when a planned revolt in Tobago was nipped in the bud. These were clear indications that the slaves were prepared to over-throw the social system by force.

The slaves also resorted to protest action when the humanitari-ans were agitating against the slave trade and slavery. Revolt and other forms of resistance occurred in Dominica in 1790, in Tobago in 1807, in all the islands in 1816, and in Dominica and Grenada in 1823. The efforts of the humanitarians to put an end to the system after 1823 were marked by periods of unrest in all the islands under study right up to the time of the Act of Emancipation in 1833.[16]

Finally, where exactly does the slave society of the British Wind-ward Islands fall within the wider context of New World Slavery? According to the postulate put forward by Tannenbaum and later ex-panded by Freyre, Elkins and Klein,[17] the slave society as analysed here would fall within the 'harsh' category, as opposed to slave soci-ety in Brazil and Spanish America where it would categorized as 'mild'. The controversy surrounding this debate has been dismissed perhaps too unreasonably by Harris as "a waste of time"[18] and it is important to note that even though we can understand why and how Harris came to such a conclusion, this does not suggest that we cannot meaningfully compare New World slave systems. As a matter of fact, this controversy can perhaps only be satisfactorily resolved when we have detailed case studies from which to draw our conclu-sions, even though the results might very well be that the similarities outweigh the differences.

Genovese has identified three categories which we might use in any comparative discussion of slave treatment. He describes the first category generally as day to day living conditions under which would fall such items as the quantity and quality of food, clothing, housing, the length of the working day and the general conditions of labour. The second category is described as conditions of life, includ-ing family security, opportunities for an independent social and re-ligious life, etcetera; while the third category deals with access to freedom and citizenship.

Our analysis of slavery in the British Windward Islands indicates that in terms of categories one and two[19] the slaves were not better off than their counterparts in the American South[20] and were in condi-tions similar to those that existed in nineteenth century Cuba.[21] In terms of category three, that is, access to freedom and citizenship, slavery in the British Windward Islands closely resembled that institution in the United States[22] and diverged slightly in Brazil. To elucidate this last point we will make a comparison of manumissions in the British Windward Islands and Brazil.

Tannenbaum has asserted that "the attitude towards manumission is the crucial element in slavery, it implies the judgement of the moral status of the slave, and foreshadows his role in the case of freedom".[23] Though critical of Tannenbaum, Davis asserts, nevertheless, that: "The ease and frequency of manumission would seem to be the crucial standard in measuring the relative harshness of slave systems."[24] Genovese has pointed out that blind adherence to such a notion might lead to the danger of confusing the extent to which a slave society is closed with the extent to which it deals severely with its slaves on a day to day basis, and further suggests that a more open system of manumissions might have necessitated tighter police control of the slave plantations.[25] But as long as these two issues are not confused, the ease and frequency of manumissions can and will be used here to determine the relative openness of slave systems.

Klein bases his conclusion that Brazilian slave society was mild partly on the rapid growth and size of the free coloured population, asserting that "only a constant process of emancipation"[26] could have accounted for this development. Working without statistics of manumissions, Klein made calculations based on census data for all of Brazil, and birth and death rates for the parish of Minas Gerais in 1814 which he assumed to be representative of Brazil for the entire nineteenth century.[27] Even though such an approach might be open to question, there seems to be general agreement that manumissions were more frequent in Brazil than in other New World slave systems. It is important to note, however, that Harris has suggested that some of the Brazilian manumissions might have been slaves who were old, incapacitated, infirm and of no productive use to the estate, implying that the generosity of the Brazilian planter in this regard could be exaggerated.[28]

But the planters in the British Windward Islands also made manumissions of this nature. In addition, they placed restrictive barriers on manumissions in the form of heavy deposits that were required on the part of the master, and it was generally hard for the slave to acquire the money necessary to buy himself out of slavery if his master would have allowed him to.[29] Again, when we look at the relatively small size of the free coloured population in these islands, allowing for death and possibilities of migration which were almost non-existent, it is evident that the restrictive legislation pertaining to manumissions was enforced. Overall, our calculations show that the frequency of manumissions was far below that of Brazil.

In the sixteen-year period 1808 to 1823 which is fairly representative of the situation in the British Windward Islands as a whole, the planters manumitted 471 slaves in St. Vincent, 1,027 in Grenada, 1,025 in Dominica, and 290 in Tobago.[30] On average, this would put yearly manumission levels at 29, 64, 64 and 18 slaves in the respective islands, with an average of 69 slaves per year for the group as a whole. When we weigh these calculations against the relative size of the slave populations over the period, taking other factors into account, we find that in St. Vincent, one slave out of every 630 gained his freedom each year; in Grenada, one out of every 408; in Dominica one out of every 290; and in Tobago one out of every 832; and an average of one out of every 460 for the group of islands as a whole.

The data presented in the preceding paragraph suggest that within the context of New World Slavery, the slave society of the British Windward Islands was, in comparison with Brazil, fairly closed. The inference need not be drawn, however, that there was any necessary connection between the closed character of this society and the harsh conditions of slavery that existed. As Cox suggests, it might be misleading to look at the situation simply in terms of numbers, since this had no a priori bearing on how the manumitted individuals and their descendants were treated as members of a 'free society'.[31] In fact, the evidence from the British Windward Islands paints a picture of harsh treatment of the free coloured and free blacks overall during the period of this study – notwithstanding the claim of an apparently more open society in eighteenth century Grenada.[32] Further, the atrocities, barbarities and other denigrating features of slavery that existed in the British Windward Islands were prevalent in the reputedly mild slave society of Brazil as well. These considerations lend support to the view that despite a few superficial differences, the slave systems of the New World were fundamentally alike.

$\mathcal{N}$OTES

CHAPTER 1

1   CO 101/1: Answers to Queries on the State of the Islands in 1763.
2   Ibid.
3   Ibid.
4   See C.S.S. Higham, "The General Assembly of the Leeward Islands," part 3, "Influence on Grenada," *English Historical Review*, Vol. 41 (1926).
5   See "Egremont Papers", P.R.O. 30/47/18/4: "Some thoughts concerning the most eligible plan of government for the new acquired Islands..."
6   *Journal of the Commissioners for Trade and Plantations, 1759-1763* Vol. 70: 396-97.
7   Ibid., Vols. 70, 71.
8   L.J. Ragatz, *The Fall of the Planter Class in the British Caribbean 1763-1833* (New York: Octagon 1928), 115.
9   F.W. Pitman, *The Development of the British West Indies 1700-1763* (New Haven: Yale Univ. Press, 1917), 359.
10 CO 102/1: Representations to His Majesty Regarding the Disposing of Lands in the Ceded Islands by the Board of Trade, November 3rd 1763.
11 Ibid.
12 CO 101/9: Lord Egremont to Commanding Officers at St. Vincent, Tobago and Dominica, August 1763.
13 CO 102/1: Representations to His Majesty Regarding the Disposing of Lands in the Ceded Islands.
14 Dated March 1st 1764, CO 102/1.
15 Ibid.
16 Ibid.
17 CO 101/9: Lieutenant Colonel Scott to Lord Egremont, January 19th 1763.
18 CO 101/9: Lieutenant Colonel Scott to Lord Egremont; Letters of March 21st and May 3rd 1763.
19 CO 101/9: Brigadier General Dalrymple to Sedgwick; January 16th 1764.
20 CO 101/9: Lord Egremont to Commanding Officers at St. Vincent, Tobago and Dominica, August 1763.
21 CO 106/9: Proceedings of the Commissioners for the Sale of Lands.
22 CO 101/9: Richard Legge to Halifax, 1764.
23 CO 101/9: Governor Melville to Sedgwick, November 13th 1764.
24 *Correspondence relating to the Estates of Sir William Young in the West Indies with Claims for Compensation 1768-1835*, 6 vols. (Oxford: Rhodes House Library), vol. 6.
25 CO 101/1: Governor Melville to the Commissioners for Trade and Plantations; January 3rd, 1765.
26 *Correspondence Relating to the Estates of Sir William Young*, op. cit., vol. 6.
27 Compiled from data in CO 106/9-12.
28 Compiled from data in CO 106/9-10.
29 CO 106/11: Extract of Letters from Dominica addressed to John Stewart and Sir William Colebroke.

30 Ibid.

31 CO 101/10: Lieutenant Colonel Scott to Lord Halifax, March 26th 1765

32 CO 106/11: Extract of Letters from Dominica, June 24th 1766.

33 Ibid.

34 CO 101/11: Copy of a Letter from the Lords Commissioners of Trade to Earl Shell-bourne, December 21st 1767.

35 Compiled from data in CO 106/9-12.

36 John Byers, *Reference to the Plan of St. Vincent* (London, 1777).

37 Elsa Goveia, *A Study on the Historiography of the British West Indies to the End of the Nineteenth Century* (Mexico: Instituto Panamericano de Geografía e Historia, 1956), 37.

38 Sir William Young, *A History of the Black Caribs in St. Vincent* (London, 1795).

39 Goveia, *A Study of the Historiography*, op. cit.,123-25.

40 Young, *A History of the Black Caribs*, op. cit., 123-25.

41 Charles Shepherd, *An Historical Account of the Island of St.Vincent* (London, 1831). He was a Chief Justice of the colony and identified with the planting interests.

42 Ragatz, *The Fall of the Planter Class*, op. cit., 117.

43 Ibid.

44 Ibid.

45 Young, *A History of the Black Caribs in St. Vincent*, op. cit., 6.

46 See for example CO 260/9, "An Account of the Island Caribs and their mode of living." Enclosed in Governor Seton's, No. 55, to Sydney, January 1789.

47 Young, *A History of the Black Caribs in St. Vincent*, op. cit., 8-11.

48 Ibid.

49 Ibid., 13-14.

50 CO 102/1: Representations to His Majesty on the method of disposing of lands in the Ceded Islands, November 1763.

51 Young, *A History of the Black Caribs in St. Vincent*, op. cit., 30.

52 CO 106/9: Instructions to the Commissioners for the Sale of Lands, March 24, 1764.

53 See for example *Correspondence relating to the Estates*, op. cit., vol. 6.

54 Compiled from data in CO 106/9.

55 CO 101/11: Sir William Young's Propositions for Surveying and Selling the Carib lands on the Windward side of St. Vincent, April 11, 1767.

56 Ibid.

57 Similar proposals dated August 13, 1765 had been put forward to the home Government by the Commissioners in their first report (see CO 106/9), in which the removal of the Black Caribs to the Grenadine Island of Bequia was also advocated. But no immediate action was taken.

58 CO 101/11: Draft of Instructions to the Commissioners for the Sale of Lands to Survey and dispose of lands on the Windward side of St. Vincent, January 1768.

59 Young, *A History of the Black Caribs in St. Vincent*, op. cit., 38.

60 Ibid., 44-45.

61 CO 101/13: Lieutenant Governor Fitz Maurice to Lord Hillsborough, No. 17, December 18, 1768.

62 CO 101/13: Lieutenant Governor Fitz Maurice's, No. 27, and enclosures, to Lord Hillsborough, May 11, 1769.

63 In a letter to the Lords of Treasury, September 4, 1770, CO 101/16.

64 CO 106/12: The Commissioners to the Committee for Trade and Plantations, August 12, 1771.

65 Ibid.

66 CO 101/16: Address of the Council and Assembly to the King, enclosed in Governor Leyborne's No. 2 to Hillsborough, November 20, 1771.

67 CO 101/16: Governor Leyborne to Hillsborough, No. 3, November 30th 1771. The alleged letter from the Governor of St. Lucia, written in French, is enclosed in that dispatch.

68 CO 101/14: Memorial of Sundry proprietors now in London to Hillsborough, January 22, 1770.

69 CO 101/16: Memorial of the Gentlemen interested in St. Vincent to Hillsborough, April 4, 1772.

70 Ibid.

71 Ibid.

72 Ibid.

73 CO 101/16: Hillsborough to Governor Leybourne, No. 4, Separate and Secret, April 18, 1772.

74 Ibid.

75 Ibid.

76 CO 101/16: Governor Leyborne to Hillsborough, No. 21, June 18, 1772.

77 CO 71/3: Governor Young to Hillsborough (St. Vincent), July 28, 1772.

78 CO 101/16: Governor Leyborne to Hillsborough, No. 26, July 30, 1772.

79 CO 101/16: Governor Leyborne to Hillsborough, No. 34, October 9, 1772.

80 Young, *A History of the Black Caribs in St. Vincent*, op. cit., 51.

81 Ibid.

82 Probus [pseud.] to Lord Dartmouth, November 30, 1772, "Injustice of the Proceedings in St. Vincent,"*Scots Magazine*, Vol. XXX1X (1772).

83 Ibid.

84 CO 101/16: Dartmouth to Major Dalrymple, December 9, 1772.

85 Ibid.

86 CO 101/16: Governor Leyborne to Hillsborough No. 34, October 9, 1772.

87 Ibid.

88 CO 101/16: Dartmouth to Major Dalrymple, December 9, 1772.

89 CO 101/17: Dalrymple to Dartmouth, December 26, 1772.

90 CO 101/16: Report of the Commissioners, July 19, 1773.

91 Compiled from data CO 106/9-12.

92 CO 101/18: Answers to Queries, 1773.

93 CO 71/4: Answers to Queries, December 24th, 1773.

94 CO 101/16: Answers to Queries, August 10th, 1772.

95 CO 101/17: State of Tobago, May 1st, 1773.

96 Ragatz, *The Fall of the Planter Class*, op. cit., Tables, 119–120.

97 For Grenada, see CO 101/17: Governor Leyborne to Dartmouth, No. 27, June 26th, 1774; Dominica, CO. 71/5: Governor Shirley to Dartmouth, March 3rd, 1775; St. Vincent, CO 101/18: Lieutenant Governor Morris to Dartmouth, May 14th, 1775.

CHAPTER 2

1 *Correspondence relating to the Estates of Sir William Young in the West Indies with Claims for Compensation 1768-1835*, 6 vols. (Oxford: Rhodes House Library), vol. 1.

2 See Richard Pares; *Merchants and Planters* (Cambridge [Eng.], 1960).

3 See for instance CO 101/17; Governor Leyborne to Dartmouth, No.15, July 17th, 1773.

4 See for instance CO 71/5; Governor Shirley to Dartmouth, March 3rd, 1775.

5 For an authoritative discussion of West Indian/North American trading relationships, see Richard Pares, *Yankees and Creoles* (London, 1956), especially chap. 2.

6 Elsa Goveia, *Slave Society in the British Leeward Islands at the End of the Eighteenth Century* (New Haven and London, 1965), p.2.

7 Enclosed in Lieutenant Governor Young's Despatch to the Earl of Dartmouth, July 26th, 1775; CO 101/18.

8 CO 260/7, Comparative Table of Prices Before and During the Revolutionary War.

9 See for example CO71/6, Governor Shirley to the Earl of Dartmouth, No. 18, February 17th 1776.

10 CO 101/20, Governor Macartney to Lord Germain, No. 34 October 1st, 1777.

11 Co 101/21, Governor Macartney to Lord Viscount Howe and Sir Williams Howe, November 26th, 1778.

12 House of Commons Accounts and Papers, Volume XXVI, 1789, No. 646a pt. v.

13 See for example CO 71/6, Governor Shirley and Enclosures to Lord Germain, July 11th 1777.

14 See for example, CO 101/20, Governor Macartney to Lord Germain, No. 28, July 3rd, 1777.

15 CO 101/24, Lieutenant Governor Ferguson to Secretary of State Ellis, March 11th, 1782.

16 See for instance CO 260/7, Answers to Queries January 1st 1785.

17 Ragatz, *The Fall*, p. 174.

18 Ibid., 176.

19 On February 20th, 1784, Governor Orde wrote from Dominica: "The people look with uncommon anxiety for the arrival of a Free Port Act." (CO 71/8).

20 CO 71/9, Governor Orde to Sydney, April 7th, 1785; CO 260/7, Governor Lincoln to Lord Sydney, No. 26, December 1st, 1785.

21 See for example CO 71/13, Governor Orde to Sydney, September 2nd,1787.

22 See S.F. Bemis, *Jay's Treaty: A Study in Commerce and Diplomacy* (New York, 1923).

23 See for instance CO 260/14, Governor Seton to the Duke of Portland No 61, 1797.

24 In Dominica for instance a proclamation admitting American vessels to the ports was renewed annually for the decade 1793-1803. See CO 71/35, Governor Prevost to Lord Hobart, No. 14, March 26th, 1803.

25 Compiled from Report enclosed in Governor Beckwith's, No. 29, to Wyndham, November 11th, 1806 (CO 260/21).

26 Ibid.

27 See for example CO 260/19, Camdem to Governor Bentinck of St. Vincent, September 1804. He was specifically cautioned not to admit American vessels except in cases of "real and very great necessity".

28 Sir William Young, *The West Indian Common Place Book* (London, 1807), p. 64.

29 Ragatz, *The Fall*, p. 165.
30 CO 101/61, Petition of the Council and Assembly of Grenada to Earl Bathurst, August 8th, 1821.
31 CO 285/11, President Balfour to William Wyndham, No. 15; December 16th, 1806.
32 CO 71/37, General Prevost to Camden, No. 57, November 15th, 1804.
33 In 1776 the duty was 6/3 per cwt.; in 1807 it was 27/-. See Ragatz, *The Fall of the Planter Class*, pp. 164, 296.
34 CO 101/44, Governor Maitland and Enclosures to Wyndham; October 27th, 1806.
35 Ragatz, *The Fall*, pp. 210-213.
36 CO 71/30, Governor Johnstone to the Duke of Portland, No. 8, May 10th, 1798.
37 CO 285/4, Governor Lindsay to the Duke of Portland, Private, March 18th, 1796.
38 Goveia, *Slave Society*, p. 14.
39 Ragatz, *The Fall*, p. 287.
40 House of Commons Accounts and Papers, Volume XXVI, 1789, No. 646a, pt. iii, "The Advantages which the French West Indies have over the British."
41 Ragatz, *The Fall*, p. 294.
42 Ibid., p.229.
43 Ibid., pp. 303-304.
44 See for instance "Imports into the Port of London 1801-1802", in *Minutes of the Meetings of West Indian Merchants* (Volume IV, Meeting April 2nd, 1802).
45 Ragatz, *The Fall*, p. 294.
46 See for instance CO101/45 – Current Prices.
47 CO 260/17, President Ottley to Lord Hobart; November 1802.
48 CO 260/23, "Memorial of the Council and Assembly of St. Vincent to the King", enclosed in Governor Becwith's, No. 22, to Lord Castlereagh, December 15th, 1807.
49 Ibid.
50 CO 71/5, Governor Shirley to the Earl of Dartmouth, March 3rd, 1775.
51 CO 260/12, Letter dated February 14th, 1793.
52 Ragatz, *The Fall*, p. 316.
53 CO 71/48, Governor Ainslie to Earl Bathurst, No. 107, October 15th, 1815.
54 CO 260/32, Governor Brisbane to Earl Bathurst, No. 129, July 10th, 1815.
55 See CO 71/44, Current Prices.
56 CO 285/ 11, Petition to the Prince Regent, December 7th, 1811.
57 See for example CO 71/46, Petition of the Planters, Merchants and Others interested in Dominica to the Prince Regent, December 24th, 1811.
58 Ragatz, *The Fall*, p. 336.
59 Ibid.
60 CO 285/23, Petition of the Two Houses of the Legislature to the House of Commons, February 4th, 1823.
61 CO 71/56, Memorial of the Colonial Agent of Dominica to Earl Bathurst, October 7th, 1819.
62 CO 260/40, Extract of a Letter from Mr. Latham to Earl Bathurst, May 12th, 1823.
63 CO 71/57, Memorial of the Colonial Agent of Dominica to Earl Bathurst, October 7th, 1819.
64 CO 260/40, The Humble Petition of the Planters, Land Owners and Others interested in St. Vincent to the King, February 28th, 1823.
65 Ibid.

66 Ragatz, *The Fall*, p. 361.
67 This was an ad valorem duty of 16.3 per cent on the Gross Sales Price. See Ragatz, *The Fall*, p. 120.
68 CO 101/61, Petition of the Council and Assembly of Grenada to the King, August 8th, 1821.
69 CO 71/60, The Humbly Petition of the Planters and Others interested in Dominica to the King, March 17, 1823.
70 Eric Williams, *Capatilism and Slavery* (Chapel Hill, 1944), ch. IX, passim.
71 CO 71/60, Petition to the King, March 17, 1823.
72 CO 71/58, Imports and Exports of Slaves, and Slaves Sold for Debt, 1808-1821.
73 CO 285/28, Petition from the Two Houses of the Legislature to the House of Commons, February 4th, 1823.
74 CO 260/40, The Humble Petition of the Planters and Land-owners and Others Interested in St. Vincent to the King, February 28th, 1823.
75 CO 261/9, St. Vincent Agency Letterbook.
76 [A Grenada Planter], A Brief Inquiry into the causes and conduct pursued by the Colonial Government for quelling the insurrection in Grenada from its commencement on the night of March 2nd to the arrival of General Nicholls on April 14th, 1795 (London, 1796), p.123.
77 Ragatz, *The Fall*, pp. 221-22.
78 As late as 1811 William Johnstone of Grenada still owed $10,000. See CO 101/50, President Adye to the Earl of Liverpool, September 4th, 1811.
79 For this controversy see Ragatz, *The Fall*, pp. 224-25.
80 CO 260/29, Petition of Lewis and John Grant to Earl Bathurst, November 7th, 1812.
81 House of Commons Reports, Volume 3, 1812-1813, No. 182: Report from the Committee on the Petition of Persons Interested in Estates in St. Vincent.

CHAPTER 3

1 Such a federation existed in the Leeward Islands. The General Assembly met regularly from 1684-1711. But the narrow selfish interests of its constituent components reduced it to ineffectiveness. After 1711 it did not meet again until 1798 and from then on it went into oblivion. But it was revived later in the 19th century. See C.S.S. Higham, "The General Assembly of the Leeward Islands," *English Historical Review* (Volume 41. 1926).
2 Egremont Papers (P.R.O. 30/47/18/4), "Some thoughts concerning the most eligible plan of government for the new acquired Islands of Grenada and the Grenadines, St. Vincent, Dominica and Tobago submitted."
3 Ibid.
4 Egremont Papers (P.R.O. 30/47/18/4), "Some reasons for a general government."
5 Ibid.
6 Ibid.
7 Ibid.
8 Ibid.
9 Ibid.

10 Shortt and Doughty, Documents relating to the Constitutional History of Canada 1759-1791, quoted in Higham, "The General Assembly," op. cit., p. 367.

11 Egremont Papers, "Some reasons", op. cit.

12 CO 102/1, Draught of a commission for Robert Melville to be Governor of Grenada, October 4th, 1763.

13 CO 102/1, Further instructions to Melville, November 3rd, 1763.

14 CO 101/1, Melville to the Board of Trade, March 1st 1766.

15 CO 101/3, Additional instructions to Governor Melville, September 3rd, 1768.

16 Higham, "The General Assembly," op. cit., p. 375.

17 See CO 101/9, Lieutenant Colonel Scott to Egremont, January 19th 1763.

18 See CO 106/9, Proceedings of the Commissioners.

19 CO 101/11, Registers of grants of lands in Dominica, St. Vincent and Tobago that have hitherto been issued – enclosed in Governor Melville's dispatch to Shellburne, January 13th, 1767.

20 CO 101/12, Governor Melville's, No. 9 and enclosure to Lord Hillsborough, May 10th, 1768.

21 Higham, "The General Assembly," op. cit., p. 370.

22 CO 101/11, The humble address of His Majesty's faithful subjects of Grenada to Robert Melville.

23 Ibid.

24 Ibid.

25 These offices are described in Chap. 4.

26 CO 101/11, The humble address of His Majesty's faithful subjects of Grenada to Robert Melville.

27 Ibid.

28 CO 101/11, Memorial of the merchants of London, and other proprietors of land in the island of Grenada by their committee to the Lords Commissioners for Trade and Plantation. Emphasis the author's.

29 CO 101/10, Melville to Halifax, April 20th 1765.

30 CO 101/10, Conway to Melville, September 12th 1765.

31 CO 101/11, Board of Trade recommendation, December 10th, 1765.

32 CO 101/10, An Ordinance for regulating the election for the General Assembly of Grenada, the Grenadines, Dominica, St. Vincent and Tobago, and for limiting the powers of that part of the said General Assembly presently to be called for Grenada and the Grenadines.

33 Ibid.

34 Acts of the Privy Council, Colonial Series, Vol. V, pp. 7-11, September 7th, 1768.

35 CO 101/10, Lieutenant Governor Scott to Lord Halifax, March 20th 1765.

36 CO 101/11, Governor Melville to Lieutenant Governor Higginson of St. Vincent, December 11th, 1765.

37 CO 101/11, Governor Melville to Lieutenant Governor Scott of Dominica, January 31st, 1766.

38 Ibid.

39 CO 101/10, Governor Melville to Conway, April 7th, 1766

40 CO 101/11, Petition for the completion of the Legislature at St. Vincent, December 19th, 1766.

41 Ibid. Emphasis the author's.

42 CO 101/11, Governor Melville to Shellburne, May 23rd, 1767.
43 CO 101/12, Memorial of the proprietors of lands in Tobago to Melville, September 16th, 1767.
44 Ibid.
45 CO 101/12, Instructions to Lt. Governor Roderick Gwyn at Tobago, February 15th, 1768.
46 CO 101/12, Governor Melville to Lord Hillsborough, No. 12, June 15th, 1768.
47 CO 101/12, Governor Melville to Lord Hillsborough, No. 13, July 15th, 1768.
48 CO 101/10, Lt. Governor Scott to Halifax, March 26th, 1765.
49 CO 101/11, Extracts of letters from Dominica – Letter 1, April 8th, 1766.
50 Ibid.
51 CO 101/11, Extracts of letters from Dominica – Letter 2, June 24th 1766.
52 Ibid.
53 Ibid.
54 Ibid.
55 CO 101/11, Extracts of letters from Dominica – Letter 1, April 8th, 1766.
56 CO 101/10, Lt. Governor Scott to Halifax, March 26th, 1765.
57 CO 101/21, Extracts of letters from Dominica – Letter dated June 24th, 1766.
58 Ibid. – Letter dated April 8th, 1766.
59 CO 101/1, Brigadier Dalrymple to Lord Egremont, July 29th, 1763.
60 Ibid.
61 CO 101/9, Brigadier Dalrymple to Lord Egremont, August 18th, 1763.
62 Ibid.
63 CO 101/10, Lt. Governor Scott to Halifax, March 26th, 1765.
64 CO 101/11, Extracts of letters from Dominica – letter dated July 24th, 1766.
65 Ibid.
66 Ibid.
67 Ibid. – letter dated August 20th, 1766.
68 CO 101/9, Lieutenant Colonel Scott to Lord Egremont, August 30th, 1763.
69 CO 101/11, Extracts of Letters from Dominica – letter dated April 8th, 1766.
70 Ibid.
71 Ibid. – letter dated August 26th, 1766.
72 Ibid. – letter dated August 20th, 1766.
73 Ibid. – letter dated August 26th, 1766.
74 Ibid. – letter dated August 20th, 1766.
75 CO 101/11, Petition of merchants, traders and inhabitants of Dominica to the King, January 19th, 1767.
76 Ibid.
77 CO 101/11, Extracts of letters from Dominica – letter dated August 20th, 1766.
78 See CO 101/9, Dalrymple to Egremont, August 18th 1763.
79 CO 101/11, Extracts of Letters from Dominica – letter dated August 20th, 1766.
80 CO 101/11, Petition of merchants, traders and inhabitants of Dominica to the King, January 19th, 1767.
81 CO 101/11, Petition of the undermentioned merchants of London to the King. There are 42 signatories to this petition.
82 Ibid.
83 Ibid.

84 Ibid.
85 CO 101/11, Memorial of merchants of Liverpool to the Rt. Hon. Earl of Shellburne – There are 86 signatures to this petition.
86 Ibid.
87 CO 101/11, Copy of a letter from the Lords Commissioners of Trade to Earl Shellburne, December 21st, 1767.
88 Ibid.
89 Ibid.
90 Ibid.
91 CO 101/11, Governor Melville to Earl Shellburne, January 15th, 1767.
92 CO 101/12, Governor Melville to Lord Hillsborough, No. 4, April 24th 1768.
93 CO 101/11, Governor Melville to Earl Shellburne, No. 21, October 7th, 1767.
94 CO 101/12, Melville to Earl Shellburne, No. 26, November 14th, 1767.
95 CO 101/12, Hillsborough to Melville, No. 4., private, February 11th, 1768.
96 CO 101/3, Lt. Governor Fitzmaurice to Hillsborough, September 23rd, 1768.
97 CO 101/12, Governor Melville to Earl Shellburne, No. 26, November 14th, 1767.
98 CO 101/12, Governor Melville to President Pringle, January 28th, 1768.
99 CO 101/12, Governor Melville to Earl Shellburne, No. 33, February 1st, 1768.
100 CO 101/12, Governor Melville to Lord Hillsborough, No. 4, April 24th, 1768.
101 CO 101/12, Governor Young to Lord Hillsborough, July 25th, 1768.
102 CO 101/12, Governor Melville to Lord Hillsborough, No. 11, May 25th, 1768.
103 CO 101/12, Memorial of Dominica Council to Lord Hillsborough, July 19th, 1768.
104 CO 101/12, Memorial of the representatives of the people of Dominica in General Assembly to Lord Hillsborough, July 4th, 1768.
105 See Dalrymple to Sedgewick, January 16th, 1764 (CO 101/9).
106 CO 101/12, Memorial of the representatives of the people of Dominica in General Assembly to Lord Hillsborough, July 4th, 1768.
107 Ibid.
108 CO 101/13, Memorial of Sir George Colebrooke, Sir James Cockburn, John Stewart and John Nelson on behalf of themselves and the other proprietors of the island of Dominica. This Petition is not dated, but it was laid before the Board of Trade, October 25th, 1768.
109 See for instance petitions for separation dated November 10th, 1769 (CO 101/3).
110 CO 101/14, Hillsborough to Melville, February 15th, 1770.
111 CO 101/21, Board of Trade to the King, March 6th, 1771, pp. 451-53, quoted in Higham, "The General Assembly," op. cit., p. 379.
112 Higham, ibid., p. 379.
113 CO 101/17, Dalrymple to Dartmouth February 22nd, 1773.
114 CO 101/17, Governor Leyborne to Dartmouth, No. 11, May 10th, 1773.
115 Ibid.
116 CO 101/17, Governor Leyborne to Dartmouth, No. 24, March 16th, 1774.
117 Ibid.
118 CO 101/18, Lieutenant Governor Morris to Dartmouth, May 24th, 1775.
119 CO 101/11, Grenada Assembly Minutes, Meeting April 18th, 1766.
120 CO 101/12, Governor Melville to Shellburne, No. 23, November 14th, 1767.
121 CO 101/16, Hillsborough to Leyborne, No. 3, March 4th, 1772.
122 CO 101/16, Hillsborough to Leyborne, No. 5, April 18th, 1772.

123 CO 101/16, Governor Leyborne to Hillsborough, No. 13, April 25th, 1772.

124 CO 101/17, Governor Leyborne to Hillsborough, No.2, January 16th, 1775.

125 CO 101/18, Governor Young to Dartmouth, January 10th, 1776.

126 CO 101/16, Governor Leyborne to Hillsborough No. 4, November 24th, 1771.

127 CO 101/16, Governor Leyborne to Hillsborough, No. 5, December 6th, 1771.

128 CO 101/16, Governor Leyborne to Hillsborough, No. 13, April 25th, 1772.

129 CO 101/16, Governor Leyborne to Hillsborough, No. 19, May 23rd, 1772.

130 CO 101/19, Grenada Council Minutes, Meeting, January 20th, 1776.

131 CO 101/16, Governor Leyborne to Hillsborough, No. 24, July 25th, 1772.

132 CO 101/16, Governor Leyborne to Hillsborough, No. 32, September 16th, 1772.

133 Bryan Edwards, *The History Civil and Commercial of the British Colonies in the West Indies*, 4 Vols. (Philadelphia, 1806), Vol. II, p. 64.

134 Ibid.

135 CO 101/17, Lieutenant Governor Morris to Dartmouth, July 11th, 1774.

136 CO 101/17, Lieutenant Governor Morris to Dartmouth, July 11th, 1774. Emphasis the author's.

137 Ibid.

138 See for instance Lieutenant Governor Morris' dispatch to Darthmouth, May 24th, 1775 (CO 101/18).

139 I. Waters, *The Unfortunate Valentine Morris* (Newport, 1964), p.36.

140 Ragatz, *The Fall*, p. 216.

141 Higham, "The General Assembly," op. cit., p. 379.

CHAPTER 4

1   See Chap. 3.

2   CO 101/18 – Answers to queries, enclosed in Lieutenant Governor Young's dispatch to Earl Dartmouth, September 1st 1775 where he gives a list of the Establishment.

3   Egremont Papers (P.R.O. 30/47/18/4), "Some reasons for a general government."

4   CO 101/18, James Gillock, Deputy, to Governor Leyborne, November 1st, 1773, enclosed in Lt. Governor Young's Dispatch to Earl Dartmouth, September 1st, 1775.

5   CO 101/14, Governor Melville to Lord Hillsborough, No. 11, September 3rd, 1770.

6   CO 71/23, Governor Orde to Dundas No. 91, July 19th, 1792.

7   CO 71/55, Governor Maxwell to Earl Bathurst, No. 92, July 30th, 1818.

8   CO 71/48, Governor Ainslie to Earl Bathurst, September 17th, 1813.

9   CO 71/49, Governor Ainslie to Earl Bathurst, No. 8, January 27th, 1814.

10 CO 71/53, Governor Maxwell to Earl Bathurst, No. 92, July 30th, 1818.

11 CO 71/55, Griffin Curtis to Henry Goulbourn, October 29th, 1818.

12 See for instance CO 260/25, "Return of Public Officers in St. Vincent", enclosed in Governor Brisbane's No. 38 to Castlereagh, September 1st, 1809.

13 CO 71/36, Governor Prevost to Lord Hobart, No. 23, July 25th, 1803.

14 CO 101/44, under 'Miscellaneous', "Function of Courts in Grenada."

15 CO 103/10, Grenada Act No. 106 of 1801, "An Act to alter and amend an Act therein mentioned for establishing a Court for hearing and determining Errors so

far as the same relates to the number of Justices necessary to compose the said Court."

16 CO 103/10, No. 105 of 1800, "An Act for establishing a Supreme Court of Judicature and uniting therein the jurisdictions of the several courts of King's Bench and Grand Sessions of the Peace and Common Pleas heretofore established in this island."

17 CO 103/2, No. 21 of 1767, "An Act to constitute a Court Merchant."

18 CO 101/9, Conway to Governor Melville, March 13th, 1776.

19 CO 260/18, President Ottley to Earl Camden, August 10th, 1804.

20 CO 260/34, Civil List.

21 CO 285/10, President Campbell to Earl Camden, No. 4, January 22nd, 1805.

22 CO 285/7, President Robley to the Duke of Portland, No. 2, November 22nd, 1800.

23 CO 285/4, Governor Lindsay to the Duke of Portland, private, October 1st, 1795.

24 CO 260/16, President Ottley to the Duke of Portland, May 17th, 1799.

25 CO 285/4, President Campbell to the Duke of Portland, No. 9, September 7th, 1796.

26 Ibid.

27 CO 285/3, Governor Lindsay to the Duke of Portland, private, October 1st, 1796.

28 CO 285/4, Memorial of John Balfour, Chief Justice of Tobago to the Duke of Portland, May 31st, 1796.

29 CO 101/29,Grenada Assembly Minutes, Meeting October 15th, 1778.

30 CO 101/54, Governor Shipley to Earl Camden, No. 4, July 12th, 1804.

31 Ibid.

32 CO 101/42, Governor Maitland to Earl Camden, No. 4, July 12th, 1804.

33 House of Commons, *The Laws of Grenada and the Grenadines from the year 1763 to 1805* (London, 1808).

34 CO 10144, Governor Maitland to Windham, No. 112, September 11th, 1806.

35 CO 101/45, "Public Papers relating to Assistant Judges." See also Council Minutes, Meeting February 19th, 1807 in the same volume.

36 Ibid.

37 Ibid.

38 Ibid.

39 Ibid.

40 Ibid.

41 It was Richard Ottley who was mainly responsible for the harsh punishments prescribed by the Courts for slaves convicted of minor offences, and who at the same time exculpated masters for brutality. See 101/50, Copies of judicial and executive proceedings regarding slaves.

42 CO 101/54, Governor Shipley to Earl Bathurst, No. 76, September 8th, 1818.

43 See for instance CO 103/2, Grenada, Act No. 13 of 1767, "An Act for establishing a militia for the defence of this island."

44 CO 101/56, Governor Riall to Earl Bathurst, No. 14, October 4th, 1816.

45 CO 101/61, Population Returns.

46 Elsa Goveia, *Slave Society in the British Leeward Islands at the End of the Eighteenth Century* (New Haven and London, 1965), p. 65.

47 Ibid.

48 CO 101/21, Governor Macartney to Lord Germain, No. 11, May 27th, 1778.

49 CO 101/21, Governor Macartney to Lord Germain, No. 12, May 31st, 1778.

50 CO 101/22, Governor Macartney to Lord Germain, No. 39, October 25th, 1778.

51 CO 260/6, Council Minutes, Meeting September 16th, 1778.

52 CO 260/6, Assembly Minutes, Meeting November 12th, 1778.

53 CO 260/6, Assembly Minutes, Meeting December 22nd, 1778.

54 CO 260/8, Enclosure 8, in Governor Seton's dispatch to Lord Sydney, November 30th, 1787.

55 CO 260/10, Lord Grenville to Governor Seton, March 31st, 1790.

56 CO 260/10, Governor Seton to Lord Grenville, June 5th, 1790.

57 CO 260/10, Lord Grenville to Governor Seton, March 31st, 1790.

58 CO 260/10, Council Minutes, Meeting July 30th, 1789.

59 CO 71/8, Governor Orde to Lord Sydney, July 6th, 1784.

60 See for instance St. Vincent Act No. 9 of 1767 (CO 262/1), "An Act for regulating the vestries in this island empowering them to raise taxes within their respective parishes and directing the application of the same"; also Act. No. 15 of 1768 (CO 262/1), "An Act for the regulating of the towns, rendering them healthy, establishing markets, etc."

61 See *Reasons for establishing a registry of slaves in the Colonies...* (London, 1815) This work was written by James Stephen, a director of the Institution.

62 Ragatz, *The Fall of the Planter Class*, op. cit, p. 390.

63 Ibid.

64 CO 260/33, Report of the committee appointed by the Council and Assembly to take into consideration the Registry Bill, enclosed in William Manning to Earl Bathurst, January 18th, 1816.

65 CO 71/52, Report of the committee of Council and Assembly on the Registry Bill, Feburary 14th, 1816.

66 CO 101/56, Joint resolutions of the Council and Assembly on the Registry Bill proposed.

67 CO 285/21, Report of the joint committee appointed by the Council and Assembly on the Registry Bill, enclosed in President Balfour's No. 8 to Earl Bathurst, April 17th, 1816.

68 Ragatz, *The Fall of the Planter Class*, op. cit., p. 398.

69 CO 260/22, Governor Brisbane to Earl Bathurst, No. 85, January 28th, 1822.

70 CO 285/9, President Campbell to Earl Camden, No. 3, August 27th, 1804.

71 CO 260/37, Governor Brisbane to Henry Goulbourn, July 23rd, 1820.

72 CO 101/15, Lord Hillsborough to Governor Melville, No. 38, August 26th, 1769.

73 CO 101/13, Lieutenant Governor Fitzmaurice to Lord Hillsborough, No. 38, August 26th, 1769.

74 CO 101/16, Governor Leyborne to Lord Hillsborough, Nos. 5 and 6, December 6th and December 19th, 1771.

75 CO 285/3, Governor Lindsay to the King, private, May 10th, 1795.

76 CO 101/18, Lieutenant Governor Morris to Earl Dartmouth, December 25th, 1774.

77 CO 71/24, Lieutenant Governor Bruce to Dundas, No. 4, December 21st, 1792.

78 CO 71/24, Council Minutes, Meeting, February 12th, 1793.

79 CO 71/55, Governor Maxwell to Henry Goulbourn, private, February 4th, 1818.

80 CO 71/55, Governor Maxwell to Henry Goulbourn, private, February 19th, 1818.

81 CO 71/56, Governor Maxwell to Henry Goulbourn, private, March 20th, 1819.

82 CO 71/60, Governor Huntingdon to the Earl of Bathurst, private, October 23rd, 1823.

83 H. H. Wrong, *Government of the West Indies* (Oxford, 1923), pp. 37-38.

84 CO 260/4, Governor Morris to Germain, September 6th, 1776.

85 Ibid.

86 CO 260/5, Governor Morris to Lord Germain, November 9th, 1777.

87 CO 260/5, Governor Morris to the Rt. Hon. Lords of the Treasury, February 2nd, 1778.

88 I. Waters, *The Unfortunate Valentine Morris* (Newport, 1964), p. 37.

89 CO 260/5, Lieutenant Governor Morris to the Rt. Hon. Lords of the Treasury.

90 CO 285/1, Lieutenant Governor Ferguson to Lord Germain, June 5th, 1780.

91 CO 101/18, Governor Young to Dartmouth, January 10th, 1776.

92 See for instance CO 101/21, Governor Macartney to Germain, No. 11, May 27th, 1778.

93 Goveia, *Slave Society*, op. cit., p. 79.

94 See for instance CO 287/1, Tobago Act No. 9 of 1770, "An Act for appointing an Agent to negotiate the affairs of this island in Great Britain for apportioning a recompense for his trouble and setting methods for the better management of that trust."

95 See Lillian Pension, *The Colonial Agents of the British West Indies: a Study in Colonial Administration, mainly in the Eighteenth Century* (London, 1924).

96 The disabilities of the free coloureds are treated at length in Chap. 7.

97 See Chap. 5.

98 Ibid.

99 House of Commons Accounts and Paper Volume XXIX 1790, No. 698 – evidence of Archibald Campbell, p.135.

100 CO 101/16, Governor Leyborne to Lord Hillsborough, No. 13, April 25th, 1772.

101 CO 101/33, President Williams to Dundas, November 10th, 1792.

102 CO 101/38, List of members of Council, January 9th 1801; CO 101/40, List of members of Council, January 28th, 1803.

103 CO 101/41, President Adye to Lord Hobart, June 10th, 1804.

104 CO 101/56, Governor Riall to Earl Bathurst, No. 14, October 4th, 1816.

105 CO 285/15, Governor Young to Earl of Liverpool, June 30th, 1810.

106 CO 260/6, enclosure in Lt. Governor Morris' dispatch to Lord Germain, February 5th, 1779.

107 CO 101/12, enclosure in Governor Melville's dispatch to the Earl of Shellburne, No. 33, February 1st, 1768.

108 CO 101/12, List of the polls for the Assembly of Grenada and the Grenadines, December 15th, 1767, enclosed in Governor Melville's No. 5 to Lord Hillsborough, May 1st, 1768.

109 CO 71/53, Governor Maxwell to Henry Goulbourn, Private, February 4th 1818.

110 CO 71/3, Governor Young to Lord Hillsborough, July 28th, 1772.

111 CO 101/27, "An Act for regulating proceedings at elections, 1786."

112 CO 103/11, No. 148 of 1812, "An Act to repeal so much of an Act entitled An Act for regulating elections as require the members of the Assembly to take an oath that they are duly qualified according to the true intent and meaning of the said Act."

113 CO 101/59, Memorial of Alexander Lumsden, a landed proprietor of Grenada to Earl Bathurst, October 7th, 1819.

114 CO 101/16, Governor Leyborne to Lord Hillsborough, No. 11, March 4th, 1772.

115 CO 71/52, Governor Maxwell to Earl Bathurst, No. 11, March 4th 1772.

116 CO 71/61, Governor Huntingdon to Earl Bathurst, January 11th, 1824.

117 CO 285/27, Governor Robinson to Earl Bathurst, No. 143, November 22nd, 1822.

118 See for example Grenada Act No. 30 of 1770, CO 103/3, "An Act to explain and amend and Act entitled An Act for establishing Courts of Common Pleas, Error, Kings Bench and Grand Sessions of the Peace."

119 CO 260/4, Governor Morris to Lord Germain, February 5th, 1779.

120 Ibid.

121 CO 260/6, Enclosures 1 and 2 in Governor Morris' dispatch to Lord Germain, February 5th, 1779.

122 See Chapter 7

123 CO 71/69, Governor Nicolay to Murray, No. 2, January 2nd 1830.

124 See Chap. 2.

125 Goveia, *Slave Society*, op. cit., p. 100.

126 See E. Williams, *Capitalism and Slavery* (Chapel Hill: Univ. of North Carolina Press, 1944), ch. 4.

CHAPTER 5

1 CO 260/9, Governor Seton to Sydney, No. 55, January 1789.

2 House of Commons Accounts and Papers, Volume XXVI, 1789, No. 646a, pt. 3: Reply of Governor Seton to query No. 31.

3 Thomas Attwood, *History of Dominica* (London, 1791), pp. 81-84.

4 Sir William Young, "Prospectus for the Institution of an Agricultural Society in Tobago" (CO 285/2, July 21st, 1807).

5 Henry Woodcock, *History of Tobago* (AYR, 1868), p. 188.

6 CO 260/10, Governor Seton to Grenville; July 2nd, 1790.

7 L.J. Ragatz, *Statistics for the Study of British Caribbean Economic History, 1763-1833* (London, 1926), Tables 15 and 16.

8 CO 101/18, Lieutenant Governor Morris to the Earl of Dartmouth, January 14th, 1775.

9 CO 261/9, St. Vincent Agency Letter Book, State of St. Vincent in 1765.

10 CO 260/28, Governor Brisbane to the Earl of Liverpool, August 17th, 1811.

11 CO 71/4, State of Dominica in 1773.

12 CO 260/11, Governor Seton to Dundas, September 27th, 1791.

13 CO 101/17, Answers to queries, Tobago, May 1st, 1773.

14 R. Pares, *Merchants and Planters* (Cambridge [Eng.]: Published for the Economic History Review at the University Press, 1960), pp. 47-48.

15 E. Goveia, *Slave Society in the British Leeward Islands at the End of the Eighteenth Century* (New Haven & London, 1965), p. 107.

16 CO 101/20, Governor Macartney to Lord Germain, No. 9, June 30th, 1776.

17 CO101/22, Governor Macartney to Lord Germain, No. 39, October 25th, 1778.

18 Mrs. A. C. Carmichael, *Domestic Manners and Social Condition of the White, Colored and Negro Population of the West Indies*, 2 vols. (London, 1833), vol. 1, pp. 34-36.

19 Ibid., p. 41.

20 *Correspondence relating to the Estates of Sir William Young in the West Indies with Claims for Compensation 1768-1835*, 6 vols. (Oxford: Rhodes House Library), vol. 4.

21 House of Commons Accounts and Papers; Volume XXVI, 1789, No. 646a, pt. 3: in reply to query No. 53.

22 Charles Peters, *Two Sermons Preached at Dominica on the 11th and 13th April, 1800, and officially noticed by His Majesty's Privy Council in that Island, with appendix containing minutes of three trials together with remarks and strictures on the issue of those trials, the Slave Trade, and the condition of the Slaves* (London, 1802), pp. 61-62.

23 House of Commons Accounts and Papers, Volume XXIX, 1790, No. 699, p. 211.

24 House of Commons Accounts and Papers, Volume XXVI, 1789, No. 646a, pt. 3: in reply to query No. 53.

25 The Library of the Royal Commonwealth Society, London MSS 745, Collection of Original Documents, Account Books and Map relating to the West India Properties of the Gregg family, notably Hillsborough Estate in Dominica, 1795-1899: "Copy of Last Will and Testament of John Gregg."

26 House of Commons Accounts and Papers, Volume XXVI, 1789, No. 646a, pt. 3: reply of Dominica proprietors to query No. 34.

27 Ibid., reply of Mr. Laing to query No. 35.

28 B. Edwards, *The History, Civil and Commercial, of the British Colonies in the West Indies*, 4 vols. (Philadelphia, 1806), vol. 3, appendix to ch. 2.

29 House of Commons Accounts and Papers, Volume XXVI, 1789, No. 646a, pt. 3: reply of both Houses of the Legislature of Grenada to query No. 30.

30 [A Resident], *Sketches and Recollections of the West Indies* (London, 1828), pp. 48-49.

31 CO 71/13, John Gregg to Nepean, November 5th, 1787.

32 CO 71/40, President Metcalfe to William Wyndham, No. 36; October 8th, 1806.

33 CO 71/50, Petition of the Council and Assembly to the Prince Regent, November 18th, 1814.

34 CO 71/56, Memorial of Colonial Agent to Earl Bathurst, October 7th, 1819.

35 CO 101/16, Governor Leybourne to Lord Hillsborough, January 30th, 1772.

36 Ibid., and enclosures.

37 Richard Madden, *A Twelve months residence in the West Indies during the transition from Slavery to Apprenticeship*, 2 vols. (Philadelphia, 1835), vol. 1, p. 68.

38 CO 71/10, Governor Orde to Sydney, April 19th, 1780.

39 CO 71/39, under 'Miscellaneous', "Detailed Statement of Losses".

40 CO 71/43, Lord Castleragh to Governor Montgomerie, No. 2, July 22nd, 1808.

41 CO 71/53, Governor Maxwell and enclosures to Earl Bathurst, No. 54, April 23rd, 1817; CO 72/11, Bathurst to Governor Maxwell, No. 19, November 8th, 1817.

42 Attwood, *History of Dominica*, op. cit., p. 283.

43 House of Commons Accounts and Papers, Volume XXVI, 1789, No. 646a, pt. 3 in reply to query No. 10.

44 CO 285/2, "Prospectus for the Institution of an Agricultural Society in Tobago", July 21st, 1807.

45 CO 101/49, Governor Maitland and enclosures to the Earl of Liverpool, August 28th, 1810.

46 House of Commons Accounts and Papers, Volume XXVI, 1789, No. 646a, pt. 3: Reply of Governor Matthew to query No. 51.

47 House of Commons Accounts and Papers, Volume XXVI, 1789, No. 646a, pt. 3: Replies to queries relating to land utilisation and agricultural techniques.

48 House of Commons Accounts and Papers, Volume XXIX, 1790, No. 698, p. 155; Statement of Archibald Campbell.

49 House of Commons Accounts and Papers, Volume XXVI, 1789, No. 646a, pt. 3: Reply of Governor Matthew to query No. 42.

50 House of Commons Accounts and Papers, Volume XXIX, 1791, Nos. 745-748, p. 130.

51 House of Commons Accounts and Papers, Volume XXIX, 1791, Nos. 745-748: Evidence of John Terry, p. 109.

52 House of Commons Accounts and Papers, Volume XXIX, 1790, No. 699, p. 232.

53 House of Commons Accounts and Papers, Volume XXIX, 1790, No. 699: Evidence of Henry Hew Dalrymple, p. 301.

54 Carmichael, *Domestic Manners and Social Condition*, op. cit., p. 104.

55 House of Commons Accounts and Papers, Volume XXVI, 1789, No. 646a, pt. 3, in reply to query.

56 Ibid., reply of Mr. Spooner to same query.

57 House of Commons Accounts and Papers, Volume XXIX, 1790, No. 698: Evidence of A.W. Byam, p. 102.

58 House of Commons Accounts and Papers, Volume XXVI, 1789, No. 646a, pt. 3, in reply to query No. 42.

59 House of Commons Accounts and Papers, Volume XXVI, 1789, No. 646a, pt. iii, in reply to query No. 47.

60 House of Commons Accounts and Papers, Volume XXVI, 1789 No. 646a, pt. 3: Reply of both houses of the Grenada Legislature to query No. 32. The replies from the other islands were similar.

61 Ibid.

62 House of Commons Accounts and Papers, Volume XXVI, 1789, No. 646a, pt. 3, in reply to query No. 42.

63 Ragatz, *The Fall*, op. cit., p. 66.

64 House of Commons Accounts and Papers, Volume XXVI, 1789, No. 646a, pt. 3: Reply to query No. 32.

65 Goveia, *Slave Society*, op. cit., p. 121.

66 House of Commons Accounts and Papers, Volume XXVI, 1789, No. 646a, pt 3: Reply to query No. 49.

67 CO 285/2, Prospectus for the institution of an Agricultural Society in Tobago.

68 House of Commons Accounts and Papers, Volume XXIX, 1790, No. 698: Evidence of Archibald Campbell, p. 138.

69 CO 285/28. See for example Petition of Both Houses of the Legislature of Tobago to the House of Commons, February 1823.

70 See Chap. 9.

71 Calculated from statistics of the slave population of the islands in 1823. See *Blue Books*: Dominica, CO. 76/14; St. Vincent, CO 265/6; Grenada, CO 105/17; Tobago, CO 290/8.

72 CO 71/58, Imports and Exports of Slaves and Slaves Sold for Debt.

73 House of Commons Accounts and Papers, Volume XXIX, 1790, No.698: Evidence of John Gregg, p. 230.

74 CO 71/44, Current Prices.

75 House of Commons Accounts and Papers, Volume X, 1804: Enclosure 2 in President Matson to Portland, January 5th, 1800.

76 CO 101/45, Population Returns.

77 House of Commons Accounts and Papers, Volume XXIX 1790, No. 698.

78 CO 103/10, Grenada Act No. 97 of 1797.

79 CO 285/16, Governor Young to Liverpool, October 12th, 1811.

80 Hilary Beckles, *Centering Woman: Gender Discourses in Caribbean Slave Society* (Kingston: Ian Randle Publishers 1999), p. 14.

81 *Blue Books of Statistics* – CO 76/14, CO 106/17, CO 290/8, CO 265/6. Population Returns: CO 285/16, CO 101/45, CO 71/38.

82 CO 260/38, Return of Slaves Imported and Exported since January 1st, 1808 enclosed in Brisbane to Bathurst, November 11th, 1821.

83 CO 71/58, Imports and Exports of Slaves 1808-1821.

84 Marrieta Morrissey, *Slave Women in the New World: Gender Stratification in the Caribbean* (University Press of Kansas, 1989), pp. 116, 152.

85 Ragatz, *The Fall*, op. cit., p. 33.

86 House of Commons Accounts and Papers, Volume XXIV, 1791, Nos. 745-748.

87 Beckles, *Centring Woman*, op. cit., p. 3.

88 In reply to query No. 28, House of Commons Accounts and Papers, Volume XXVI, 1789, No. 646a, pt. 3.

89 CO 101/28, Imports of Slaves 1784-88.

90 House of Commons Accounts and Papers, Volume XXIV, 1791, Nos. 745-748.

91 CO 101/61, Population Returns, enclosed in Governor Riall to Bathurst, October 11th, 1821; Blue Books of Statistics, House of Commons Accounts and Papers, Volume XXXI, 1830, No. 582.

92 CO 76/14, CO 290/8, CO 265/6, Blue Books of Statistics, House of Commons Accounts and Papers, Volume XXXI, 1830, No. 582.

93 Beckles, *Centring Woman*, op. cit., p. 15.

94 House of Commons Accounts and Papers, Volume XXVI, 1789, No. 646a, pt. 3, in reply to query No. 7.

95 Morrissey, *Slave Women*, op. cit., p. 117.

96 House of Commons Accounts and Papers, Volume XXVI, 1789, No. 646a, pt. 3, in reply to query No. 7.

97 Ibid.

98 House of Commons Accounts and Papers, Volume XXIV, 1791, Nos 745-748, p179.

99 Ibid., p. 110.

100 Ibid., p. 101.

101 Beckles, *Centring Woman*, op. cit., p. 11.

102 House of Commons Accounts and Papers, Volume XXIV, 1791, Nos. 745-748: Captain Hall at p 101.

103 See Beckles, *Centring Woman*, op. cit., p. 103

104 House of Commons Accounts and Papers, Volume XXIV, 1791, Nos. 745-748: Captain Hall at p. 101.

105 Ibid., Matthew Terry at p. 84.

106 House of Commons Accounts and Papers, Volume XXVI, 1789, No. 646a, pt. 3: Replies to queries relating to mortality and longevity of slave population.

107 House of Commons Accounts and Papers, Volume XXIX, 1790, No.698: Evidence of Dr. John Castles, p 201.

108 Ibid., at p. 110.

109 Ibid., at p. 230.

110 CO 71/10, Orde to Sydney, October 4th, 1788.

111 House of Commons Accounts and Papers, Volume XXIX, 1790, No. 698: Evidence of Dr. John Castles, p. 211.

112 Franklyn Knight, *Slave Society in Cuba during the Nineteenth Century* (University of Wisconsin Press, 1970), p. 82.

113 Beckles, *Centring Woman*, op. cit., p. 13.

114 Morrissey, *Slave Women*, op. cit., p. 117.

115 House of Commons Accounts and Papers, Volume XXIV, 1791: Captain Hall at p. 101.

116 CO 285/16, Governor Young to Liverpool, October 12th, 1811.

117 See for instance, Petition of the Council and Assembly of Grenada to Earl Bathurst, August 10th, 1821 (CO 101/61).

118 Calculated from list of slaves imported into St. Vincent (CO 260/9).

119 Calculated from Slave Imports, Dominica (CO 71/38); Grenada (CO 101/42).

120 CO 288/10, Petition to Parliament, July 17th, 1823.

121 CO 101/63, President Paterson to Earl Bathurst, No. 16, October 10th, 1823.

122 CO 260/40, Governor Brisbane to Earl Bathurst, No. 119, September 26th, 1823.

123 House of Commons Accounts and Papers, Volume XXIX, 1790, No.698: Evidence of Mr. A.W. Byam, p. 124.

124 House of Commons Accounts and Papers, Volume XXIX, 1790, No.698: Evidence of Archibald Campbell, p. 139.

125 Attwood, *History of Dominica*, op. cit., p. 78.

126 House of Commons Accounts and Papers, Volume XXIX, 1790, No. 698: Evidence of Archibald Campbell, p. 138.

127 House of Commons Accounts and Papers, Volume XXIX, 1790, No.698: Evidence of Mr. A.W. Bryam, p. 102.

128 House of Commons Accounts and Papers, Volume XXIX, 1790, No. 698: evidence of Mr. Archibald Campbell, p. 138.

129 House of Commons Accounts and Papers, Volume XXIX, 1790, No. 698: Evidence of Mr. Archibald Campbell, p. 139.

130 House of Commons Accounts and Papers, Volume XXX, 1790, No. 699, p. 231.

131 House of Commons Accounts and Papers, Volume XXVI, 1789, No. 646a, pt. 3: Replies to query No.1.

132 CO 71/55, Governor Maxwell to Earl Bathurst, No. 85, June 25th, 1818.

133 House of Commons Accounts and Papers, Volume XXVI, 1789, No. 646a, pt. 3, in reply to query No. 2.

134 House of Commons Accounts and Papers, Volume XXIX, 1790, No. 698, p.101.

135 Carmichael, *Domestic Manners*, op. cit. p. 96.

136 Peters, *Two Sermons Preached at Dominica*, op. cit., pp. 20-29.

137 Ibid., p. 30.

138 House of Commons Accounts and Papers, Volume XXVI, 1789, No. 646a, pt. 3: Reply of Mr. Robinson to query No. 10.

139 CO 73/13, Dominica Act, No. 293 of 1821: "An Act for regulating the government and conduct of Slaves and for the more effectual protection, encouragement and general melioration of their condition", Clause 3.

140 CO 260/40, Governor Brisbane's No. 119, and enclosures to the Earl of Bathurst, September 26th, 1823.

141 Ibid.

142 Carmichael, *Domestic Manners*, op. cit., pp. 177-79.

143 Ibid. p. 201.

144 House of Commons Accounts and Papers, Volume XXIX, 1790, No. 698, p. 145.

145 House of Commons Accounts and Papers, Volume XXIX, 1790, No. 698: Evidence of Mr. A.W. Bryan, p. 108.

146 House of Commons Accounts and Papers, Volume XXVI, 1789, No. 646a, pt. 3: Reply of Mr. Laing to query No. 6.

147 House of Commons Accounts and Papers, Volume XXIV, 1790, No. 698: Evidence of Mr. A.W. Byam, p. 108.

148 House of Commons Accounts and Papers, Volume XXVI, 1789, No. 646a, pt. 3: Replies to query No. 40.

149 [A Resident?], *Sketches and Recollections*, op. cit., p. 76.

150 "An Act to oblige the owners of negroes...usually attending and plying as public porters, canoe and boatmen ... to give in the names of such negroes to regulate their conduct and hire...", Clauses 2, 3 and 4, in House of Commons Accounts and Papers, Volume XIX, 1816, No. 226.

151 CO 73/12, Dominica Act, No. 241 of 1816.

152 Carmichael, *Domestic Manners*, op. cit., p. 144.

153 Ibid., p. 154.

154 House of Commons Accounts and Papers, Volume XXIX, 1790, p.232.

155 House of Commons Accounts and Papers, Volume XXVI, 1789, No. 646a, pt. 3: Reply of Mr. Spooner to query No. 7.

156 Ibid., Reply of Both Houses of the Grenada Legislature to the same query.

157 CO 260/7, Answers to queries January 8th, 1785; CO 260/9 to 260/15, CO 260/23, Current Prices.

158 See Chap. 2, this volume.

159 CO 101/63, President Paterson to Earl Bathurst, No. 16; October 10th, 1823.

160 CO 101/53, George Whitfield to Governor Shipley, December 11th, 1813.

161 CO 71/52, Governor Maxwell to Earl Bathurst, No. 13, August 16th, 1816.

162 See CO 260/40, Reply of the Legislature of St. Vincent to Earl Bathurst's Despatches of May 28th and July 9th, 1823.

163 See for instance, CO 101/61: Petition from both houses of the Grenada Legislature to Parliament, August 8th, 1821.

164 Adam Smith, *The Wealth of Nations*, 2 vols. (London: Meuthen, 1961), vol. 1, pp. 411-12.

165 Goveia, *Slave Society*, op. cit., p. 146.

166 Carmichael, *Domestic Manners*, op. cit., p 120.

167 CO 285/16, Governor Young to the Earl of Liverpool, October 12th, 1811.

168 Carmichael, *Domestic Manners*, op. cit., p. 121.

169 House of Commons Accounts and Papers, Volume XXVI, 1789, No. 646a, pt. 3: Reply of both Houses of the Legislature to query No. 48.

170 House of Commons Accounts and Papers, Volume XXIX, 1790, No. 698, p. 154.

171 See for example CO 260/13, Governor Seton to the Duke of Portland, March 28th, 1795.

172 CO 101/34, President Mackenzie to the Duke of Portland, March 28th, 1795.

173 CO 71/28, Governor Hamilton to the Duke of Portland, No. 44, December 14th, 1795.

174 For a discussion of Maroon activity, see Chap. 9.

CHAPTER 6

1   House of Commons Accounts and Papers, Volume XXVI, 1789, No. 646a, pt. 3: "A General View of the Principles upon which this System of Laws appears to have been originally founded."

2   For an authoritative discussion of these ideas and techniques, see Elsa Goveia, "The West Indian Slave Laws of the Eighteenth Century," *Revista De Ciencas Sociales*, Volume 1, No. IV, 1960.

3   See for instance, CO 287/1, Tobago Act, No. IV of 1768, "An Act declaring slaves, mules, boilers, stills, and still heads and other plantation utensils belonging to Mills, Boiling Houses and Still Houses to be Real Estate."

4   CO 262/1; St. Vincent Act, No. 7, of 1767; 'An Act for making slaves Real Estate and for the better government of slaves and free Negroes; Clause IV.

5   Ibid., and Clause V.

6   Ibid.

7   Goveia, "The West Indian Slave Laws", op. cit., p. 86.

8   CO 287/1, Tobago Act, No. 1, of 1768: "An Act for the good order and government of slaves and for keeping them under proper restraint, for establishing the method of trial in capital cases and other regulations for the greater security of that part of the inhabitants' property."

9   CO 73/5, Dominica Act, No. 9, of 1770: "Copy of an Act for the Suppression of Runaway Slaves...and of Five Acts since passed reviving, continuing and amending the same."

10 CO 103/2, Grenada Act, No. IV, of 1766: "An Act for the better government of Slaves and for the more speedy and effectual suppression of Runaway Slaves."

11 CO 262/1, St. Vincent Act, No. 7, of 1767.

12 Ibid., Clause XXXIX.

13 Ibid., Clause XL.

14 Ibid., Clause VIII.

15 Ibid., Clause XLII.

16 Ibid., Clause XXXI.

17 Ibid., Clause XVIII.

18 Ibid., Clause IX.

19 Ibid., Clause XLIV.

20 Ibid., Clause XII.

21 Ibid.

22 CO 103/2, Grenada Act, No. 9 of 1767: "An Act to prevent persons from hawking and peddling and carrying goods about the town and country, from house to house, to sell and dispose of." Clause 1.

23 CO 103/7, Grenada Act, No. 13, of 1784: "An Act to establish regular markets in the different towns of this island…" Clause XVII.

24 Ibid., and Clause XXI.

25 CO 73/5, Dominica Act. No. 9 of 1770, Clause 1.

26 Ibid., Clause iii.

27 Ibid., Clause V.

28 Ibid., Clause XIII.

29 CO 103/2, Grenada Act, No. 4 of 1766, Clause XII.

30 CO 73/5, Dominica Act, No.9, of 1770, Clause X.

31 Ibid., Clause XVIII.

32 Ibid., Clause XIII.

33 See for instance CO 73/10, Dominica Act, No.150, of 1794.

34 CO 73/11, Dominica Act, No. 166, of 1798: "An Act to make the testimony of slaves admissible in certain cases and under certain restrictions for a limited time, to forfeit runaway slaves who have been absent from the service of their masters a certain time…and to prevent persons from harboring or employing slaves on their plantations or in their houses without a written permission from the owner or person having charge of such slaves and for other purposes."

35 Ibid., Clause VI.

36 Ibid., Clause VIII.

37 Ibid., Preamble.

38 Ibid., Clause ii.

39 CO 287/1, Tobago Act, No. 1, of 1768, Clause XVII.

40 CO 262/1, St. Vincent Act, No. 7, of 1767, Clause XXI.

41 CO 73/5, Dominica Act, No. 9, of 1770, Clause XV.

42 "An Act for regulating the manumission of slaves, for better preventing slaves so manumitted become burdensome to the colony, and for punishing free negroes, free mulattoes and mustees in a more summary and speedy manner than heretofore for any offences by them committed not being capital and for invalidating their evidences in capital cases against white persons", in *The Laws of the Colony of Dominica commencing from its early Establishment to the close of the year 1818, and Tables of Several Acts* (Roseau, 1818).

43 Ibid., Preamble.

44 House of Commons Accounts and Papers, Volume XXVI, 1789, No.646a, pt. iii: 'A General View of the Principles…'

45 CO 262/1, St. Vincent Act, No. 7, of 1767, Clause LI.

46 CO 73/5; Dominica Act, No.9, of 1770; Clause XVIII.

47 CO 287/1, Tobago Act, No. 1, of 1768, Clause 1.

48 CO 73/5, Dominica Act, No.9, of 1770, Clause XVII.

49 Ibid., Clause XXV.

50 See for instance, CO 287/1, Tobago Act, No. 1, of 1768, Clause XXXII.

51 CO 73/9, Dominica Act, of December 23rd 1788: 'An Act for the encouragement, protection, and better government of slaves', Clause XIII.

52 House of Commons Accounts and Papers, Volume XXVI, 1789, No. 646a, pt. iii: 'A General View of the Principles…'

53 Goveia, "The West Indian Slave Laws", op. cit., p. 86.

54 For Dominica see CO 73/9: "An Act for the encouragement, protection and better government of slaves. For Grenada see House of Commons Accounts and Papers, Volume XXXVI, 1789, No. 646a, pt. iii: 'An Act for the better protection and for promoting the increase and population of the slaves and for repealing the 1st, 2nd, and 3rd Clauses of "An Act to prevent the further sudden increase of free negroes and mulattoes and such part of all and every law and laws now in force relative to the trial and punishment of slaves as relate to their trial and punishment for the sole offence of running away and for substituting another mode of trial and punishment in lieu thereof, and for appointing Guardians to carry this Act into execution'." November 3rd, 1788. This Act will hereafter be cited as The Grenada Guardian Act of 1788.

55 The Grenada Guardian Act of 1788, Clauses i and ii.

56 Ibid., Clause VIII.

57 Ibid., Clause IX.

58 Ibid., Clause XVIII.

59 Ibid., Clause X.

60 See for example, House of Commons Accounts and Papers, Vol. XXIX, No. 698, Statement of Mr. H.H. Dalrymple, p. 301.

61 The Grenada Guardian Act of 1788, Clause iii.

62 House of Commons Accounts and Papers, Volume XXIX, 1790; No. 698: Evidence of Mr. H.H. Dalrymple, p.301.

63 The Grenada Guardian Act of 1788, Clause XII.

64 House of Commons Accounts and Papers, Volume XXX, 1790, No. 698: Evidence of H.H. Dalrymple, p. 301.

65 Ibid.

66 House of Commons Accounts and Papers, Volume XXVI, 1789, No. 646a, Pt. iii: Extract of a letter from Mr. Chief Justice Ottley to Sir William Young, August 6th, 1788.

67 House of Commons Accounts and Papers, Volume XXIV, 1791, Nos. 745-748: Evidence of Drewrey Ottley of St. Vincent, p. 101.

68 House of Commons Accounts and Papers, Volume XXIX, 1790, No. 698: Evidence of Sir Ashton Warner Byam, p. 100. See also CO 101/28: Extract from the Minutes of the Court of King's Bench and Grand Sessions of the Peace for the Island of Grenada.

69 House of Commons Accounts and Papers, Volume XXX, 1790, No. 699, p.34.

70 Ibid., p. 300.

71 House of Commons Accounts and Papers, Volume XXIX, 1790/91, Nos. 745-748, p. 161.

72 Goveia, *Slave Society in the British Leeward Islands*, op. cit., p. 198.

73 Ibid., p. 95

74 See Chapter 9.

75 House of Commons Accounts and Papers, Volume XLVIII, No. 967a, 1798/99: Copy of a Circular Letter to His Majesty's Governors of the West Indian Islands, April 23rd, 1798.

76 House of Commons Accounts and Papers, Volume XLVIII, No. 967a, 1798/99: Copy of a Circular Letter to His Majesty's Governors of the West Indian Islands.

77 House of Commons Accounts and Papers, Volume XLVIII, No. 967b: Report of the Committee of both Houses of the Legislature on the Slave Trade.

78 CO 285/6, Governor Master and enclosure to the Duke of Portland, April 3rd, 1800.

79 See Edward Brathwaite, *The Development of Creole Society in Jamaica* (Oxford: Clarendon Press, 1971), p. 251.

80 House of Commons Accounts and Papers vol xlv, No. 931, Enclosure 1, in Governor Seton to the Duke of Portland, July 12th, 1799.

81 An Act to punish those who shall murder or maim slaves in the island of St. Vincent and its dependencies; in House of Commons Accounts and Papers, Volume XIX, 1816, No. 226.

82 House of Commons Accounts and Papers, Volume XLVIII, No. 967b, 1798/99: The Duke of Portland to President Matson, March 21st, 1799.

83 House of Commons Accounts and Papers, Volume X, No. 119, 1804: President Matson and enclosures to the Duke of Portland, July 20th, 1799.

84 House of Commons Accounts and Papers, Volume XLV, No. 931, 1798; Enclosure C, in Governor Green to the Duke of Portland, July 25th, 1797.

85 CO 103/10, Grenada Act, No. 97 of 1797, 'An Act for the better protection, and for promoting the natural increase and population of the slaves within the island of Grenada, and such of the Grenadines as are annexed to the Government thereof; for compelling an adequate provision for and care of them as well as in sickness and old age, as in health; and for constituting and appointing Guardians to effectuate and carry into execution the regulations and purposes of this Act'. Clauses VI, XIV.

86 Ibid., Clause X, XI.

87 Ibid., Clause XIII.

88 Ibid., Clause X, XX, XXII.

89 CO 101/51, President Adye to the Earl of Liverpool; February 1st, 1812.

90 CO 101/ 58, Governor Riall to the Earl of Bathurst, No. 14; August 27th, 1818.

91 Fortunatus Dwarris, *Substance of Three Reports of the Commissioners of Enquiry into the Administration of Civil and Criminal Justice in the West Indies* (London, 1827), pp. 176-178.

92 Ibid., p. 177.

93 House of Commons Accounts and Papers, Volume XVII, 1818, No. 251: Governor Maxwell to Earl Bathurst, September 3rd, 1817.

94 House of Commons Accounts and Papers, Volume XXII, 1818, No. 251, p.267.

95 House of Commons Accounts and Papers, Volume XVII, 1818, No. 251: 'Copy of the Presentment of the Grand Jury', August 20th, 1817.

96 CO 262/11, St. Vincent Act, No. 243 of 1821: An Act to repeal an Act entitled 'An Act for making slaves Real Estate, and to ameliorate the condition of slaves, and for other purposes.'

97 CO 73/13, Dominica Act No. 293, of 1821: 'An Act for regulating the Government and conduct of slaves, and for their more effectual protection, encouragement, and general amelioration of their condition', Clause XIII.

98 See Preambles.

99 Williams, *Capitalism and Slavery*, op. cit., pp. 197-98.
100 CO 285/28, Governor Robinson to Earl Bathurst, No. 181, October 9th, 1823.
101 CO 260/40, Governor Brisbane's, No. 119, and Enclosures to Earl Bathurst, September 20th, 1823.
102 Ibid.
103 Ibid.
104 Ibid.
105 CO 71/61, Circular, Roseau, May 30th, 1823.
106 CO 71/60, 'Report of the Committee of the Legislature appointed to inquire into and report on certain queries relating to the treatment, rights and privileges of the negro population of this island.'
107 Goveia, *Slave Society*, op. cit., p. 202.

CHAPTER 7

1 The estimates for Grenada, Tobago and Dominica are calculated from Blue Books of Statistics, CO 106/17, CO 290/8 and CO 76/13, respectively. For St. Vincent, see House of Commons Accounts and Papers, Volume 21,1830, No. 582.
2 Calculated from Population Returns, 1820, enclosed in Governor Riall to Earl Bathurst, October 11th, 1821, CO 101/61.
3 CO 101/27, "An Act for regulating proceedings at elections 1786"; CO 101/32, Dundas to Lieutenant Governor Home, October 5th, 1792.
4 See for instance CO 260/4, Governor Morris to Lord Germain, February 5th, 1799.
5 See for instance CO 71/69, Dominica Act No. 367 of 1830, "An Act for the relief of His Majesty's Roman Catholic Subjects of this island."
6 CO 101/1, Petition of the French inhabitants to Melville, February 14th, 1766.
7 Gad Heuman, *Between Black and White: Race, Politics and the Free Coloured in Jamaica 1792-1865* (Westport, Conn: Greenwood Press, 1981), p. 5.
8 See for example, Grenada Election Act of 1786; CO 101/27.
9 CO 285/9, President Campbell to Earl Camden, No. 3; August 27th, 1804.
10 CO 103/11, No. 148 of 1812, An Act to repeal so much of an Act entitled 'An Act for regulating elections as require the members of the Assembly to take an oath that they are duly qualified according to the true intent and meaning of said Act'.
11 CO 101/59, Memorial of Alexander Lumsden to Earl Bathurst; October 7th, 1819.
12 CO 71/52, Governor Maxwell to Earl Bathurst, No. 26, November 10th, 1816; CO 71/61, Governor Huntingdon to Earl Bathurst, January 11th, 1824.
13 Verene Shepherd, Bridget Brereton, & Barbara Bailey, eds., *Engendering History: Caribbean Women in Historical Perspective* (Kingson: Ian Randle Publishers, 1995), p. 131.
14 See for instance House of Commons Accounts and Papers, Volume XXIX (1790), No. 698: Evidence of Archibald Campbell.
15 For instance, Governor Seton of St. Vincent paid his overseers $200 p.a. See West India Committee Archives, Letters to Colonel Seton from various agents in Grenada.
16 House of Commons Accounts and Papers, Volume XXIV, 1790, No. 698, p. 147.

17 For instance, Sir William Young paid his managers in St. Vincent $250 p.a. See *Correspondence relating to the Estates of Sir William Young*, Volume V.

18 House of Commons Accounts Papers, Volume XXIX, 1790, No. 698.

19 CO 285/16, Governor Young to Liverpool, October 12th, 1811.

20 CO 71/20, Council Minutes.

21 CO 71/21, Council Minutes: Meeting, June 18th, 1791.

22 CO 71/8, "At a Committee of Dominica Proprietors assembled in London", November 25th, 1783.

23 CO 71/9; Governor Orde to Sydney, August 24th, 1785.

24 CO 71/8, Governor Orde to Lord North, February 27th, 1784.

25 CO 71/10, Governor Orde to Sydney, 1786.

26 These percentages are calculated from *Blue Books of Statistics for 1823, Grenada*, CO106/7; Dominica, CO 76/13; Tobago, CO 290/8; St. Vincent, CO 265/6.

27 See Heuman, *Between Black and White*, op. cit., Table I, p. 2.

28 For the 1823 statistics see CO 76/13; for 1788, see CO 71/15.

29 The population statistics on which these percentages are based are to be found in Williams, *Capitalism and Slavery*, op. cit., p. 59; and CO 290/8.

30 See Knight, *Slave Society in Cuba*, op. cit.

31 House of Commons Accounts and Papers, Vol. 23-24, 1824, Return of Apprenticed Africans.

32 House of Commons Accounts and Papers, Vol. 23, 1821, Return of Apprenticed Africans.

33 James Walker, *Letters on the West Indies* (London, 1818).

34 Heuman, *Between Black and White*, op. cit., p.4

35 Attwood, *History of Dominica*, op. cit., p. 210.

36 See Williams, *Capitalism and Slavery*, op. cit. p. 59.

37 CO 285/27, Manumission Returns 1808-1821.

38 Heuman, op. cit., p. 8.

39 Carmichael, *Domestic Manners and Social Condition*, op. cit., Volume I, pp. 91-94.

40 Attwood, op. cit., p. 214.

41 Sheperd et al., op. cit., p. 135.

42 Carmichael, op. cit., p. 273.

43 For colonial Brazil, see for example A.R. Russel Wood, "Colonial Brazil", in *Neither Slave nor Free: the Freedom of African Descent in the Slave Societies of the New World*, edited by D. Cohen & J.P. Greene (Baltimore: Johns Hopkins Univ. Press, 1972), pp. 84-133; p. 90.

44 House of Commons Accounts and Papers, Volume XXIX, 1970, No. 698, p. 153.

45 Attwood, op. cit., p. 272.

46 CO 260\16, President Ottley to Hobart January 1802.

47 Heuman, op. cit., p. 4.

48 See H. Klein, "Nineteenth century Brasil", in Cohen & Greene, *Neither Slave nor Free*, op. cit., p. 319.

49 Carmichael, op. cit., pp. 91-94.

50 At this time all the islands enacted legislation placing restrictions on manumissions by requiring large sums of money to be deposited in the Treasury before a Deed could be effected; see for example, CO 262/1, St. Vincent Act No. 7 of 1767, Clause XXV. This was similar to the restrictive legislation of North America; see

E.V. Genovese, "The Slave States of North America", in Cohen and Greene, op. cit., pp. 259-60.

51 See for instance St. Vincent Slave Law of 1767, in House of Commons Accounts and Papers, Vol. XXIV 634 (1789).

52 CO 71/58, Governor Maxwell to Earl Bathurst, 1818.

53 See House of Commons Accounts and Papers, Vol. XXVI (1789), No. 646a, pt. iii: Statement of Laws in Force, Grenada. For a similar practice in North America, see Genovese, op. cit., p. 261.

54 Heuman, op. cit., p. 5.

55 CO 318/76, Grievances of the Free People of Color, Dominica Papers.

56 These statistics are compiled from data in CO 71/58, CO 101/61, CO 260/38, and House of Commons Accounts and Papers, Volume XXII (1826).

57 See Carmichael, op. cit., pp. 82-83.

58 House of Commons Accounts and Papers, Volume XXIX (1790), No. 698, p. 53.

59 CO 318/76, Grievances of the Free People of Color.

60 By an Act passed on September 7th, 1774.

61 Heuman, op. cit., p. 12.

62 CO 262/11, St. Vincent Act, No. 224 of 1820: An Act to repeal an Act entitled 'An Act to regulate vestries in this island', Clause VI.

63 CO 318/76, Grievances of the Free People of Color, Dominica Papers.

64 A.C.C.W.M., I. Purkis to David Bogue, November 1st, 1809.

65 CO318/76, Grievances of the Free People of Color, Dominica Papers.

66 See Russell Wood, "Colonial Brazil" loc. cit., p. 110.

67 CO 71/59, The humble petition of the Free Colored Inhabitants to Earl Bathurst, January 10th, 1822.

68 CO 73/8, Dominica Act No. 66 of 1784, "An Act for the preservation of Game and Fish".

69 CO 262/1, St. Vincent Act No. 7 of 1767, Clauses XXIX, XXX.

70 Co 71/55, Governor Maxwell to Earl Bathurst; Letters of February 4th, and June 2nd, 1818.

71 CO 103/4, No. 53 of 1766. "An Act for establishing a regular night watch in the town of St. George and the suburbs thereof and for erecting a public cage and watch house on the public parade", Clauses V, VI.

72 CO 103/9, No. 53 of 1789. "An Act for the better regulation of the Police of the town of St. George and its neighborhood, and for the more effectual prevention of the sale of rum and other spiritous liquors to the slaves", Clauses 1, 2, 3, 5, 6.

73 Carl Campbell, *Cedulants and Capitulants: The Politics of the Coloured Opposition in the Slave Society of Trinidad 1783-1838* (Port of Spain: Paria Publishing Company, 1992), p1.

74 See H. Klein, "Nineteenth century Brasil", in Cohen and Greene, op. cit., p. 311.

75 CO 260/28, Governor Brisbane of St. Vincent to the Earl of Liverpool; August 17th, 1811.

76 See Goveia, *Slave Society*, op. cit., p. 219.

77 CO 262/3, No. 37of 1776, "An Act for arming the free of this island and forming a Militia".

78 Campbell, op. cit., p. 67.

79 CO 103/2, No. 13 of 1767, "An Act for establishing a Militia for the defence of this island."

80 Heuman, op. cit., p. 27.

81 For Grenada, CO 103/5, No. 64 of 1778, "An Act for establishing...a Militia in this island and the islands of Bequia, Canouan, Union; Dominica"; CO 73/6, No. 19 of 1771, "An Act for forming and establishing and regulating a militia in this island and the islands of Bequia, Canouan, Union, Tobago"; CO 287/3, No. 47 of 1804, "An Act for establishing and regulating a Militia in the island of Tobago".

82 CO 262/9, No. 180 of 1806, "An Act for establishing and regulating a Militia in the islands of St. Vincent, Bequia, Canouan, and the Union".

83 CO 318/76, Grievances of the Free People of Color, Tobago Papers.

84 Knight, *Slave Society in Cuba*, op. cit., p. 97.

85 In a Despatch to the Earl of Bathurst, October 30th, 1823; CO 285/28.

86 House of Commons Accounts and Papers, Volume XXVI (1789), No. 646a pt. iii, in Reply to Query No. 37.

87 House of Commons Accounts and Papers, Volume XXIX (1790), No. 698, p. 153.

88 Knight, op. cit., p. 97.

89 CO 73/8, Dominica Act No. 74 of 1784, Clauses iii, viii.

90 CO 318/76, Grievances of the Free People of Color, St. Vincent Papers.

91 Ibid.

92 See for instance CO 260/29, Population Returns, St. Vincent.

93 Heuman, *Between Black and White*, op. cit., p. 5.

94 CO 287/3 – No. 46 of 1804: An Act to encourage the further introduction of White Inhabitants in the island.

95 In a despatch to Henry Goulbourn, April 6th, 1819; CO 285/24.

96 Campbell, op. cit., p. 62.

97 Goveia, *Slave Society*, pp. 181-82.

98 CO 262/1, St. Vincent Act, No. 7, of 1767, Clause XXVII.

99 CO 318/76, Grievances of the Free People of Color.

100 Campbell, op. cit., p. 68.

101 CO 71/59, Comparative Statement of the slaves, produce, and the annual income of the white and free colored population of Dominica in 1820.

102 See for example CO 71/59, Resolutions at a meeting of the principal free colored inhabitants of Dominica. The executive at the meeting were the large slave plantation owners.

103 CO 71/59, "Comparative Statement..."

104 House of Commons Accounts and Papers, Volume XXVI (1789), No. 646a, pt. iii, in Reply to query No. XXXVII.

105 This information is compiled from Statistical Report for Tobago in 1811; Enclosed in Governor Young to the Earl of Liverpool, October 12th, 1811, CO 285/16.

106 Ibid.

107 Ibid.

108 Ibid.

109 See Anon., Resident, p. 231.

110 House of Commons Accounts and Papers, Volume XXIII (1821); Return of apprenticed Africans.

111 Carmichael, op. cit., pp. 78-79.

112 Heuman, op. cit., p. 9.
113 See Cohen and Greene, op. cit.
114 Heuma, op. cit., p. 9.
115 Campbell supra p. 68.
116 CO 260/29, Population Returns.
117 Evidence of this has been found for Dominica only.
118 See CO 101/34, President MacKenzie to the Duke of Portland, March 1795.
119 Edward Cox, *Free Coloureds in the Slave Societies of St. Kitts and Grenada 1763-1833* (Knoxville: University of Tennessee Press, 1984), p. 150.
120 Ibid.
121 See for example the Petition from the Free Colored inhabitants of Dominica in CO 318/76.
122 Jerome Handler and Arnold Sio, "Barbados" in Cohen and Greene, op. cit., pp. 214-57; p. 256.
123 Heuman, op. cit., p. 30.
124 In a despatch to the Duke of Portland, June 5th, 1800; CO 260/16.
125 Carmichael, op. cit., p. 75.
126 See Campbell, op. cit., p. 56.
127 Charles Peters, *Two Sermons preached at Dominica on the 11th and 13th of April 1800...* (London, 1802), p. 56.
128 CO 318/76, Grievances of the Free People of Colour, Tobago Papers.
129 Ibid., Grenada Papers.
130 Peters, op. cit., p. 57.
131 Anon., A Resident, p. 231.
132 CO 285/8, President Robley to Lord Hobart, January 2nd, 1802.
133 In a petition submitted in 1776, see CO 101/1.
134 CO 71/59, Resolutions of planters and merchants resident in Great Britain and interested in Dominica to the Earl of Bathurst, February 4th, 1822.
135 Ibid.
136 See Carmichael, op. cit., p. 244.
137 Ibid. p. 83.
138 Ibid., pp. 83-84.
139 House of Commons Accounts and Papers, Volume XXVI (1789), No.646a, pt. iii: Replies to queries on slave mortality and longevity.
140 House of Commons Accounts and Papers, Volume XXVI (1789), No. 646a, pt. iii; in reply to Query No. 13.
141 Ibid.
142 CO 101/61, Reverend Nash to Earl Bathurst, October 11th, 1821.
143 See for instance J.D. Fage, *An Introduction to the History of West Africa* (U.K.: Cambridge University Press, 1962), p. 77.
144 CO 285/16, Governor Young to Liverpool, October 12th, 1811.
145 Calculated from Population Returns, 1813; CO 71/48.
146 Sir William Young, "A tour through the several islands of Barbados Antigua and Grenada in the Years 1791 and 1792"; in Bryan Edwards, The History, Civil and Commercial, of the British Colonies in the West Indies, vol. 3 (Philadelphia, 1806), pp. 268-69.
147 Carmichael, op. cit., chap. XII passim.

148 See CO 101/15, 16,17.

149 Goveia, *Slave Society*, op. cit., pp. 244-49.

150 Orlando Patterson, *The Sociology of Slavery: Jamaica 1544-1838* (London: MacGibbon & Kee, 1967), chaps. 6, 7 passim.

151 Edward Brathwaite, *The Folk Culture of the Slaves in Jamaica* (London: New Beacon, 1970).

152 Attwood, *History of Dominica*, op. cit., p. 268.

153 Ibid., pp. 262-63.

154 Ibid.

155 A.W.M.M.S., *Methodist Magazine*, Volume XLV, 1822, pp. 543-45: Extract from Mr. Smedley's Journal.

156 See M.G. Smith, *Kinship and Community in Carriacou* (New Haven and London, 1962), chap. 7.

157 See *Methodist Magazine*, op. cit.

158 Attwood, op. cit., p. 263.

159 See Chapter 8.

160 Carmichael, op. cit., p. 252.

161 House of Commons Accounts and Papers, Volume XXVI (1789), No. 646a, pt. iii: reply of Mr. Spooner to Query No. 22.

162 Attwood, op. cit., p. 263.

163 See *Methodist Magazine*, op. cit.

164 Ibid.

165 House of Commons Accounts and Papers, Volume XXVI (1789), No. 646a, pt, iii: reply of Mr. Spooner to queries, Nos. 22, 23,24,25.

166 Carmichael, op. cit., p. 254.

167 Attwood, op. cit., pp. 269-72.

168 House of Commons Accounts and Papers, Volume XXVI (1789), No. 646a, pt. iii: reply of Mr. Spooner to Queries, Nos. 22,23,24.

169 Brathwaite, *Folk Culture of the Slaves*, p. 10.

170 House of Commons Accounts and Papers, Volume XXVI (1789), No. 646a, pt. iii: reply of Mr. Spooner to queries, Nos. 22,23,24.

171 Ibid.

172 Attwood, op. cit., p. 261.

173 Brathwaite, *Folk Culture*, p. 10.

174 Carmichael; op. cit., p. 293.

175 Sir William Young, "A tour through the Several Islands..." in Bryan Edwards, *The History, Civil and Commercial of the British Colonies...* (London: John Stockdale, 1801), p. 276.

176 Carmichael, op. cit., pp. 292-93.

177 Sir William Young, "A Tour", p. 276.

178 Ibid.

179 Carmichael, op. cit., p. 292.

180 House of Commons Accounts and Papers, Volume XXX (1790), No. 699, p.32.

181 Ibid.

182 House of Commons Accounts and Papers, Volume XXIX (1790), No. 698, p.146.

183 Carmichael, op. cit., p. 77.

184 Goveia, *Slave Society*, p. 249.

185 Carmichael, op. cit., p. 73.

186 Heuman, op., cit., p. 14.

187 Carmichael, op. cit., p. 73.

188 Heuman, op. cit., p. 14.

CHAPTER 8

1 V.L. Oliver, ed., *Caribbeana; Being Miscellaneous Papers Relative to the History, Geneal-ogy, Topography, and Antiquities of the British West Indies* Vol. 3 (London, 1909-1919). See p. 324 for a list of persons licensed to the plantations by the Bishop of London, 1735-1792.

2 Answers to Queries on the State of Religion in 1823: Dominica, CO 71/60, Governor Huntingdon to Earl Bathurst, No. 79 (December 8th); Grenada, CO 101/63, President Paterson to Earl Bathurst, No. 17 (November 6th); St. Vincent, CO 260/40, Governor Brisbane to Earl Bathurst (September 23rd); Tobago, CO 285/28, Governor Robinson to Earl Bathurst (September 29th).

3 Rev. Thomas Coke, *A History of the West Indies containing the Natural, Civil, and Ec-clesiastical History of each Island, with an account of the missions instituted in the islands, from the commencement of their civilizations; but more especially of the missions which have been established by the society late in connection with Rev. John Wesley*, vol. III (Liverpool, 1808), pp. 63-64.

4 CO 71/30, Governor Johnstone to the Duke of Portland, No. 8, May 10th, 1798.

5 CO 260/28, Reverend Guilding of St. Vincent to Governor Brisbane, February 4th, 1811.

6 CO 101/47, Governor Maitland to Castlereagh, No. 23, February 23rd, 1808.

7 CO 71/16, Lieutenant Governor Bruce to Grenville, September 8th, 1789.

8 CO 101/29, Etat de Cures au Services des Catholiques Romans en la present Isle Grenade, August 29, 1789.

9 CO 260/9, Governor Seton to Grenville, No. 76, August 28th, 1789.

10 CO 71/46, Lieutenant Governor Barnes to the Earl of Liverpool, November 19, 1811.

11 CO 71/20, Governor Orde to Grenville, No. 25, February 14th, 1791.

12 CO 71/13, Lieutenant Governor Barnes to Castlereagh, December 8, 1808.

13 CO 71/58, Thimoty Kelly to Earl Bathurst, June 27th, 1821.

14 William Doyle, *An Account of the British Dominions Beyond the Seas* (London, 1770), pp. 38-39.

15 Coke, *History*, vol. I, p. 406.

16 Charles Peters, *Two Sermons preached at Dominica*, pp. 5-6.

17 Ibid., p. 2.

18 *Mrs. Brown's Roseau Gazette, and Dominica Chronicle*, Thursday, April 17th, 1800, quoted in Peters, op. cit., pp. 5-6.

19 *The Dominica Journal or Weekly Intelligencer*, quoted in Peters, op. cit., pp. 5-6.

20 Peters, op. cit., pp. 57-58.

21 F.P. Volume XXXII: Ordination Papers, Windward Islands; *Gentleman's Magazine and Historical Chronicle*, vol. 82, January to June 1812, p. 603.

22 The First Moravian mission in the British West Indies was established in Jamaica in 1754 at the estate of New Carmel in Black River. See Revd J.E. Hutton, *A History of the Moravian Missions* (London, 1923), pp. 51-53.

23 A.M.C.: Copy of Subscriptions for the support of the Moravian Brethren, March 15th, 1789.

24 *Periodical Accounts Relating to the Missions of the... United Brethren*(London, 1790-1831), vol. I: James Walker to La Trobe, February 16th, 1790. An earlier attempt to establish this mission failed (see ibid., pp. 119-20).

25 Ibid., Sir William Young to La Trobe, October 29th, 1798.

26 *Periodical Accounts*, vol. II, 1797.

27 A.M.C.: Diary of the Negro Congregation at Tobago, July 1800 to April 1802.

28 A.M.C.: John Hamilton, Jr to La Trobe, June 23rd, 1803: Minutes of Conferences of the Mission in Tobago, Meeting April 22nd, 1802.

29 "Instructions for the members of the *Unitas Fratrum* who minister in the Gospel among the Heathen" (London, 1784), quoted in Goveia, *Slave Society*, pp. 275-77.

30 Ibid.

31 A.M.C.: Diary of the Negro Congregation at Tobago, July 1800 to April 1802.

32 Minutes of Conferences: Meetings, April 5th, 1800; July 6th, 1800; August 3rd, 1800; August 31st 1800; September, October, November, December, 1800, January 1801.

33 Ibid., Meeting, March 1801.

34 Ibid., House of Commons Accounts and Papers, Volume XXVI, 1789, No. 646a, pt. iii; detached pieces of evidence, No. 2, "An account of the missionary work of the Church of the United Brethren among the slaves in the West Indies".

35 Ibid.

36 A.M.C., Minutes of Conferences: Meeting, November 23rd, 1801.

37 Hutton, op. cit., chap. XIII, passim.

38 House of Commons Accounts and Papers, Volume XXVI, 1789.

39 A.M.C., Diary of the negro congregation at Tobago, July 1800 to April 1802.

40 *Periodical Accounts*, Volume ii: extract from Brother Schirmer's Diary.

41 A.M.C., Diary, July 1800 to April 1802.

42 *Periodical Accounts*, Volume iii: Extract of a letter from Brother Church, January 8th, 1802.

43 Richard Lovett, *History of the London Missionary Society, 1795-1895*, 2 vols. (London, 1899), vol. i, p. 3.

44 Ibid., p. 30.

45 Ibid., pp. 38-39.

46 A.C.C.W.M. Box: West Indies - Tobago, Letter No. IV: George Baines to Joseph Hardcastle, Treasurer of the Missionary Society, August 28th, 1807.

47 Ibid., No. VI: Memo of a Conversation between Mr. George Baines and Mr. Robley, on the subject of a mission in Tobago; December 9th, 1807.

48 A.C.C.W.M. Box 3: Board Minutes 1805-1809. Meeting, December 21st, 1807, pp. 175-76.

49 A.C.C.W.M. Box: West Indies - Tobago; Folder i, Jacket B, No. VIII; Elliott to Reverend Burder, June 26th, 1808.

50 Ibid., Elliott to Joseph Hardcastle, August 8th, 1808.

51 Ibid., Elliott to the Directors, July 1808.

52 A.C.C.W.M., Purkis to the Directors, August 7th, 1809.

53 Ibid.

54 Ibid.

55 Ibid.

56 A.C.C.W.M., Board Minutes, Book No. 5, 1809-1813.

57 A.C.C.W.M., Elliott to Reverend Burder; June 27th, 1810.

58 A.C.C.W.M., Reverend Burder to Elliott; February 18th, 1812.

59 A.C.C.W.M., *Considerations and Regulations respecting Missionaries in connection with the Missionary Society*, February 11th, 1811; Rule ii.

60 A.C.C.W.M., Elliott to the Directors, December 7th, 1808 (*emphasis mine*).

61 A.C.C.W.M., A continuance of my journal from July 26th to December 7th, 1808.

62 A.C.C.W.M., Elliott to Reverend Burder and Joseph Hardcastle, January 28, 1812.

63 A.C.C.W.M., *Reports of the London Missionary Society from its formation in the year 1795 to 1812 inclusive*, reprinted from the original Reports, volume I, 1795-1814; Report at sixteenth meeting, May 10th, 1810.

64 Coke, *History*, Volume iii, p. 64.

65 Ibid., pp. 253-57.

66 Ibid., pp. 353-55.

67 Coke, *History*, Volume ii, pp. 72-73.

68 Ibid., pp. 259-66.

69 A.W.M.M.S., *Methodist Magazine*, Volume XXIII, 1800: Extract of a letter from Mr. Hallett to Dr. Coke.

70 A.W.M.M.S. Thomas Coke, *An Account of the Rise, Progress and Present State of the Methodist Missions* (London, 1804).

71 Ibid.

72 A.W.M.M.S., *Ariminian Magazine,*Volume XVII, 1794: Extract of a letter from Mr. Bishop, April 19th, 1793.

73 Coke, *An Account of the Rise*, op. cit.: Extract of a letter from Mr. Shipley, January 14th, 1804.

74 Coke, *History*, Volume ii, pp. 353-57.

75 *A Continuation of the Rev. Dr. Coke's Third Tour through the West Indies in a letter to the Rev. J. Wesley* (London, 1791): Letter dated January 4th, 1791.

76 CO 260/12, Dundas to Governor Seton, No. 9, October 27th, 1793; Dr. Coke to Pitt, January 27th, 1793.

77 A.W.M.M.S., *The Report of the Executive Committee for the Management of the Missions* (London, 1816).

78 Ibid.

79 A.W.M.M.S., *The Report of the Wesleyan Methodist Missionary Society, 1819*.

80 A.W.M.M.S., *The Report of the Wesleyan Methodist Missionary Society, 1823*.

81 A.W.M.M.S., *The Report of the Wesleyan Methodist Missionary Society, 1820*.

82 A.W.M.M.S., *The Report of the Wesleyan Methodist Missionary Society, 1823*.

83 A.W.M.M.S., *Methodist Magazine*, Volume XXXVIII (1815): 714-16.

84 A.W M.M.S., *The First Report of the General Wesleyan Methodist Missionary Society, 1818*.

85 See, for instance, Thomas Coke, *To the Benevolent Subscribers for the Support of the Missions Carried on by Voluntary Contributions in the British Islands in the West Indies for the Benefit of the Negroes and Caribs* (London, 1789).

86 A.W.M.M.S., *Reports of the Wesleyan Methodist Missionary Society 1820 and 1821*: Account of donations and subscriptions.
87 A.W.M.M.S., *The Report of the Executive Committee for the Management of the Missions, 1816*: Letter from Mr. Dace, June 22nd, 1816.
88 A.W.M.M.S., *The Report of the Wesleyan Methodist Missionary Society, 1820*.
89 Ibid.
90 Ibid.
91 Ibid.
92 A.W.M.M.S., *Methodist Magazine*,Volume XLIII (1820): Extract of a letter from Messrs. Shrewsbury and Goy, Grenada, January 22nd, 1810.
93 A.W.M.M.S., *Methodist Magazine*, Volume XLII (1819): Letter of October 7th, 1818.
94 A.W.M.M.S., *The Report of the Wesleyan Methodist Missionary Society, 1820*.
95 Richard Watson, *A defence of the Wesleyan Methodist Missions in the West Indies* (London, 1817).
96 A.W.M.M.S., *Instructions delivered by the Committee to the Wesleyan Missionaries*, No. 1.
97 Ibid., No. VI (*emphasis mine*).
98 In 1816 after the Barbados Slave Insurrection the St. Vincent Legislature passed a Law requiring each missionary to put up $500 with two sureties while swearing that he would preach no doctrines subversive of the Establishment. But the Act was disallowed – see CO 260/3, Legislative Council Minutes, May 3rd, 1816.
99 A.W.M.M.S., *The Report of the Wesleyan Methodist Missionary Society, 1820*.
100 A.W.M.M.S., *The Report of the Wesleyan Methodist Missionary Society, 1822*.
101 A.W.M.M.S., *The Report of the Wesleyan Methodist Missionary Society, 1823*.
102 A.W.M.M.S., *Methodist Magazine*, Volume XXXIX (1816): Letter from Mr. Thomas Dakin to Mr. Wood, Dominica, July 22nd, 1816.
103 Goveia, *Slave Society*, p. 308.
104 A.W.M.M.S.,*The Report of the Wesleyan Methodist Missionary Society, 1820*.
105 A.W.M.M.S., *The Report of the Wesleyan Methodist Missionary Society, 1819. Methodist Magazine*, Volume XLII (1819).
106 C.O. 71/57, Governor Whittingham to Henry Goulbourne, August 22nd, 1820.
107 A.W.M.M.S., *The Report of the Wesleyan Methodist Missionary Society, 1819*.
108 Ibid.: Extract of a Letter from a proprietor in St. Vincent (*emphasis mine*).
109 A.W.M.M.S., *The Report of the Executive Committee for Management of the Missions, 1816*.
110 A.W.M.M.S., *The Report of the Wesleyan Methodist Missionary Society, 1820*: Extract of a Letter from Mr. Ross at Grenada, July 20th, 1820 (*emphasis mine*).
111 George Rose, *A Letter on the Means and Importance of Converting the Slaves to Christianity* (London, 1823).
112 A.W.M.M.S., *The Report of the Wesleyan Methodist Missionary Society, 1820* : Extract of a Letter from Mr. Larcum, September 23rd, 1820.
113 George Rose, *A Letter on the Means and Importance*, op. cit.
114 See, for instance, CO 285/28, Petition from the Legislature of Tobago to the House of Commons, April 1823.
115 See Kenneth Stamp, *The Peculiar Institution, Slavery in the Antebellum South* (New York: Alfred Knopf, 1956), pp. 156-62.

CHAPTER 9

1 Hilary Beckles, *Black rebellion in Barbados: The struggle against slavery 1627-1838* (Bridgetown: Antilles Publications, 1984), p. 6.

2 Elsa Goevia, *Slave Society in the British Leeward Islands* (New Haven: Yale Univ. Press, 1965), p. 198.

3 D. B. Gaspar, *Bondsmen and rebels: A study of master-slave relations in Antigua* (Baltimore: Johns Hopkins University Press, 1985), p. 172.

4 John Blassingame, *The slave community: Plantation life in the antebellum South* (Oxford University Press, 1972), chap 5 passim.

5 M. Morrisey, *Slave women in the New World: Gender stratification in the Caribbean* (KA: Univ Press of Kansas, 1989), pp. 153-56.

6 B. Bush, *Slave women in Caribbean society 1650-1838* (Kingston: Heinemann Publishers, 1990), p. 56.

7 CO 260/40, Report of both houses of the legislature in answer to Earl Bathurst dispatches of May 28th and July 9th, 1823: .enclosed in Governor Brisbane's No. 119 to Bathurst, September 20th 1823

8 See Beckles, *Black rebellion*, op. cit. See also Beckles, "Caribbean anti-slavery: The self-liberation ethos of enslaved Blacks", in Beckles and Shepherd, eds. *Caribbean slave society and economy: A student reader* (Kingston: Ian Randle Publishers, 1991), pp. 363-71.

9 See CO 101/18, Report on State of Tobago, June 1771 to December 1775; CO285/13, Statistical report.

10 G.K. Lewis, *Main currents in Caribbean thought: The historical evolution of Caribbean society in its ideological aspects 1492-1900* (Baltimore: Johns Hopkins Univ. Press, 1983);see also Beckles, "Caribbean anti slavery", op. cit..

11 R.T. Gurr, *Why Men Rebel* (Princeton, NJ: Princeton University Press, 1970).

12 Ibid., p. 11.

13 Ibid., p. 4.

14 Ibid.

15 Ibid.

16 Ibid., pp. 3-13 passim.

17 Ibid.

18 See McKillan, "Social movements: A review of the field", in Robert R. Evans, ed., *Social movements: A reader and source book* (Chicago: Rand McNally College Pub. Co., 1973), p. 5.

19 Ibid.

20 Mckillan, "Social movements", in Evans, op. cit. passim

21 Ibid., pp. 16-19.

22 J.E. Greene, "Contradictory aspects of protest and change in the Caribbean". Paper presented at International Studies Association Conference, Los Angeles California.

23 Beckles, "Caribbean anti-slavery", op. cit., p. 363.

24 Bush, *Slave women*, op. cit., p. 74.

25 Gaspar, *Bondmen and rebels*, op. cit., p. 175.

26 CO 101/15, Governor Melville to Hillsborough, No. 28, January 1st, 1771.

27 T. Attwood, *History of Dominica* (London, 1791), pp. 48-49.

28   CO 71/9 Governor Orde to Sydney, December 15th,1785.

29   Ibid.

30   CO 71/50, President Lucas and enclosures to the Earl of Bathurst, August 28th, 1815.

31   CO 71/30, Captain Monroe to Governor Johnstone, December 12th, 1797.

32   M. Craton, *Testing the chains: Resistance to slavery in the British West Indies* (Ithaca, NY: Cornell University Press, 1982), p. 231.

33   R. Price, ed., *Maroon societies: Rebel slave communities in the Americas* (New York Anchor Books, 1973).

34   CO 71/9, Governor Orde to Sydney, 1785.

35   CO 71/32, Governor Johnstone to the Duke of Portland, September 4th, 1800.

36   CO 71/9, Governor Orde to Sydney, December 15th, 1785.

37   Ibid.

38   CO 71/49, Governor Ainslie to the Earl of Bathurst, March 21st, 1814.

39   CO 71/9, Governor Orde to Sydney, December 15th, 1785.

40   Ibid.

41   CO 71/9, Sydney to Governor Orde, February 7th, 1786.

42   CO 71/10, Governor Orde to Sydney, April 16th, 1786.

43   CO 71/27, Minutes of Meetings of the Dominica Council, October 15th and December 9th, 1794.

44   CO 71/30, Governor Johnstone and enclosures to the Duke of Portland, December 16th, 1797.

45   Ibid.

46   Ibid.

47   [A Resident], *Sketches and recollections of the West Indies* (London, 1828), pp. 86-89.

48   CO 71/30, Governor Johnstone to the Duke of Portland, February 10th, 1798.

49   CO 71/32, Governor Johnstone to the Duke of Portland, September 4th, 1800.

50   CO 71/33, Governor Johnstone to the Duke of Portland, January 7th, 1801.

51   Craton, *Testing the chains*, op. cit., p.231.

52   CO 71/49, Governor Ainslie to the Earl of Bathurst, June 26th, 1814.

53   This proclamation is to be found in CO 71/49.

54   CO 71/49, Governor Ainslie and enclosures to the Earl of Bathurst: Letters of March 21st and June 26th, 1814.

55   CO 71/49, Governor Ainslie to the Earl of Bathurst, March 21st, 1814.

56   CO 71/49, Proclamations of June 1st and October 3rd, 1813.

57   CO 71/50, Return of slaves killed, taken and surrendered between May 10th, 1813 and November 22nd, 1814.

58   Craton, *Testing the chains*, op. cit. p. 232.

59   CO 71/32, Governor Johnstone to the Duke of Portland, September 4th, 1800.

60   CO 71/49, Governor Ainslie to the Earl of Bathurst, March 21st, 1814.

61   CO 71/49, Address of Governor Ainslie to the Council and Assembly, March 2nd, 1814.

62   Craton, op. cit., p. 232.

63   CO 101/33, President Williams to Dundas, December 28th, 1792.

64   CO 101/33, Lieutenant Governor Home to Dundas, August 1st, 1794.

65   CO 71/26, Lieutenant Governor Bruce to the Duke of Portland, No. 3; October 18th, 1794.

66 See CO 71/27, Privy Council Minutes, October 9, 1794.

67 CO 71/27, Governor Hamilton to the Duke of Portland, No. 15, March 27th, 1795.

68 House of Commons Accounts and Papers, Volume 19 (1816), No. 226: An Act for establishing regulations respecting slaves arriving in this island, or resident therein, except such as are imported direct from the coast of Africa.

69 CO 285/3, Governor Lindsay to the King, April 18th, 1795.

70 See [A Grenada Planter?], *A brief enquiry into the causes of and conduct pursued by the colonial government in quelling the Insurrection in Grenada from its commencement on the night of March 2, to the arrival of General Nicholls on April 14, 1795* (London, 1796).

71 CO 101/34, President MacKenzie to the Duke of Portland, March 28th, 1795.

72 Ibid.

73 See, for instance, CO 260/3, Governor Lincoln to Lord North, August 6th, 1783.

74 CO 101/34, Arretts: Les commissaries délégués par la convention nationale aux isles du vent.

75 See for instance, C.O. 260/17, President Ottley to the Duke of Portland, No. 29, July 8th, 1795.

76 CO 71/27, Governor Hamilton to the Duke of Portland, No. 29, July 8, 1795.

77 CO 71/27, Governor Hamilton to the Duke of Portland: Letters of July 8 and July 23, 1795.

78 V. Shepherd, B. Brereton, B. Bailey, *Engendering history: Caribbean women in historical perspective* (Kingston: Ian Randle Publishers, 1995), pp. 149-50.

79 CO 285/8; President Robley to Lord Hobart; January 2, 1802.

80 CO 285/2, *The Tobago Gazette*, January 1st, 1802; CO 285/7, Brigadier Carmichael to Lord Hobart, January 15th, 1802.

81 CO 285/8, Report of a Court appointed for the trial of prisoners concerned in the late insurrection.

82 Ibid.

83 Ibid.

84 CO 71/20, The examination of Polinaire, a free mulatto at the Chambers of the President of the Council, February 7th, 1791.

85 Ibid.

86 *The Caribbean Register*, March 26th, 1791, CO 71/20.

87 CO 71/19, Governor Orde to Grenville, No. 12, February 3rd, 1791.

88 CO 71/20, Governor Orde to Grenville, March 27th, 1791.

89 In Minutes of Meetings of the West India Merchants and Planters, Volume 1, April 5th, 1791.

90 CO 71/23, Governor Orde to Sydney, April 13th, 1788.

91 C. O. 71/14; Governor Orde to Sydney, April 13th, 1788.

92 A.C. Carmichael, *Domestic manners and social condition of the white, colored, and Negro population of the West Indies*, 2 vols (London, 1833), p. 244.

93 CO 285/2, Governor Young and enclosures to Castlereagh, November 16th, 1807.

94 Ibid.

95 Ibid.

96 CO 71/52, Report of the Committee of the Council and the Assembly on the Registry Bill, February 14th, 1816.

97 See Beckles, *Black Rebellion in Barbados*, op. cit.

98 CO 260/33, Governor Brisbane to Earl Bathurst, No. 153, March 14th, 1816.

99   CO 101/56, Governor Riall to Earl Bathurst, No. 14, October 4th, 1816.

100 See, for example, CO285/21, President Campbell of Tobago to Earl Bathurst, No. 2, August 17th, 1816.

101 See, for example, CO 260/40, Report of both houses of the Legislature of St. Vincent in answer to Earl Bathurst's despatch of May 28th and July 9th, 1823.

102 Carmichael, *Domestic manners*, op. cit., p. 246.

103 CO 71/61, Governor Huntingdon to Earl Bathurst; January 11th, 1824.

CHAPTER 10

1   F.W. Knight, *Slave society in Cuba during the nineteenth century* (Madison: Univ. of Wisconsin Press, 1970), pp. 13, 53, 70.

2   See chap. 1.

3   The discussion of the social structure of the British Windward Islands which follows is based on some of the main findings of chap. 7.

4   Knight, *Slave society in Cuba*, op. cit., pp. 76, 82-83.

5   For the detailed evidence on which this conclusion is based see chap. 6.

6   J. Blassingame, *The slave community: Plantation life in the antebellum south* (NY: Oxford Univ. Press, 1995), p. 125.

7   See chap. 8 passim.

8   See, for example, Goveia, *Slave society in the British Leeward islands to the end of the eighteenth century* (New Haven: Yale Univ. Press, 1965), cf. chapter. on the Christian missions.

9   R.W. Fogel and S.L. Engerman, *Time on the cross: The economics of American Negro slavery* (Boston: Little Brown, 1974).

10   H.G. Gutman, *Slavery and the numbers game: A critique of 'Time on the Cross'* (Urbana: University of Illinois Press), 1975.

11   See chap. 5 passim.

12   Knight, op. cit., pp. 30-34.

13   See chap. 9.

14   See chap. 2.

15   Goveia, *Slave Society*: Introduction.

16   See chap. 9.

17   See Tannenbaum, *Slave and Citizen The Negro in the Americas* (NY: Alfred Knopf, 1946). For this debate see Foner and Genovese, eds.,*Slavery in the new world: A reader in comparative history* (NJ: Prentice Hall, l969).

18   M. Harris, "The Myth of the Friendly Master", in Foner & Genovese, *Slavery in the new world*, op. cit., pp. 38-47, p. 43.

19   E.V. Genovese, "The treatment of slaves in different countries: Problems in the application of the comparative method", in Foner and Genovese, *Slavery in the new world*, op. cit., p. 202, pp. 302-310.

20   For authoritative discussions of slavery in the American South, see Blassingame, *The slave community*, op. cit.; and Genovese, *'Roll Jordan Roll': The world the slaves made* (NY: Pantheon Books, 1974).

21   See Knight, *Slave society in Cuba*, op. cit., chap. IV. passim.

22 According to Genovese, in the period 1831–1861, "the condition of the slaves worsened with respect to access to freedom and the promise of citizenship" (Genovese, 1974), pp. 50-51.

23 Tannenbaum, *Slave and citizen*, op. cit., p. 69.

24 D.B. Davis, *The problem of slavery in Western culture* (Ithaca, New York: Cornell Univ. Press, 1966), p. 54.

25 Genovese, "The treatment of slaves", in Foner and Genovese, *Slavery in the new world*, op. cit., pp. 203-204.

26 H. Klein, "Nineteenth century Brasil", in Cohen & Greene, *Neither Slave nor Free*, op. cit., p. 317.

27 Ibid., pp. 313-17.

28 Harris, "The origin of the descent rule", in Foner and Genovese, *Slavery in the new world*, op. cit., pp. 48-59, 52-53.

29 See chap. 7.

30 These totals are calculated from:
CO 71/57: Report on Slaves manumitted, 1808-1821.
CO 71/57: Return of Manumissions, 1817-1830.
CO 285/27: Report on Manumissions effected, Negro. marriages, Slaves escheated to the Crown and other Manumissions, 1808-1821.
CO 285/39: Return of Manumissions, 1807-1830.
CO 260/38: Manumissions, 1808-1821.

31 Cox, op. cit., p. 154

32 Ibid., p. 147.

SELECT BIBLIOGRAPHY

Guides:

Ragatz, L.J. *A Guide to the Official Correspondence of the Governors of the British West Indies with the Bibliography*. Secretary of State 1763-1833. London, n.d.

_____. *A Check List of House of Commons Sessional Papers relating to the British West Indian Slave Trade and Slavery 1763-1834*. London, 1923.

_____. *A Guide for the Study of British Caribbean History 1763-1834*. Washington, D.C., 1932.

Ragatz, L.J., and Mary P. Ragatz. *A Guide for the Study of British Caribbean History 1763–1834, Including the Abolition and Emancipation Movements*. Washington, US Govt Print. Off., 1932.

Work, M.N. *A Bibliography of the Negro in Africa and America*. New York: The H.W. Wilson Company, 1928.

The following guide proved useful for information on clergymen and missionaries of the established Church:

Manross, W.W. *The Fulham Papers in the Lambeth Palace Library: American Colonial Section, Calendar and Indexes*. Oxford: Clarendon Press, 1965.

Standard Modern Works

Of the modern books, articles and pamphlets consulted, those which proved the most useful were:

Beckles, H. *Black Rebellion in Barbados: the Struggle against Slavery, 1627-1838*. Bridgetown, Barbados: Antilles Publications, 1984.

_____. *Centering Woman: Gender Discourses in Caribbean Slave Society*. Kingston, Jamaica: Ian Randle Publishers, 1999.

_____, and V. Shepherd. *Caribbean Slave Society: a Student Reader*. Kingston, Jamaica: Ian Randle Publishers, 1991.

Bemis, S.F. *Jay's Treaty: a Study in Commerce and Diplomacy*. Westport, Conn.: Greenwood Press, 1962.

Blassingame, J. *The Slave Community: Plantation Life in the Antebellum South*. New York: Oxford University Press, 1972.

Boxer, C.R. *The Golden Age of Brazil: Growing Pains of a Colonial Society, 1695–1750*. New York: St Martin's Press, 1995.

Braithwaite, E. *Folk Culture of the Slaves in Jamaica*. London: New Beacon, 1970.

_____. *The Development of Creole Society in Jamaica*. Oxford: Clarendon Press, 1971.

Bush, B. *Slave Women in Caribbean Society, 1650–1838*. Kingston: Heinemann Publishers (Caribbean); Bloomington: Indiana University Press; London: J. Currey, 1990.

Campbell, C. *Cedulants and Capitulants: the Politics of the Colored Opposition in the Slave Society of Trinidad 1783-1838*. Port of Spain: Paria Publishing Company, 1992.

Cohen, D., and J.P. Greene, eds. *Neither Slave nor Free: the Freedman of African Descent in the Slave Societies of the New World*. Baltimore: Johns Hopkins University Press, 1972.

Cox, E. *Free Coloureds in the Slave Societies of St. Kitts and Grenada 1763–1833*. Knoxville: University of Tennessee Press, 1984.

Craton, M. *Testing the Chains: Resistance to Slavery in the British West Indies*. Ithaca, N.Y.: Cornell University Press, 1982.

Davis, D.B. *The Problem of Slavery in Western Culture*. Ithaca, N.Y.: Cornell University Press, 1966.

Evans, R.R., ed. *Social movements: A reader and source book*. Chicago: Rand McNally College Pub. Co., 1973.

Fage, J.D. *An Introduction to the History of West Africa*. Cambridge [Eng.] University Press, 1962.

Fogel, R.W., and S.L. Engerman. *Time on the Cross: the Economics of American Negro Slavery*. Boston: Little, Brown, 1974.

Foner, L., and E.D. Genovese, eds. *Slavery in the New World: a Reader in Comparative History*. Englewood Cliffs, N.J.: Prentice Hall, 1969.

Gaspar, D.B. *Bond men and Rebels: a Study of Master-Slave Relations in Antigua with Implications for British-America*. Baltimore: Johns Hopkins University Press, 1985.

Genovese, E.V. *Roll Jordan Roll: the World the Slaves Made*. New York: Pantheon Books, 1974.

Goveia, E.V. *Slave Society in the British Leeward Islands to the End of the Eighteenth Century*. New Haven: Yale University Press, 1965.

_____. *A Study on the Historiography of the British West Indies to the End of the Nineteenth Century*. Washington, D.C.: Howard University Press, 1956.

_____. *The West Indian Slave Laws of the Eighteenth Century*. Barbados: Caribbean Universities Press, 1970.

Gurr, R.T. *Why Men Rebel?* Princeton, NJ: Princeton University Press, 1970.

Gutman, H.G. *Slavery and the Numbers Game: a Critique of Time on the Cross*. Urbana: University of Illinois Press, 1975.

Herskovits, M. *The Myth of the Negro Past*. Boston: Beacon Press, 1956.

Heuman, G. *Between Black and White: Race, Politics and the Free Coloreds in Jamaica 1792–1865*. Westport, Conn: Greenwood Press, 1981.

Higham, C.S.S. The General Assembly of the Leeward Islands. *English Historical Review* XLI (1926): 190-209.

Hutton, J.E. *A History of the Moravian Missions*. London, 1923.

James, C.L.R. *The Black Jacobins: Toussaint L'Ouverture and the San Domingo Revolution*. New York: Vintage Books, 1963.

Knight, F.W. *Slave Society in Cuba during the Nineteenth Century*. Madison: University of Wisconsin Press, 1970.

Le Page, R.B. *Jamaican Creole: an Historical Introduction to Jamaican Creole.* London: Macmillan; New York: St Martin's Press, 1960.

Marx, K. Preface and Introduction to *A Contribution to the Critique of Political Economy.* Peking: Foreign Languages Press, 1976.

Marx, K., and F. Engels. *Das Kapital: a Critique of Political Economy.* Chicago: H. Regnery, 1970.

Morrissey, M. *Slave Women in the New World: Gender Stratification in the Caribbean.* Lawrence, Kan.: University Press of Kansas, 1989.

Pares, R. *Merchants and Planters.* Cambridge [Eng.]: Published for the Economic History Review at the University Press, 1960.

_____. *Yankees and Creoles: the Trade between North America and the Caribbean before the American Revolution.* Cambridge: Harvard University Press, 1956.

Patterson, O. *The Sociology of Slavery: Jamaica 1655-1838.* London: MacGibbon & Kee, 1967.

Penson, L.M., Dame. *The Colonial Agents of the British West Indies: a Study in Colonial Administration, mainly in the Eighteenth Century.* London: University of London Press, 1924.

Pitman, F.W. *The Development of the British West Indies, 1700-1763.* New Haven: Yale University Press, 1917.

Price, R., ed. *Maroon Societies: Rebel Slave Communities in the Americas.* New York: Anchor Books, 1973.

Ragatz, L.J. *The Fall of the Planter Class in the British Caribbean, 1763-1833: a Study in Social and Economic History.* New York: Octagon Books, 1928.

_____. *Statistics for the Study of British Caribbean Economic History 1763-1833.* London: Bryan Edwards Press, 1927.

Rousseau, J-J. *The Social Contract, and Discourses.* New York: Dutton, 1950.

Shepherd, V. et al. *Engendering History: Caribbean Women in Historical Perspective.* Kingston, Jamaica: Ian Randle Publishers, 1995.

Smith, A. *The Wealth of Nations* Vol. 1. London: Meuthen, 1961.

Smith, M.G. *Kinship and Community in Carriacou.* New Haven and London: Yale Univ. Press, 1962.

_____. *The Plural Society in the British West Indies.* London: Yale Univ. Press, 1965.

Stampp, Kenneth M. *The Peculiar Institution: Slavery in the Ante-bellum South.* New York: Alfred Knopf, 1956.

Tannenbaum, F. *Slave and Citizen: The Negro in the Americas.* New York: A. A. Knopf, 1946.

Thomas, Aquinas Saint. *Summa Theologica.* Romae: Ex Typographia Forzani et S., 1922.

Williams, E. *Capitalism and Slavery.* Chapel Hill: Univ. of North Carolina Press, 1944.

_____. *A History of the People of Trinidad and Tobago.* Port of Spain: P.N.M. Publishing Company, 1962.

Wrong, H. H. *Government of the West Indies* Oxford: The Clarendon Press, 1923.

Manuscript Records

The basic materials for this study were collected from among the records available in the Public Record Office, London. My most important sources were the volumes of original correspondence, sessional papers, acts, and entry books of commissions, instructions and correspondence. About 300 volumes were consulted. Of these, the most important were:

Original Correspondence – Board of Trade

Dominica, Grenada, St. Vincent – CO 101/1, CO 101/3

Tobago – CO 101/1, CO 101/3, CO 285/1

Original Correspondence – Secretary of State

West Indies: CO 318/76. This volume contains papers dealing with the disabilities and grievances of the free people of color and is of invaluable aid to the researcher of British West Indian social history during the period of slavery.

Dominica: CO 101/9 to CO 101/15; CO 71/2 to CO 71/61; CO 71/69, CO 71/75

Grenada: CO 101/9 to CO 101/63,CO 101/66, CO 101/75

St. Vincent: CO 101/9 to CO 101/23; CO 260/3 to CO 260/40; CO 260/42.

Tobago: CO 101/9 to CO 101/24; CO 285/1 to CO 285/28; CO 285/39.

Sessional Papers – Minutes of Councils and Assemblies

Dominica: Papers bound in separate volumes:

CO 74/9

Papers also bound in the following volumes of original correspondence:

CO 71/8

CO 71/9

CO 71/16

CO 71/21

CO 71/24

CO 71/25

CO 71/27

CO 71/40

Grenada: Papers bound in the following volumes of original correspondence:

CO 101/19

CO 101/29

CO 101/45

St. Vincent: Papers bound in separate volumes:

CO 260/3

Papers also bound in the following volumes of original correspondence:

CO 260/6

CO 260/10

CO 260/11

CO 260/12

CO 260/18

CO 260/20

Tobago: Papers bound in separate volumes:

CO 288/10

Papers also bound in the following volumes of original correspondence:

CO 101/14

Acts

Dominica: CO 73/5, CO 73/6, CO 73/8, CO 73/9, CO 73/10, CO 73/11, CO 73/12, CO 73/13

Grenada: CO 103/2, CO 103/3, CO 103/4, CO 103/5, CO 103/6, CO 103/9, CO 103/11

St. Vincent: CO 262/1, CO 262/3, CO 262/4, CO 262/5, CO 262/6, CO 262/9, CO 262/11

Tobago: CO 287/1, CO 287/3, CO 287/4

Copies of acts are also to be occasionally found bound in the volumes of original correspondence.

Entry books of commissions, instructions and correspondence

Dominica: CO 72/11

Grenada: CO 102/1

St. Vincent: CO 261/9/. This volume covering the period 1763 to 1804 also contains records of correspondence between the planters and the Colonial Agent and between the Agents and the last administration. A large section is devoted to representations from the planters to the administration concerning the cultivation of lands made vacant by the expulsion of the Black Caribs and the reactions of British policy makers.

The records of the proceedings of the Commissioners for the sale and disposal of lands are also preserved in the Public Record Office. The following volumes were consulted:

CO 76/9, CO I06/9, CO 106/10, CO 106/11, CO 106/12

Blue Books of Statistics

Dominica: CO 76/13, CO 76/14

Grenada: CO 106/17

St. Vincent: CO 265/6

Tobago: CO 290/8

West India Committee records

Minutes of the Meetings of the West Indian Merchants, Volume 1 (April 1769 to April 1779)

Minutes of the Meetings of West India Merchants, Volume 1V (March 1794 to December 1802)

Minutes of the Meetings of West India Merchants and Planters, Volume 1 (May 1785 to December 1792)

Private papers

P.R.O. London: Papers relating to the government of Dominica, Grenada, St. Vincent and Tobago 1761-1763, by Lord Egermont.

West India Committee Archives, London: Letters to Colonel Seton, Governor of St. Vincent, from various agents in Grenada

The Library of the Royal Commonwealth Society, London:

MSS 745 – Collection of original documents, account books and map relating to the West India Properties of the Gregg Family notably Hillsborough Estate in Dominica, 1795-1899

Rhodes House Library, Oxford:

Correspondence relating to the Young Estates in the West Indies and claims for compensation, 1768-1835. 6 Vols. of which Vols. 1, IV, V and VI proved the most useful

Printed Sources

Parliamentary papers:

House of Commons Accounts and Papers:[on microfilm and microfice at University of West Indies Library Mona Jamaica]

Vol. XXVI (1789), No. 646a

Vol. XXIX (1790), No. 698

Vol. XXX (1790), No. 699

Vol. XXIV (1790-91), Nos. 745-748.

Vol. XLV (1798), No. 931

Vol. XLVIII (1798-1799), Nos. 967a, 967b

Vol. X (1804), No. 119

Vol. XIX (1816), No. 226

Vol. XVII (1818), No. 251

Vol. XXVI (1826-27)

Vol. XXI (1830), No. 582

Of these the most important single volume for my purposes was Vol. XXVI (1789), No. 646a, part 111 which contains the Report of the Lords of the Committee of the Privy Council which investigated the slave trade and the condition of slaves in the British West Indies. This report along with the evidence of witnesses before Parliamentary Committees in Vols. XXIX and XXX

(1790), and XXIV (1790-91), is of invaluable aid for an understanding of the treatment and condition of slaves in the British West Indies.

House of Commons Reports

Vol. II (1801-1802), No. 25:

Report from the Select Committee to whom the proprietors of estates in the island of Grenada was referred.

Report from the committee on the petition … respecting losses by fire at Roseau.

Vol. III (1812-1813), No. 182:

Report from the Select Committee of persons interested in estates in St. Vincent.

Laws and legal commissions

The Laws of Grenada and the Grenadines from 1763 to 1805. London, 1808.

The Laws of the Colony of Dominica commencing from its earliest establishment to the close of the year 1818, and tables of several Acts. Rousseau, 1818.

Sir Fortunatus Dwarris, Substance of three reports of the Commissioners of Enquiry into the Administration of civil and criminal justice in the West Indies. London, 1827.

Materials on Jurisprudence

Dworkin, R.M. *Taking Rights Seriously.* London: Duckworth, 1978.

Freeman, M.D., and D. Lloyd of Hampstead, Baron. *Lloyd's Introduction to Jurisprudence.* 6th edn. London: Sweet and Maxwell, 1994.

Gibson, M. Pluralism, social engineering and some aspects of law in the Caribbean. *Bulletin of Eastern Caribbean Affairs* 10, no. 3 (1984): 56-87.

Harris, J.W. *Legal Philosophies.* London: Butterworths, 1980.

Kelsen, H. *General Theory of Law and State.* Cambridge, Mass.: Harvard University Press, 1946.

Marx, K. Preface to *Contribution to a Critique of Political Economy.* New York: International Publishers, 1967.

Pound, R. *An Introduction to the Philosophy of Law.* New Haven: Yale University Press, 1974.

_____. *Outlines of Lectures on Jurisprudence.* Cambridge: Harvard University Press, 1943.

_____. The scope and purpose of sociological jurisprudence. *Harvard Law Review* 25 (1911).

_____. *Social Control through Law.* New Haven [Conn.]: Published for Indiana University [by] Yale University Press, 1942.

Quinney, R. *Criminal Justice in America: a Critical Understanding.* Boston: Little, Brown, 1974.

Sumner, C. *Reading Ideologies: an Investigation in to the Marxist Theory of Ideology and Law.* London; New York: Academic Press, 1979.

Contemporary historical and descriptive accounts, articles, and later nineteenth century works. Of these, the most important was Volume 1 of the following work:

Carmichael, A.C., Mrs. *Domestic Manners and Social Condition of the White, colored, and Negro Population of the West Indies.* 2 Vols. London, 1833.

The other works which proved useful, some for general and others for particular points of reference, were as follows:

[A Grenada Planter]. *A brief enquiry into the causes of and conduct pursued by the Colonial government for quelling the insurrection in Grenada from its commencement on the night of March 2nd, to the arrival of General Nicholls on April 14th 1795.* London, 1796.

[A Resident]. *Sketches and Recollections of the West Indies.* London, 1828.

A general return of the number of slaves and the quantity of Produce made on the several estates in St. Vincent 1801–1824, Compiled from official returns. Kingston, 1825.

Attwood, T. *History of Dominica.* London, 1791.

Byers, J., *Reference to the plan of St. Vincent,* London, 1777.

Coleridge, H.N. *Six Months in the West Indies in 1825.* New York, 1826.

Doyle, W. *Some Account of the British Dominions beyond the Seas.* London, 1770.

Edwards, Bryan. *The History, Civil and Commercial, of the British Colonies in the West Indies.* 4 Vols. Philadelphia, 1806.

Lovell, Langford. *A letter to a friend, relative to the present state of Dominica.* London,1818.

Madden, Richard. *A twelve month Residence in the West Indies during the transition from slavery to apprenticeship.* 2 Vols. Philadelphia: Carey, Lea and Banchard, 1835.

Peters, Charles. *Two Sermons preached at Dominica on the 11th and 13th of April 1800 and officially noticed by His Majesty's Privy Council of that island, with appendix containing minutes of three trials together with remarks and strictures on the issue of those trials, the slave trade, and the condition of the slaves.* London, 1802.

Probus [pseud.]. Injustice of the proceedings in St. Vincent. *The Scott Magazine* (Nov. 1772). (This periodical was published monthly in Edinburgh from 1739.)

Walker, James. *Letters on the West Indies.* London, 1818.

Wells, Septimus. *Historical and descriptive sketch of the island of Grenada.* Kingston, Jamaica, 1890.

Woodcock, Henry. *History of Tobago.* Ayr, 1868.

Young, William, Sir bart. *Considerations which may tend to promote the Settlement of Our new West India Colonies, by Encouraging Individuals to Embark in the Undertaking....* London: Printed for James Robson (49 pages 21 cm 8vo pamph), 1764.

_____. "A tour through the Several Islands of Barbados, St. Vincent, Antigua, Tobago and Grenada in the years 1791 and 1792." In Bryan Edwards, *The History, Civil and Commercial of the British Colonies in the West Indies. Third edition, with considerable additions.* Vol. 3. London: John Stockdale, 1801.

_____. *The West India Common Place Book: compiled from parliamentary and official documents, showing the interest of Great Britain in its Sugar Colonies, &c. &c. &c.* London, 1807.

Manuscript sources for the established Church and the Christian missions

a) Established Church:

Church commissioners records

These are chiefly letters and papers concerning candidates for ordination which are located in Lambeth Palace Library, London SW1. They are classified under the heading "Fulham Papers".

The most important volume of my purpose was Volume XXXII – Ordination Papers, Windward Islands.

b) Moravians:

The records of the Moravians missions are located at the headquarters of the Moravian Mission agency, 5 Muswell Hill, London N10.

Two important parcels were consulted:

Parcel 1: Diaries and minutes of the Conferences of the mission in Tobago, 1799-1803.

Parcel 2: Letters from and relating to the Tobago mission, 1784-1803.

c) The London Missionary Society:

The records of this Society are located in the Archives of the Congregational Council for World Missions at 11 Carteret St., London, SW1.

Two boxes were consulted:

Box 1 West Indies – Tobago:

This box contains correspondence concerning the establishment of the mission, correspondence between the missionaries and the directors of the Society, and a Journal of a resident missionary, all covering the period 1807-1812.

Box 3:

This box contains the minutes of the meetings of the meetings held by the board of directors, covering the period 1805-1809. Author consulted Minute Books Nos. IV and V.

d) The Methodists 25 Marleybone Road, London:

The only important manuscript for the author's purpose was a journal of Mr. Thomas Richardson who was a missionary stationed n Dominica. It covers the year 1803.

Printed sources for the Christian Missions

a) The Methodists – 25 Marleybone Rd.:

An invaluable source work is Reverend Dr. Thomas Coke's *A History of the West Indies, containing the natural civil and ecclesiastical history of each island, with an account of the Missions instituted in the islands, from the commencement of their civilization; but more especially of the missions which have been established in the Archepelago by the Society late in connection with the Rev. John Wesley*. 3 Vols. Liverpool, 1808; London, 1810, 1811.

Other useful works by the same author included:

A journal of Rev. Dr. Coke's third tour through the West Indies in two letters to the Rev. John Wesley. London, 1791.

A continuation of Dr. Coke's third tour to the West Indies in a letter to the Reverend John Wesley. London, 1791.

A Statement of the Receipts and disbursements for the support of the Missions established by the Methodist Society for the instruction and conversion of the negroes in the West Indies... addressed to the benevolent subscribers. London, 1794.

An account of the Rise, Progress and present State of the Methodist Missions. London, 1804.

The information in these works by Dr. Coke is supplemented by the following:

The Annual Report of the State of the Missions which are carried on both at home and abroad by the society late in connection with the Reverend John Wesley. London, 1811.

The Annual Report of the State of the Missions foreign and domestic, conducted by the Conference and supported by the members and friends of the United Societies late in connection with the Reverend John Welsey. December 31st, 1812 to December 31st, 1813. London, 1814.

The Report of the Executive Committee for the Management of the Missions. London, 1818.

The first Report of the Wesleyan Methodist Missionary Society. London, 1818; and subsequent reports for the years 1819, 1820, 1821, 1822 and 1823.

Instructions delivered by the Committee to the Wesleyan Missionaries. These are to be found in the Appendix to the Report of the Society for the year 1820.

The above reports of the society are bound in two separate volumes:

Volume 1 covering the period 1804 to 1820.

Volume II covering the period from 1821.

A fairly useful work for the activities of the Methodists in the West Indies is provided by Richard Watson in *A defense of the Wesleyan Missionaries in the West Indies* (London, 1817).

In addition, extracts of letters from missionaries working in the West Indies were published in Methodist periodicals. The author used extracts from the volume covering the period 1789–1823:

The Ariminian Magazine(London), Vol. 17, 1778-1797.

This periodical was continued as *The Methodist Magazine*, which was published in London from 1798 onwards on a yearly basis. The following volumes were consulted:

Vols. 23, 25 26, 27, 30, 38, 39, 42 and 43.

b) The London Missionary Society, 11 Carteret St. London SW1:

Considerations and regulations respecting missionaries in connection with the Missionary Society. London, 1811.

Reports of the London Missionary Society from its formation in the year 1795 to 1814 inclusive; reprinted from the original reports. London, 1814.

c) The Moravians, 5 Muswell Hill, London N10:

Periodical accounts relating to the Missions of the Church of the United Brethren, London, 1790 - 1831, of which I used Vols. I, II and III.

A good account of the work of the Brethren in the West Indies is to be found in *House of Commons Accounts and Papers* Vol. XXVI (1789) No. 646a, part 111, detached pieces of evidence no. 2.

Registers, Almanacs and other works consulted on particular points of reference

The Gentleman's Magazine and Historical Chronicle

This was published monthly in London from 1731. The most important issue for the author's purpose was volume 82 covering the period January–June 1812.

Oliver, Vere Langford (ed.). *Caribbeana: being Miscellaneous Papers relating to the History, Genealogy, Topography and Antiquities, of the British West Indies*. London.

This was published quarterly from 1909 to 1919.

7NDEX

Page numbers in italics indicate illustrations and maps